ROUTLEDGE LIBRARY EDITIONS:
LIBRARY AND INFORMATION SCIENCE

Volume 20

# CONFLICTS IN REFERENCE SERVICES

# CONFLICTS IN REFERENCE SERVICES

Edited by
BILL KATZ AND RUTH A. FRALEY

LONDON AND NEW YORK

First published in 1985 by The Haworth Press, Inc.

This edition first published in 2020
by Routledge
2 Park Square, Milton Park, Abingdon, Oxon OX14 4RN

and by Routledge
52 Vanderbilt Avenue, New York, NY 10017

*Routledge is an imprint of the Taylor & Francis Group, an informa business*

© 1985 The Haworth Press, Inc.

All rights reserved. No part of this book may be reprinted or reproduced or utilised in any form or by any electronic, mechanical, or other means, now known or hereafter invented, including photocopying and recording, or in any information storage or retrieval system, without permission in writing from the publishers.

*Trademark notice*: Product or corporate names may be trademarks or registered trademarks, and are used only for identification and explanation without intent to infringe.

*British Library Cataloguing in Publication Data*
A catalogue record for this book is available from the British Library

ISBN: 978-0-367-34616-4 (Set)
ISBN: 978-0-429-34352-0 (Set) (ebk)
ISBN: 978-0-367-37425-9 (Volume 20) (hbk)
ISBN: 978-0-367-37427-3 (Volume 20) (pbk)
ISBN: 978-0-429-35437-3 (Volume 20) (ebk)

**Publisher's Note**
The publisher has gone to great lengths to ensure the quality of this reprint but points out that some imperfections in the original copies may be apparent.

**Disclaimer**
The publisher has made every effort to trace copyright holders and would welcome correspondence from those they have been unable to trace.

# Conflicts in Reference Services

Edited by
Bill Katz and Ruth A. Fraley

The Haworth Press
New York • London

*Conflicts in Reference Services* has also been published as *The Reference Librarian*, Number 12, Spring/Summer 1985.

© 1985 by The Haworth Press, Inc. All rights reserved. No part of this book may be reproduced or utilized in any form or by any means, electronic or mechanical, including photocopying, microfilm and recording, or by any information storage and retrieval system, without permission in writing from the publisher. Printed in the United States of America.

The Haworth Press, Inc., 12 West 32 Street, New York, NY 10001
EUROSPAN/Haworth, 3 Henrietta Street, London WC2E 8LU England

**Library of Congress Cataloging in Publication Data**
Main entry under title:

Conflicts in reference services.

   Has also been published as the Reference librarian, no. 12, spring/summer 1985.
   Includes bibliographies.
   1. Reference services (Libraries)—Addresses, essays, lectures. I. Katz, William A., 1924- . II. Fraley, Ruth A.
Z711.C64 1985    025.5'2    84-25147
ISBN 0-86656-385-7

# Conflicts in Reference Services

The Reference Librarian
Number 12

## CONTENTS

| | |
|---|---|
| **Introduction**<br>*Ruth Fraley* | 1 |

### IN THE LIBRARY

| | |
|---|---|
| **Academic Reference Departments and User Groups: A Preliminary Survey**<br>*John W. Berry* | 5 |
| Survey Results | 6 |
| Consideration | 8 |
| Observations | 10 |
| Improving the Quality of Reference Services | 11 |
| **The Reference Librarian as Middleman: Conflicts Between Catalogers and Reference Librarians**<br>*Gillian M. McCombs* | 17 |
| Confusion | 19 |
| Search | 20 |
| Nature of the Job | 22 |
| Steps Taken | 23 |
| Total Control | 25 |
| Need for Involvement | 26 |
| **Conflicts Between Reference and Interlibrary Loan**<br>*Marcia L. Sprules* | 29 |
| Copyright | 29 |
| Bibliographic Instruction | 32 |
| Fees for Service | 33 |
| Lending Restrictions | 34 |
| Document Delivery | 35 |
| Conflict Resolution | 36 |
| Conclusion | 37 |

**Check Your Catalog Image**     39
    *Marcia J. Myers*

  Leverence Study     40
  Dennison Study     41
  Procedures     42
  Findings     43
  Implications     46

**Uneven Reference Service: Approaches for Decreasing This Source of Conflict at the Reference Desk**     49
    *Fred Batt*

**Yours, Mine and Ours: Reference Service and the Non-Affiliated User**     65
    *Debbie Masters*
    *Gail Flatness*

  Higher Reference Use     66
  Little Guidance     67
  Limitation Policies     69

**Conflicts in Reference Service: A Personal View**     73
    *George R. Bauer*

  How to Fill the Slack Time at the Reference Desk and Still Be Alert to Needs     74
  For Whom the Bell Tolls: Juggling In-Person and Telephone Questions     75
  The Reference Librarian as Factotum     76
  Further Animadversions on the Concept of Maxi-Service/Mini-Staff     76
  The Over-Demanding Patron—Where Do You Draw the Line?     77
  Jargonry and Acromania     78
  Muscling Up for the Future     80
  Pedal Point and Coda     80

**Reference Philosophy vs Service Reality**     83
    *Larry D. Benson*
    *H. Julene Butler*

  Causes of the Dilemma     84
  Solutions     86

# FEES AND CHARGES

## Fee vs Free in Historical Perspective — 93
*Margaret F. Stieg*

| | |
|---|---|
| Economic Argument | 95 |
| Assumptions | 96 |
| Tax Support | 97 |
| Favor Fees | 98 |
| Fiction Debate | 99 |
| Measures | 100 |

## Fee or Free: The Data Base Access Controversy — 105
*Dean Burgess*

| | |
|---|---|
| Goals | 106 |
| The Rights of Access | 109 |
| Discrimination | 110 |
| Financial Questions | 111 |
| Realities | 113 |
| Conclusion | 113 |

# ABOUT INSTRUCTION

## Conflicts Between Reference Librarians and Faculty Concerning Bibliographic Instruction — 117
*David Isaacson*

| | |
|---|---|
| Working Together | 119 |
| Status Conflicts | 120 |
| Third Group | 121 |
| Fourth Group | 122 |
| Good Advice | 123 |
| Internal Disputes | 124 |
| Justification | 126 |

## Help Your Administration Support Bibliographic Instruction — 129
*Robert E. Brundin*

| | |
|---|---|
| Pressures | 130 |
| Fully Informed | 132 |
| Enlist Support | 132 |
| Program Information | 133 |

**Promoting a Positive Image: Hints for the New
Reference Librarian in Dealing With Faculty**     **135**
    *Eric W. Johnson*

Perceptions     136
Good Image     138

**A Collection of Books: The College Professor
vs the Reference Librarian**     **141**
    *Melissa Watson*

No Win     142
Another Area     143
The Issue     144
Relationships     146
Conflicts     146

## ABOUT THE ROLE OF THE PROFESSIONAL

**Nonprofessionals on Reference Desks in Academic
Libraries**     **149**
    *Nancy J. Emmick*

Definition of Terms     150
Reference Desk Staffing Alternatives     151
The Consequences of Using Nonprofessionals
   at the Reference Desk     153
Academic Library Reference Service Practices     155
Conclusions and Observations     157

**Self-Conflict in the Academic Reference Librarian:
Or Help! We Need a Better Word for What We Do!**     **161**
    *Paul B. Weiner*

Background     162
What is Help?     163
Personality     164
What Is Reference Work?     165
Self-Conflict Peculiar to Reference Work     166
Lurching Toward Happiness     169

**Why Didn't They Teach Us That? The Credibility Gap in Library Education**    171
*Michael McCoy*

| | |
|---|---|
| Ethics | 173 |
| Conflicts | 174 |
| Trivia Questions | 175 |
| Possibilities | 177 |

**Role Conflict and Ambiguity in Reference Librarianship**    179
*Henry N. Mendelsohn*

| | |
|---|---|
| Literature Review | 180 |
| Examples | 181 |
| Organizational Process in Role Strain | 183 |
| Boundary Roles | 183 |
| Innovative Roles | 184 |
| Consequences | 185 |
| Conclusions | 185 |

## ABOUT THE RESOURCES

**In This Conflict of Opinions and Sentiments I Find Delight**    187
*Donald Davinson*

| | |
|---|---|
| Conflict in Reference Service | 188 |
| Periodical Research | 190 |
| Image Bolster | 190 |
| Proud Possessor | 192 |

**Access to Consumer Health Information**    195
*Robert Berk*

| | |
|---|---|
| Public Libraries and Consumer Health Information | 196 |
| Hospital Libraries and Consumer Health Information | 196 |
| Academic Health Sciences Libraries and Consumer Health Information | 198 |
| University Libraries and Consumer Health Information | 199 |

Health Information Centers and Consumer Health
   Information   200
Legal Implications of Providing Consumer Health
   Information   201
A Model for Library Provision of Consumer Health
   Information   202
Conclusion   204

**Academic Library Service to Physically Disabled Students and Faculty**    **207**
   *Gerald Jahoda*
   *Paula Faustini*

Discussion of Results   210

**Abstract Thinking: Considerations for the Provision of Statistical Data in Evaluation**    **213**
   *Juri Stratford*
   *Jean S. Stratford*

Definitions   214
Comparability and Bias   216
Basic Level   218
Experiences   220
Reference Considerations   221
Reference Interview   222
Sources   223
Personal Contacts   224

**The NASA Industrial Applications Centers: Fee Based vs Free Information Services**    **227**
   *Lynn Heer*

RECON Database   229
Operation   230
Competition   233
Summary   234

# Introduction

Ruth Fraley

This issue of *The Reference Librarian* evolved from a discussion about conflict. Is conflict something to be avoided or is it interwoven in the professional life of all librarians? Should a career be directed by attempts to make everything smooth, placid, and without disturbances? On one side of the discussion, this was the case and there was heavy criticism of anyone who is involved in a conflict. Conflict, according to this view is a force for disturbance, it never yields progress, and always reflects negatively on those involved who are unable to communicate and unworthy of being professional librarians. The other view in the discussion is that some conflict is inherent in most aspects of library work and is especially evident in public services. The tensions in a conflict situation encourage originality, lead to new solutions to old problems and foster creative evolution of the profession. A librarian can be evaluated on his or her ability to function in and understand a conflict situation and be able to react in the best interest of the library and the profession. A library without some conflict, opined a participant in the discussion, is either dead or doomed, and probably not fulfilling its mission. At least one author in this collection points out that a lack of conflict often represents the behavior of the burnt out—the apathetic reaction of an individual to a situation which is no longer a challenge, of interest or of value to them. Creativity, new thoughts, growth of the profession and of libraries depends on the skillful evolution of conflicts.

The librarian without conflicts and stress is a throwback to the stereotype we have all worked so long to abolish; the quiet library free from problems and the librarian reigning supreme amidst rows and rows of suitable, intellectually adequate books perturbed only when the right patron, with clean hands borrows these gems and returns them on time. The librarian of the stereotype is missing the best, the most intellectually challenging, and, admittedly, the most frustrating parts of librarianship.

Conflicts exist in all types of libraries, and are not without precedent nor do they exist in isolation from the concerns of society in general. Stieg sets the stage with her discussion of the issue of fee versus free in historical perspective. Burgess continues the discussion and examines present day goals and rationales for charging for on-line searches. Part of this controversy is the argument that charging fees disenfranchises the group of users who cannot pay. Are we an egalitarian profession? Berry has studied the question of quality of reference services to different groups of users in an academic setting and presents some interesting conclusions.

McCombs discusses the conflicts that have evolved between the reference librarian and the cataloger. Her discussion of the function of the role of the card catalog and its rather bumpy qualities provides an excellent summary and argues effectively that the library must determine whether the card catalog is intended as an access tool or as a perfect bibliographic document. Conflicts between reference and other library departments are also brought out. Sprules looks at the conflicts between reference and interlibrary loan. Myers' research showed a relationship between the way in which an academic library is perceived and presented to the outside world by the college administration and the quality of service.

How to provide quality service and who is best suited to provide it are two other issues for discussion and conflict. Benson and Butler look at the issue from the perspective of the public services librarian in a library whose budget is materials oriented as opposed to service oriented. Emmick conducted research into the numbers of libraries which include nonprofessionals on the reference desk, another topic of concern for many in the profession.

Conflict exists between librarians and faculty and among librarians about bibliographic instruction. Image is important here, the image of the librarian in the academic community as well as a self-image. The reference desk is described by Batt as the mirror of the library, a reflection of its image and its importance in its community and to the individuals who toil there daily. Batt has well thought out suggestions for the reference administrator.

There is also conflict about the collections, not only the type but also the use of the materials that are in place. Davinson points out the interesting, and sometimes apparently inconsistent materials in library collections that do not relate to the service demands of the library. The Stratfords discuss the possibility of conflicting answers to patrons from information in standard statistical resources.

New conflicts, and growing concerns for all types of libraries are found in the conflicts between libraries and specialized information brokers that evolved with the flood of information in recent years. This area is discussed not only from the perspective of the new technology and information sources but also from the existence of types of information such as medical and legal information. Berk examines the question of health information in public libraries.

References services is the front line for most of the professional conflicts in librarianship. The reference librarian at the desk is regularly identifying alternatives in conflict situations and makes quick decisions relating to these issues on a daily basis. These decisions are the products of values, roles, and education for the profession, topics examined by McCoy, Mendelsohn, and Weiner.

Just think how crushingly boring our libraries would be without these on-going impetus to thought and self examination—the conflicts.

## IN THE LIBRARY

# Academic Reference Departments and User Groups: A Preliminary Survey

John W. Berry

Considerable attention has been devoted to examining the reference process in libraries in recent years. This increase in critical studies has been due, in part, to a need to understand more fully the fundamental nature of what has long been considered an imprecise, mysterious, almost artistic library function, and to help provide administrative justification for relatively large monetary expenditures for personnel. The library manager's need to be accountable for expenditures has been, at times, a source of conflict with reference librarians who may have felt threatened by close scrutiny of their work.

Nevertheless, the results of some of these studies have been quite revealing, not to say shocking, to the library public service community. In a recent "unobtrusive" study of the quality of reference services for academic library government depository collections, librarians were able to provide correct answers to a set of pretested inquiries only 37 percent of the time.[1] Other studies of a similar nature in both academic and public library settings have shown that general reference departments tend to provide correct answers to between 50 and 60 percent of test questions asked in person or by telephone. Although most reference librarians admit to being occa-

---

The author is Assistant Director for Public Services, The University Libraries, Northern Illinois University, DeKalb, IL 60015. Peggy Sullivan, also of Northern Illinois University, worked with the author on all phases of the development of this article.

© 1985 by The Haworth Press, Inc. All rights reserved.

sionally "stumped" by a question, few like to believe they provide correct answers only about half the time.

With this background, the present writer was curious about another aspect of the provision of reference services. To what extent do academic reference departments differentiate among user groups in providing various types of services? Do faculty members, administrators and graduate students get more complete attention for their information requests than do undergraduate students and other library users? Or, put another way, are academic library reference services essentially egalitarian or elitist?

A search of the literature produced very little information that directly addresses this question, although some studies have dealt with it peripherally. A short telephone survey instrument was developed (See Appendix A) and used with reference departments in academic libraries with particular emphasis on medium to large-size libraries. An attempt was made to survey libraries of both private and public institutions from various geographic regions in the United States. (See Appendix B for a list of libraries surveyed).

## *SURVEY RESULTS*

Twenty-two academic libraries were contacted by telephone during February, 1984. In most instances, respondents were reference department heads, although in a few cases another professional member of the reference department answered the survey questions.

The average number of professional librarians in the reference departments surveyed was almost nine (8.72); non-professionals accounted for about four (4.27) additional staff members. In most cases, non-professionals did participate in staffing the reference desk, usually in conjunction with a librarian. Most of the libraries double-staff (or occasionally triple-staff) during prime daytime hours, typically 10 a.m. to 3 p.m. Fewer departments double-staff evenings and weekends.

Determining the existence of a reference policy manual was considered a key element in assessing the treatment of various user groups in the present study since a written manual might indicate "official" department policy, or at least a philosophy of service priorities.

In 1980-81, Bill Katz and Anne Clifford compiled materials for a handbook on reference and online services in academic, public and special libraries. Of the fifty-three academic libraries contacted, only five, or about 10 percent were found to have written policy or procedure manuals providing the essential guidelines, procedures, and policies deemed necessary for the daily provision of effective reference services.[2]

Of the twenty-two libraries surveyed for the present study, six reported having a reference policy or procedure manual (28 percent). Significantly, of the sixteen respondents who indicated they had no policy manual, five said they were presently compiling one, while several others noted they were "thinking about a policy manual." Four respondents provided the author with copies of their department's policy manual upon request.

Another question asked whether students (undergraduate and graduate) tend to ask reference questions in numbers proportional to their numbers on campus. Or, if seventy-five of one hundred library users are undergraduates, do they ask about seventy-five percent of the reference questions? Answers to this question revealed that no institution surveyed attempted to count users by group affiliation, but most respondents felt that such information would reflect a roughly proportionate percentage of user group and numbers of questions asked. A few respondents suspected that graduate students would be overrepresented by reference inquiries when compared to their numbers on campus.

The loan period for circulating materials to various user groups was also felt to be significant information, although the results provided few surprises. Faculty loan periods are usually longer than loan periods for other user groups. Ten institutions reported a one-year faculty loan period, eight reported a semester or quarter loan, and four indicated loan periods of shorter duration. Loans of materials to graduate students showed a predominance of two- to four-week loans, with ten institutions reporting a semester or quarter loan. A few institutions granted faculty borrowing privileges to doctoral students who were writing dissertations. Without exception, circulation to undergraduates fell within a two- to four-week time frame. It was somewhat surprising to find that several reference department heads did not readily know what their library's current circulation policies were.

The central question in the survey asked if there were any services provided to faculty that were not provided to other patrons. Two examples of such services were mentioned to respondents: 1) not charging faculty for online searches and 2) limiting interlibrary loan requests to faculty and graduate students only.

The overwhelming response revealed that no differentiation is made between user groups in the provision of such reference services, thus indicating a strong apparent tendency toward an egalitarian service posture for affiliated user groups. One institution indicated that faculty members were provided with one free library computer search each year. Three other institutions reported that partial or full subsidies were made for undergraduate student computer searches one or more times each academic year. Four institutions responded that undergraduates were restricted in interlibrary borrowing, indicating that requests must be approved by faculty members or librarians; another institution noted that interlibrary loan activity for undergraduates was restricted to in-state or in-region only. Finally, several institutions reported that special privileges for faculty included access to locked library study carrels and no assessment of overdue fines.

## *CONSIDERATION*

Another consideration in determining the kinds and extent of reference services provided to various user groups was the existence of any recommendations or policy on the amount of time spent on reference questions from faculty, graduate and undergraduate students. As was the case above, the typical response was that "no distinction is made between user groups." Many respondents indicated they would not want to make such distinctions in any case. Two department heads said that each professional staff member does as "he or she sees fit." Three respondents indicated something to the effect that "if the President's Office calls, we'll go all out," while only two said they would be likely to pursue a question further if it were asked by a faculty member.

In response to this question, several respondents mentioned that unaffiliated users (e.g., the general public) may be treated differentially. One respondent said that once a lack of affiliation with the university is determined, "we tend to refer these requests elsewhere more quickly." Other factors also affected treatment of non-university users. Public institutions tended to feel an obligation to serve all users, while private institutions were much more likely to actively restrict services to unaffiliated users. As might be expected, urban institutions were more likely to identify service to unaffiliated users as a significant problem than were suburban or rural-based institutions.

Another question in the survey shed further light on the issue of unaffiliated users. The question asked if users were asked to identify themselves either in person or over the telephone before a reference question was answered. Again, uniformly the answer was no, sometimes emphatically stated. A number of respondents indicated that some attempt was made to determine university affiliation before proceeding to do in-depth telephone reference work. This determination was left largely to the individual discretion of the reference librarian answering the question. Two of the four institutions which sent copies of their reference department's policy manual specifically address the need to determine the institutional affiliation of telephone callers. Nearly all institutions have a policy limiting telephone look-up service to three items, whether formally or informally stated. In many cases, telephone reference service was considered a somewhat lower priority than in person service by reference department heads.

The question that provoked some of the most interesting responses asked if (and if so, how) respondents dealt with the evaluation of reference services provided to different user groups, and more generally, what procedures or criteria do reference departments use to determine the effectiveness of reference services? Nearly all respondents identified this as a definite problem area or concern. No institution claimed the ability to measure effectively the quality of reference services provided to users. Most reference departments in the survey regularly evaluate the performance of reference librarians providing services, typically through direct observation or informal discussions. One institution has a "tough question bulletin board" which serves as a forum for staff communication on the quality of questions and answers. Direct patron feedback is very rare indeed, with the exception of formal evaluation of reference librarians teaching in a formal classroom program. The use of evaluation forms for online reference services was also found to be quite common. Most reference department managers admit this is an area they have thought about a great deal, but that it remains difficult to address. The opinion was offered by several respondents that reference librarians tend to regard the evaluation of reference services as a potential threat to their autonomy, if not to their academic freedom.

The final question asked simply for the optimum length of time (in minutes) for a reference interaction in the respondent's opinion. There was a nearly unanimous response that this question could not be answered since there were so many variables involved—the nature of the request, person seeking the information, staff member responding to the user's need, and so on. Eight respondents ventured opinions beyond this response. Three of them gave a ten- to fifteen- minute maximum as ideal; one said three minutes, another two to thirty minutes. One respondent indicated that graduate assistants in the department were instructed not to spend more than five minutes on a question before referring it to a librarian. Another respondent answered that most questions could be handled in less than five minutes, but that some could require ten minutes or more; still another gave a thirty-second minimum and a two- to three-minute maximum.

## *OBSERVATIONS*

A number of observations come to mind in analyzing the results of this preliminary survey. The question of time duration of the reference interview and search process is an intriguing one. Although relatively little data exists on this issue, one recent study is worth mentioning in some detail on this and several other points raised here. In a study referred to earlier, Charles McClure and Peter Hernon studied government depository reference services in academic libraries in the Northeast and the Southwest regions of the United States. The average duration of the interview and search process (I & S) for test questions asked in person of librarians in the Northeast was seven minutes for a correct answer and five minutes for an incorrect answer. The opposite situation was found to be true in the Southwest, where an average of four minutes was spent finding a correct answer and six minutes for an incorrect answer to questions asked in person. Furthermore, Northeastern librarians increased their overall percentage of correct answers given during the six minutes of I & S, with correct answers rapidly declining thereafter. Southwestern staff members, on the other hand, gave the greatest percentage of correct answers with only one to two minutes I & S, and their success rate decreased the longer the search proceeded.[3]

A somewhat different pattern was evidenced by answers to telephone questions. Both Northeastern and Southwestern depository reference staff increased their correct answer performance until the five or six minute mark, after which the number of correct answers supplied quickly decreased the longer the search continued.[4] Among the variables not considered in the study, but important for our purposes, were: staff workload at the time questions were asked; other activities occurring at the reference point; the number of other patrons waiting for reference service; the extent of use of non-professionals; the sophistication of the user in presenting the question; and the competency of library staff members and their knowledge of the reference interview and question negotiation.[5]

McClure and Hernon confirm the results of other studies that show a positive relationship between correct answers given by reference librarians and reference questions asked by telephone. That is, users tend to get a higher percentage of correct answers through telephone inquiries than through in person requests. To the extent that the present survey found a tendency to give telephone questions a somewhat lower priority than in person requests, one may reasonably question such written or unwritten policy by reference departments in this regard. McClure and Hernon speculate that reference staff may, in fact, pay more attention to telephone requests, that the question can be answered as time permits, that staff may work harder to answer the question in order to return to other work, and so on. Finally, it is possible that since student "proxies" delivered both the telephone and in person questions "they may have been perceived as 'less important' for the receipt of extensive reference services . . . because they may have 'looked like students' or 'acted like students' "[6] when questions were delivered in person. Again, is a philosophy of egalitarian or elitist service a significant factor in the delivery of reference services? Data of this kind generate a great many questions of this type, most of which remain unanswered.

## *IMPROVING THE QUALITY OF REFERENCE SERVICES*

One fact emerges from all reference services studies in recent years—we simply do not yet know enough about the reference process to fully understand its subtleties and complexities. The present writer therefore urges reference managers and librarians to continue to address these questions in much greater depth in two primary areas. First, attempt the rigorous measurement of the quality of reference services provided, to various user groups, and second, develop guidelines, policies and procedures that address staffing, user priority, extent of services provided, and so on. Let us consider for a moment some of the ways in which reference departments may proceed in these areas.

The tremendous power of the computer and a trend toward the development of in-house "management information systems" offer great possibilities for the improvement of information services through the systematic examination of the reference process. Furthermore, library managers, reference librarians, and above all, library users stand to benefit from such a process.

The widely available Statistical Package for the Social Sciences (SPSS) offers the potential for gaining significant information from the routine statistics that many library reference departments collect. Such factors as time of day of an information inquiry, day of the week, mode of inquiry (telephone or in person), type of question (reference or directional) are commonly recorded. Linking these factors with the status of the library staff member (professional or non-professional), user status (undergraduate, graduate, faculty, unaffiliated), time duration (in minutes) of a transaction and sources used to answer a question, all of which could be easily collected, and could provide an enormous amount of evaluative information on the reference process. By "pairing" or "cross-tabulating" various groups of data on SPSS, reference departments could learn whether they, in fact, tend to offer what we have called elitist or egalitarian reference services (by pairing user status with library staff member status), or whether librarians are handling the time-consuming questions and non-professionals the briefer questions (by pairing time duration with library staff status). The possibilities for manipulating reference data are practically endless.[7]

Apparently, significant progress has been made in the last two or three years in the development of guidelines, policies and procedures in academic reference departments, if the present survey is representative of national trends in this area. Still, fewer than one third of all academic libraries appear to have written reference policies. Some of those manuals that are written are guidelines rather than policies. Statistics-gathering and analysis of the kind described above could form the basis for writing, reviewing or updating policy statements. Clearly, the need to exists to undertake or continue such work.

Among the questions or issues that should be addressed by reference policies that significantly affect the overall quality of reference services are:

— How much time should be spent in answering a typical reference inquiry?

— To what extent will non-professionals be utilized at the reference desk? What kinds of questions should they answer? Which questions should be referred?
— Should professionals deal primarily with graduate students and faculty or should their efforts be directed toward undergraduates and other library users as well?
— What kinds of reference requests should be referred to other librarians or other libraries, networks, etc.?

Of course, there are many other questions that could be asked in devising policies and guidelines for individual reference departments.

Enhancing our knowledge of the reference process through more careful statistical analysis, and writing policies and procedures based, at least in part, on that analysis, are quite likely to cause tension between reference managers and some members of their departments. These conflicts should be recognized and openly addressed. The clear goal, after all, is improving the ability of reference departments to offer high quality, effective reference services to users, a goal shared by the entire public service community of the library.

## APPENDIX A

### The Reference Process: An Assessment and Opinion Survey

Name of Interviewer:
Name of Respondent:
Position (Title):
Institutional Affiliation:
Telephone:
1. Number of professional librarians in your reference department _____.
2. Number of non-professional staff _____.
3. Do you double-staff the reference desk? _____ If so, during what hours _____.
4. Does your reference department have a policy manual? _____ If yes, would you be willing to send a copy? _____
5. Do students (either undergraduate or graduate) account for about the same proportion of reference questions asked when compared to their number on campus? (i.e. if 75 out of 100

library users are undergraduates, do they ask about 75% of the reference questions?)
6. Is your circulation loan period the same for students and faculty? If not, what is the loan period for faculty? _____, for graduate students? _____, for undergraduates? _____.
7. Are services provided to faculty that are not provided to other patrons? Examples: (1) not charging faculty for online searches and (2) limiting interlibrary loan requests to graduate students and faculty only.
8. How do you (if you do) make recommendations or set policy on the amount of time spent on reference questions from undergraduate, graduate students, and faculty?
9. Are users asked to identify themselves either in person or over the telephone before a reference question is answered?
10. How do you evaluate the quality of reference services provided to different groups of users? What procedures or criteria are used to determine the effectiveness of reference services?
11. What is the optimum length of time (in minutes) for a reference interview in your opinion?

## *APPENDIX B*

### *Institutional Respondents*

The writer is grateful to the following institutions for participating in the telephone survey utilized here.

The University of California/Irvine
The University of California/Riverside
Colgate University
Colorado State University
University of Delaware
Duke University
Georgia State University
University of Illinois/Chicago
University of Michigan
University of Nebraska/Omaha
University of New Mexico
State University of New York/Stony Brook

Northern Illinois University
University of Notre Dame
University of Pennsylvania
Pennsylvania State University
Rutgers University/Camden
Southern Illinois University
Syracuse University
Texas A & M University
Vanderbilt University
University of Wisconsin/Madison

## REFERENCES

1. Charles McClure and Peter Hernon, *Improving the Quality of Reference Service for Government Publications.* (Chicago: American Library Association, 1983), p. 54.
2. William A. Katz and Anne Clifford, eds., *Reference and Online Service Handbook: Guidelines, Policies and Procedures for Libraries.* (New York: Neal Shuman, 1982), p. xx-iii.
3. Charles McClure and Peter Hernon, p. 47.
4. McClure and Hernon, p. 51.
5. McClure and Hernon, p. 52.
6. McClure and Hernon, p. 33.
7. For a detailed treatment of the uses of SPSS in evaluating reference work see: Howard D. White, "Measurement at the Reference Desk," *Drexel Library Quarterly,* 17 (1981): 3-35.

## BIBLIOGRAPHY

American Library Association, Reference and Adult Services Division, Standards Committee. "A Commitment to Information Services: Developmental Guidelines 1979," *RQ,* 18 (Spring 1979): 277-278.
Chen, Ching-Chih, and Peter Hernon. *Information Searching: Assessing and Anticipating User Needs.* New York: Neal-Shuman, 1982.
Halperin, Michael and Maureen Strazdon. "Measuring Students' Performance for Reference Services: A Conjoint Analysis," *Library Quarterly,* 50 (April 1980): 208-224.
Howell, Benita J. and Others. "A Technical Report on a Role Analysis Prepared for the Reference Department of Margaret I. King University Library, University of Kentucky." Lexington: University of Kentucky, 1977. ED 138244.
Jirjees, Jassim Muhammed. "The Accuracy of Selected Northeastern College Library Reference/Information Telephone Services in Responding to Factual Inquiries." Ph.D. dissertation, Rutgers University, 1981.
Johnson, Kerry A. and Marilyn Domas White. "The Cognitive Style of Reference Librarians," *RQ,* 21 (Spring 1982): 239-246.
Kantor, Paul B. "Quantitative Evaluation of the Reference Process," *RQ,* 21 (Fall 1981): 43-52.
Katz, William A. and Anne Clifford, eds. *Reference and Online Services Handbook: Guidelines, Policies and Procedures for Libraries.* New York: Neal-Shuman, 1982.

Katz, William A. "Uncertain Realities of Reference Service," *Library Trends,* 31 (Winter 1983): 363-374.

Lancaster, F.W. *The Measurement and Evaluation of Library Services.* Washington, D.C.: Information Resources Press, 1977.

Lederman, Linda Costigan. "Fear of Talking: Which Students in the Academic Library Ask Librarians for Help?," *RQ,* 20 (Summer 1981): 382-393.

Markham, Marilyn J., Keith H. Stirling, and Nathan M. Smith. "Librarian Self-Disclosure and Patron Satisfaction in the Reference Interview," *RQ,* 22 (Summer 1983): 369-374.

Martyn, John and F. Wilfrid Lancaster. *Investigative Methods in Library and Information Science: An Introduction.* Washington, D.C.: Information Resources Press, 1981.

McClure, Charles R., and Peter Hernon. *Improving the Quality of Reference Services for Government Publications.* Chicago: American Library Association, 1983.

Myers, Marcia Jean. "The Effectiveness of Telephone Reference/Information Services in Academic Libraries in the Southeast." Ph.D. dissertation, Florida State University, 1979.

Rettig, James. "A Theoretical Model and Definition of the Reference Process," *RQ,* 17 (Fall 1978): 19-29.

Schmidt, Janine B. "Evaluation of Reference Service in the College of Advanced Education Libraries in New South Wales." University of New South Wales, Australia, 1979. ED 197707.

Vathis, Alma Christine. "Reference Transaction and End Product as Viewed by the Patron," *RQ,* 23 (Fall 1983): 60-64.

White, Howard D. "Measurement at the Reference Desk," *Drexel Library Quarterly,* 17 (Winter 1981): 3-35.

Wilkinson, Billy R. "The Undergraduate Library's Public Service Record: Reference Services." San Diego: University of California/San Diego Library, 1970. ED 042473.

# The Reference Librarian as Middleman: Conflicts Between Catalogers and Reference Librarians

Gillian M. McCombs

How does a patron locate a specific title or body of work in the library? Usually by searching in the card-catalog or online catalog. Who is responsible for getting that information into the catalog? The cataloger. How successful are catalogers in giving patrons access to the library's collection? It is often only the reference librarian—who in many instances must act as interpreter of the card-catalog for the patron—who can judge the success of technical services. Does the cataloger provide or deny access to the collection?

In addressing these potential conflicts, I am going to limit myself to discussing academic or research libraries which have distinctly separate Technical Services and Reference Divisions, and which have holdings large enough to cause card-catalog confusion. Naturally these conflicts are not as great when librarians' functions are not defined quite so narrowly and when the card catalog is small enough (and the support staff large enough) to make whatever changes new cataloging rules and decisions require.

I would also like to presume that, although the direction is definitely towards the online catalog, most of us have still to get there, dragging behind us closed card-catalogs, unfunded retrospective conversion projects and the knowledge that one way or another, all these various data-bases will have to be fed and probably by Technical Services.

The fact that there are numerous conflicts is demonstrated not only by what we all know and are experiencing—as librarians and patrons—but by the number of critical issues to be addressed in the

---

The author is Head, Catalog Maintenance Unit, University Libraries, State University of New York at Albany 12222.

Fall/Winter Technical Services and Cataloging issue of the *Reference Librarian*. Unfortunately that publication will not appear in time for its discussion to have any bearing on this article. However, just a rundown of some of the topics to be discussed gives an idea of some of the concerns we have: What do reference librarians want from Technical Services? What is wrong with cataloging? Effects of user considerations on Reference and Technical Services. Integrating AACR1 and 2. The impact of Technical Services decisions on public services, and so on.

In November 1975, Michael Gorman, in his humorous but apt followup to Andrew Osborn's much cited "The Crisis in Cataloging", stated that "Catalogs are instruments of communication between the library user (and library staff) and the documents the library can make available. Anything increasing this communication is good, and anything detracting from this is bad."[1] Mr. Gorman then went on to play an important role in the compilation of AACR2, and, to my way of thinking, to lead us forever into a confusion of piggyback catalogs, split files, interfile notices, arbitrary cutoffs (cataloged before or after December 1980), bibliographic flips and so on.

The card catalog may be obsolete, but, like it or not, most of us still use one, contribute to one or spend countless hours deciding how, when and if to replace one. Cooperative cataloging is perpetuating the card-catalog, not replacing it, merely increasing the level of detail we can bring to our work. The majority of our online catalogs are reproducing catalog cards on the screen, with varying levels of description. Instead of opening new vistas in cataloging, providing freer and more flexible access, the computer is being used merely as a larger place to store catalog cards. Is this potential not being utilized because catalogers cannot imagine anything but a 3 × 5 card? The ability to make global changes (our magic phrase) has in many cases complicated instead of simplifying changes in name or subject headings. The Library of Congress is afraid to use its global change capacity because of its experiences so far, and the Washington Library Network found several surprises in making global changes—when the subject heading "Graves" was changed to "Burials", Graves County (Kentucky) became Burials County (Kentucky). Is this because we are as yet unsophisticated in programming, or does it reflect on a basic lack of system capability?

It seems to me that almost ten years after Mr. Gorman's article, communication between the library user and the library's holdings, via the card catalog, has deteriorated to a point where even the simplest forms of access—author and title—are being denied. A senior librarian, book in hand, finds trouble in locating catalog entries, never mind an undergraduate student experiencing for the first time in his life a card-catalog outside that of his school library or local public library. Who sees these struggles and conflicts on a daily basis? The reference librarian, the "Middleman" of my article, the person who must not only interpret the card-catalog for the patron, but must interpret the patron's needs to the cataloger who, for better or worse, is working (usually in the basement) in a vacuum without any direct contact with the patron. And after all, the avowed goal of all our daily striving is, indeed, to serve the patron better.

## CONFUSION

When I asked one reference librarian how he dealt with post-AACR2 confusion, he replied, "Well, we just muddle through". Are we really reduced to standing in front of the card-catalog and saying, as Celia and Rosalind did to Touchstone in "As You Like It", "Celia: How prove you that in the great heap of your knowledge? Rosalind: Ay, marry, now unmuzzle your wisdom."[2] Does the card-catalog prove to be any less of a fool than Touchstone?

Examples of the card-catalog either denying access to or providing obstacles to a library's holdings are not hard to find. There are many different categories, some specific to a particular library, many stemming from changes affecting the whole library field. Patrons and librarians alike have difficulty in forgetting that works about the U.S. Constitution were located under the heading *UNITED STATES. CONSTITUTION.* and are now located several drawers away under

*UNITED STATES.*
*CONSTITUTION.*

Even with book in hand, it is hard to locate a corporate main entry in the New York or United States section of the card catalog. For instance, what is the difference between New York (N.Y.), New York (State), and New York State as preliminary filing factors? Several drawers of difference. Why is the Attorney General's Office treated one way—*New York (State). Attorney General's Of-*

*fice*—and the Advisory Council on Vocational Education another—*New York State Advisory Council on Vocational Education.*

Cross-references, you say? The syndetic structure of the catalog? Catalogers are never happier than when talking about the syndetic structure of the card-catalog, especially to reference librarians, who are surprised to find this phrase does not refer to the wood, glue, brass etc. that holds the whole thing together. These days, the latter structure is certainly more useful than the former. Who has the support staff available to maintain the syndetic structure of the card-catalog in full? Who has not started to at least re-evaluate if not already cut down on all the cross-references predicated by strict adherence to Library of Congress Cataloging authorities i.e. the automated LC NAF files and the Library of Congress Subject Headings (Redbooks, microfiche or whatever). If you are lucky(?) enough to have a "piggyback" catalog, it is unlikely that you will find cross-references from old to new or vice versa, only from old to old and new to new. How many patrons become confused when they mistakenly go from old to new or the reverse?

Several pre-AACR2 library surveys have revealed that readers are quite incapable of using a library catalog without help of some sort, written or oral. One problem is that a reader does not always realize he needs help. Not surprisingly, he is unaware of the various revolutions in the cataloging world. A card-catalog is a card-catalog is a card-catalog after all, and there are certain basic principles that apply to all of them (a mistaken view I hasten to add, especially in the era of machine filing, which puts 10 before 2 and a space before a character).

## *SEARCH*

I recently watched a college graduate search the card-catalog in a library unfamiliar to him for two specific items the library did possess, without scoring a hit. One was a new acquisition—the on-order slip was filed under title and the patron had searched under author. This particular library at least had some access to new acquisitions not yet cataloged—not all research libraries do—however there were no signs to indicate how new acquisitions were filed, if at all. The reference librarian must act as interpreter. The second book in question was part of a series in which each volume had a unique author and title. The library had cataloged all the volumes as a series with no separate author/title access. Again, the reference librarian must intervene. The patron was about to leave the card-catalog, his search unsuccessful and the presumption being not that his searching techniques were inadequate but that the library holdings were. In statistical jargon, this would be labelled a Type I or alpha error—the rejection of a true hypothesis. However, most statistical analysts would agree that the card-catalog is a prime example of a Type II or beta error—the acceptance of a false hypothesis, the hypothesis being in this case the assumption that other people i.e., anybody not a cataloger, can understand what is going on in the card catalog. The patron was asked if he had looked for these items in the front as well as the back of the catalog drawer. The fact that this was a "piggyback" catalog had escaped his notice. The signs indicating this were placed on top of the catalog itself, above eye level. The dividers themselves in the catalog drawers were highly visible if that was what you were looking for, but failed to catch the eye of the unfocussed user.

Obviously, the piggyback catalog—one way of dealing with AACR2—is not completely successful. These examples just quoted should not reflect harshly on this particular library or any other. This is but an imperfect world, and few libraries have staff time to change tracings on several million cards and their automated counterparts. However, what these examples should reflect upon is the validity of the original cataloging decisions, made on a multinational level.

How many reference librarians were part of the nitty-gritty, decision making process during the revising of AACR? Of course, the Reference and Adult Services Division of ALA took part in the review process, but by that time certain concepts seemed to already have become engraved in stone.

Mary George and Sharon Hogan in their recent article on the card catalog ("What's 3 × 5 and full of holes?) quote the card-catalog as being "probably the single greatest obstacle to library research for all but the most experienced patrons."[3] They observed the response once given in answer to a question asked of prospective Reference/Bibliographic Instruction candidates—what is the most complicated reference tool to explain to users? The answer was " 'Why the catalog of course. Isn't it awful everywhere?' " It would seem that somewhere along the line we catalogers are falling down in at least one of our avowed goals—providing easy access to our library resources. Whatever else a card-catalog could or should provide, this at least it should do.

It is conceivable that the consequences of AACR2 were not envisaged in 1975, when C. Sumner Spalding, editor AACR 1967, commented "I doubt that general reference librarians and readers will find the cataloging under the new edition much changed in substance from present cataloging . . . That should greatly reduce cataloging costs in research libraries everywhere. Our readers will find it easier to use catalogs in foreign countries and their nationals will find it easier to use ours."[4] But have we achieved this objective, succinctly stated as the primary purpose of the ISBD(M), aiding the "international communication of bibliographic information," and if so, have we done it at the expense of the everyday patron of the card-catalog, the native as opposed to the foreign national?

## *NATURE OF THE JOB*

Because of the nature of the job, and the infra-structure within which a cataloger works, these conflicts are often shielded from the very people who, inadvertently or otherwise, cause them. We are all very quick to point out that a misfiled catalog card denies access to the patron, how about an overlooked or badly conceptualized access-point? The Library of Congress has recently discontinued the practice of not making title-added entries for works starting with the name of a person, the presumption having been that these works would be located under this name as a subject heading. Nobody would think to explain this to a patron looking for the book "Marilyn Monroe" in the Author/Title section of a non-dictionary catalog. Another Type I error.

According to Donald Davinson in his much-quoted book "The Reference Librarian", it is the job of the reference librarian "to comprehend the structures of recorded knowledge where they exist and assist in the structuring process where they do not."[5] They are in the position of being "the interface between the mass of recorded knowledge and the potential users of that knowledge to whom, at the start of their quest, the mass must often appear totally unstructured and unfathomable." Needless to say Mr. Davinson was not just speaking of the card-catalog. However, the card-catalog is often the first reference tool that patrons use when visiting the library, and they expect their experiences with it to provide an indication of how the library will be able to serve their individual needs. An incomplete or poor catalog does nothing to enhance the reputation of the library, misguides users and reference librarians alike, makes the latter look like mere fools and discourages use of the library.

Why are there so many conflicts? What are the larger issues that catalogers are struggling with, resulting in the morass of confusion that now purports to be a card-catalog?

One basic area of conflict is confusion over the function of the card-catalog. Is it a simple finding tool for the location of specific works, or a bibliographical instrument assembling groups of books under uniform headings? Should the card-catalog be regarded as a means of finding books, or a series of irreproachable bibliographical documents? There is a constant dichotomy. The Library of Congress and the cataloging codes tend to promulgate the latter view, thereby taking the catalogers with them. The reference librarian inclines to the view that patrons should be able to find what they want in the card-catalog with a minimum of help, especially on the one-to-one basis. This is perfectly natural, since if a reference librarian had to help with every request on this basic level, there would be no time to spend giving the in-depth service which is also part of the job. A catalog entry should never be a substitute for looking at the book.

Robert H. Burger, in his article on the decline of cataloging quality, discusses this problem—the fact that catalogers see cataloging as an end to a means instead of vice versa. As a cataloger himself, he brings up the fear that greater attention to the wrong kind of detail in cataloging in MARC format has become a "real subversion of the goal of cataloging: the best access possible to works via their author, title, or subject, broadly defined."[6] He cites the increased "emphasis on the channel of communication, on the format in which the cataloging information is communicated." For instance, more time is spent on trying to construct online authority files than on trying to improve the headings themselves.

## *STEPS TAKEN*

The Library of Congress in the last eighteen months, has taken steps to try to improve this situation. It has given a series of excellent three day Subject Headings Institutes throughout the nation, dealing with all facets of LCSH. Topics include history and basic application, special problems, free-floating subdivisions, geographical features, law headings and so on. The participants come away from these sessions with large red manuals (Redbooks perpetuated) explaining and giving examples of some of the idiosyncrasies of LCSH practice, and feeling that they are now privy to national secrets. Sometime in 1984 LC will be publishing a subject headings manual that will consist of most of the memos published as part of the Cataloging Service Bulletin, and also include most of their in-house memos. I hope they will pay especial attention to the index. It is very hard to justify looking in 25 different locations (Redbooks, updates, Microfiche, CSB etc.) when establishing or verifying subject headings.

One side effect of these Institutes is that the participants come away with possibly more knowledge and awareness of the intricacy of LCSH than we can deal with, especially when for most of us only a small portion of our day is spent dealing with subject headings. Few of us are allowed the luxury of concentrating on one facet of cataloging, itself only one small part of librarianship. When is a cancellation not a cancellation? When should the form subdivision PERIODICALS come before PLACE and not after? When the periodicals are not merely informative but contain scholarly legal articles. Has anybody told a reference librarian about this legal nicety, or indicated the scholarly differences in periodical content to a patron? How many times at the Subject Headings Institutes did we point out inconsistencies in corporate or other names used as subject headings, only to be told that this was because the heading had first been established by the descriptive catalogers at LC. Dividing up the world, as it is referred to "in-house", seems to be done rather unevenly. For instance, El Salvador contradicts the basic rule of not using initial articles for names of geographic entities because it was established by the descriptive catalogers and not the Board on Geographic Names. If catalogers themselves are overwhelmed by these details, where does this leave the reference librarian, and, in turn, the patron?

The misemphasis on bibliographical control instead of bibliographical access discussed by Mr. Burger may have a lot to do with the infinite possibilities that librarians see in online catalogs, and the misconception that computers save us time and money. Whilst ever catalog cards were handwritten, the entries were brief, to the point and limited in number. Now that there are no physical limits to the information we can put on a catalog card, or the number of access points we can give, we are defeating our original goals of time-saving and easy access.

## TOTAL CONTROL

In theory, the card-catalog will provide the basis for a totally automated, integrated system with the capability for total physical as well as bibliographical control of all items. One will always know where a book is—on-order, being cataloged, processed, shelved, whatever. Keeping total physical control of books in the short period before they go to the shelves may be an admirable goal, but is it worth it? Control is lost once the book is on open shelving and available for browsing, slipping behind larger books, dropping down the stacks and propping open the doors of graduate students' carrels. Do we really need all the bibliographical minutiae available in MARC format? Is it essential to the ability of the library to serve the patron better that we be able to produce, on demand, lists of technical reports in Korean and Polish published between 1970 and 1980? Are we generating too much "fake" or secondary information? Libraries are becoming known as information warehouses, but it seems that computer storage capacity for information about books is becoming more of a hotly discussed issue than physical storage space for the books themselves. However, it may be that the golden age of detailed bibliographical description is over. How many libraries have started to discuss minimum-level cataloging as an option for dealing with back-logs, reduced cataloging staff and the inability to keep up with current processing? LC has started minimum-level cataloging of selected materials, and is working with OCLC on ways to market these abbreviated records. It could be that catalogers have cataloged themselves out of business. If it becomes generally possible to access full texts online, what will become of catalogers and cataloging? The reference librarians of the future will be information retrieval specialists with not a catalog or cataloger left to bother them.

Meanwhile, back at the reference desk, the reference librarian must still perform his role as mediator. What can be done in view of these basic conflicts, to improve communication between catalogers and reference librarians and by extension, between reference librarians and patrons?

Firstly, there must be communication lines in existence between the two divisions before they can be improved. In some library situations there is very little contact at all. There have to be channels through which catalogers can express their frustration with these nitty-gritty issues, and through which the reference librarians can express their difficulties in interpreting the card-catalog to the patrons. These channels do not have to be formal—a joint goal of working together for the good of the patron should be enough.

The reference staff should form part of the decision-making process when important cataloging decisions or rule changes are made. A session on how the card-catalog works should be part of every new reference librarian's training program. He shouldn't just have to "muddle through". The reference staff should be involved in continuing staff orientations and refresher filing/revising sessions in the card-catalog. It is perfectly feasible for reference librarians to revise in the card-catalog whilst doing reference duty on quiet days at the desk, although the majority of reference librarians I have discussed this suggestion with are against it. I know of one exception to the general rule, and she is a part-time cataloger. However, it is one way for a reference librarian to look at a catalog drawer the same way a cataloger does, and helps to find those blind cross-references before they mislead a patron. Technical Services staff should make sure that new subject headings, cancellations, rule changes etc. are circulated to the reference staff. Do not expect the reference librarian to be avidly reading the latest edition of the CSB over a hurried cup of coffee. Be sensible, xerox or underline the most appropriate passages. Reference librarians should make an effort to attend these orientation/refresher sessions. It is no excuse that they have to be "on the desk", when 3 people are on the desk, 20 librarians on the reference staff and only 4 people attending the sessions. This is part of a prevailing attitude that the reference librarian has little to learn from his colleague in the basement. Both have a lot to learn from each other.

## *NEED FOR INVOLVEMENT*

By the same token, catalogers should be more involved in reference activities. If they knew how hard it was for a reference librarian to explain the library's definition of a serial and periodical, perhaps they would concentrate on ways of treating the two formats similarly rather than otherwise. Catalogers should participate in Bibliographic Instruction. It would give them some insight into how little basic knowledge of the card catalog an undergraduate brings with him into the library. Be wary though, in case the cataloger overwhelms the students with the peculiarities of this particular card-catalog and of AACR2 in general. That would be an excellent way to kill any desire a student might have for opening catalog drawers.

Reference librarians and catalogers alike should keep abreast of new developments which would help each other. For instance, the new CONSER Abstracting and Indexing Coverage project, which will be adding to the CONSER database information about title coverage by abstracting and indexing services, will be a big help to reference librarians and provide a needed link between library catalogs and A & I services.

Split positions—part-time reference librarian, part-time cataloger, is another way of improving the perspective each brings to his job. However, this concept tends to work better in smaller libraries where the degree of specialization is not as rigid or inbred. Many catalogers feel that if they had wanted to be reference librarians, that is what they would be, and the same from the reference librarian's standpoint. However, there are some librarians who enjoy cataloging, but also like some interplay with the general public and this kind of cross-over should be encouraged.

Communication should not be one-way i.e., catalogers telling the reference staff that because LC is changing a heading this is the way it is going to be. The reference librarian should feel free to make suggestions on cross-references, forms of entry, extra notes etc., anything they have noticed a patron lacks. After all, it is these things a cataloger never sees, and which can often make the difference between rendering a cataloger and his work useful or obstructionist. If a cataloger himself ever had to look up a conference proceedings, it is unlikely that he would have revised his cataloging procedures to have twenty five years of proceedings classified together and the subsequent twenty five years classified all over the ball park in the name of better bibliographical access.

Girja Kumar in his "Theory of Cataloging", said "A cataloger should feel satisfied, if the catalogue is able to meet the requirements of ordinary users".[7] How many of us can feel that satisfaction today?

## REFERENCES

1. Michael Gorman, "Osborn Revisited," *American Libraries*, November 1975.
2. William Shakespeare, *"As You Like It,"* I:2.
3. Mary George and Sharon Hogan, "What's 3 × 5 and Full of Holes?" *Research Strategies*, Summer 1983.

4. C. Sumner Spalding, "Notes from the Notable Editor, AACR, 1st Ed.," *American Libraries*, November 1975.

5. Donald E. Davinson, (1979) *"Reference Service."* C. Bingley, London.

6. Robert H. Burger, "Data definition & the decline of cataloging quality," *Library Journal,* October 15, 1983.

7. Girja Kumar, (1975), "Theory of Cataloging." Vikas Pub. House, Delhi.

# Conflicts Between Reference and Interlibrary Loan

Marcia L. Sprules

Budget cuts and reduced appropriations for new library materials in recent years have meant that libraries are only able to buy a small (and shrinking) percentage of the total number of new books (or other information sources) published per year. Therefore, it is increasingly likely that library users will need to request additional materials through interlibrary loan in order to satisfy their information needs. Many libraries have offered interlibrary loan to their borrowers for years and have a well-established method for dealing with such requests.

In spite of this experience, however, conflicts arise with distressing frequency between the reference staff who deal most directly and most often with the public and the interlibrary loan staff who will actually fill the request. Five areas seem to be the most frequent cause of conflict: copyright restrictions on what may be borrowed, bibliographic instruction vs. excessive reliance on interlibrary loan, fees for service in the so-called "Free Library," circulation restrictions, and document delivery delays which impinge upon the user's deadline. Reference librarians who handle these conflicts clumsily or inadequately may adversely affect the public impression of the library and undo previous efforts at public relations and marketing. This paper will point out the nature of these conflicts and the pitfalls which threaten the library if they are poorly handled.

## *COPYRIGHT*

A new responsibility has been placed on already hard-working interlibrary loan departments by the current U.S. copyright law, and the associated CONTU guidelines. As is well known, the library is

---

The author is Computer Assisted Bibliographic Service Coordinator, The University of South Dakota, Vermillion.

now limited to requesting no more than five recent articles from one journal title, if they were published within the preceeding five years. Books may be borrowed only if a copy is not available for purchase at a fair price. Clearly, these restrictions could result in a significant paperwork burden for the interlibrary loan staff if each request to borrow a book must be checked for availability at least in *Books in Print* and possibly in the catalogs of out-of-print specialists as well. The record keeping necessary to stay within the CONTU guidelines has added to the work necessary to fill a loan, but as the Register of Copyright report suggests, the record keeping is a bearable if burdensome task.[1]

Between the passage of the law in 1976 and its effective date of January 1, 1978, there were many educational materials published by the American Library Association, by state and regional associations, and by private groups. For the most part, this educational campaign was aimed at the interlibrary loan librarian, although the issue affects many more people than just them. Not all librarians read and absorbed the available information. Comments overheard at professional conferences within the past year or so suggest, however, that the educational effort has not been completely successful yet, that some librarians are only now realizing that "You know, that (copyright law) really has implications for my library!"

In any individual library, the person or persons who work with the copyright law most closely are probably the interlibrary loan staff (professional or technician). They are the ones who have the records of previous requests to borrow from a particular journal title, for example. It is very confusing to some poor student or borrower when the reference librarian at the desk suggests that the interlibrary loan office will be able to obtain an article, only to have the interlibrary loan person say that the quota has already been used up on that title. How is the patron to decide whom to believe? The reference librarian has probably established his/her credibility with the patron over many positive experiences at the desk. This conflict in the patron's mind may have the effect of undermining the credibility of the interlibrary loan staff, even though they are right in such a case. What does that do to the overall credibility of the library?

Reference librarians already have a great deal to keep up with in order to do their job well; they undoubtedly have myriad projects of their own to work on while away from the desk. Thus it is unreasonable to expect them to add copyright concerns to their list. It is enough to remember that most published material is probably protected by copyright, and therefore interlibrary loan may be restricted. The best reference service for a patron inquiring about interlibrary loan is a referral to the appropriate office. A good reference librarian provides referrals to appropriate community services; the same principle should apply to referrals within the library building.

There is an inherent conflict between authors and librarians, caused by the principle of copyright. Authors have a right, guaranteed by the Constitution, to the advantages of their work. In most cases, this means a right to receive royalties for the copies sold. Under our free-market economy, the publishers (and their shareholders) have the right to a profit if their product sells well. Librarians, on the other hand, believe that information is a public good and should be available to all citizens equally, regardless of ability to pay. The South Dakota Interlibrary Loan Code, under which I work, states that "It is the right of every South Dakotan, no matter where such citizen may live within the state, to have access to whatever that person wants, to read, view or hear and whatever that person wants to know within a reasonable time; . . ."[3] Such statements sound glorious, but do ignore the economics of information. Librarians would give away what the authors and publishers would sell.

Explained in these terms, it's no wonder that the publishers wanted a new law to replace the 1909 statute. And it is no wonder that they still feel hurt by the current statute and guidelines. The Register of Copyright's five-year review of the 1976 law very definitely sided with the publishers, against the librarians when it concluded: "Provision of nonreturnable photocopies in lieu of a true loan of the material requested is 'systematic' copying within the meaning of the statute."[2]

It is not always easy to keep the personal interests separate from the professional interests when discussing copyright and royalties. In hours away from the reference desk, librarians may also be authors, receiving royalties of their own. If the publishers cannot make the profit they desire, author-librarians will have no outlet for their writings. And where would libraries get their information sources if there were no (or fewer) publishers? Some librarians are also stockholders in publishing or other corporations, at least through a pension fund, collecting dividends paid from publishing profits. Under these circumstances, it is difficult to live up to the level of altruism expressed by the national and state library organizations. Reference librarians are accustomed to providing a specific fact out of a book for a library patron without thinking of royalties to the author or compiler of the book. This same mind-set seems to carry over to interlibrary loan.

## BIBLIOGRAPHIC INSTRUCTION

A new emphasis for some reference librarians (at least in academic libraries) has emerged over the last ten years or so. It is bibliographic instruction, the formal teaching of courses in library use by librarians. Orientation tours to new students (at all levels) have been an established feature in academic libraries for many more years. It is certainly fitting that such an introductory tour should mention that the library provides an interlibrary loan service. When this service is mentioned will often affect the student's impression of the entire library. If mention is made too early during the tour, the lecturer risks creating the impression that the library itself does not have much, that interlibrary loan will be of paramount importance to the student. If at the end, the listeners may have lost interest before then and not hear the remarks at all. My own preference is to mention interlibrary loan nearer the end, stressing resources in-house at the beginning of the tour.

When the week for writing term-papers arrives (as it must each semester), the librarians at the reference desk will soon know it. This is true in public libraries as well as in academic libraries. At such busy times it is difficult to give each question at the desk the attention that it requires. Other students clamor for help, and the telephone is probably ringing every few seconds. It's one of those days when there isn't enough staff to help everyone at once. One shortcut which is very tempting to the harried reference librarian is to suggest that the student request through interlibrary loan the first few references found in a periodical index or other printed bibliography. This allows the reference librarian to mark another question on the statistics sheet and turn attention to the next person waiting at the desk. It certainly makes the student happy, because he/she thinks that the research for the paper is now done.

But is this effective bibliographic instruction? Perhaps if the student looked through a few more years of the same periodical index, he/she might find listed articles that are available in the library. Perhaps another index would be equally appropriate to the topic;

perhaps there is a book in the reference collection that might help as well. Although explaining these other avenues means more work for both the librarian and the student, it is better for both in the long run. Good bibliographic instruction should help the student jump over the hurdles of unfamiliar information sources, not detour around them; only by doing so will he/she learn to use the library effectively.

The most blatant example of this point is the use of the *Reader's Guide to Periodical Literature* in the academic library. *Reader's Guide* is a very useful tool in some reference situations, but it is not appropriate for use by college students for research papers. Its attractions are many: students were used to using it in high school, it indexes magazine titles which are familiar to many readers, and in most cases the articles are short and not excessively difficult to read. But which is the better source for a paper on alcohol abuse: an article in a women's magazine from *Reader's Guide* or a paper from the *Journal of Alcohol Abuse*, indexed in *Social Sciences Index?* This ability to discern good sources and to recognize authority and bias is something which students should be cultivating. Because classroom faculty do not always take the time to teach this skill, the reference librarians have a responsibility (especially if they have faculty status) to foster such discernment. Therefore, to suggest that a student request copies of popular articles through interlibrary loan instead of changing to a more appropriate index is not in the student's best interest. It may make both feel good for the moment, but has no long-term benefit.

## *FEES FOR SERVICE*

Much has appeared in the professional literature in recent years on the subject of charging fees for extra services, such as interlibrary loan. It is not the purpose of this paper to contribute to that discussion, but merely to point out that charging fees will cause additional conflict. Reference librarians are used to providing their services without thinking of the cost. Patrons are used to thinking of their library as the (City) Free Public Library; many assume that the library has no costs or no budget, that the staff are all volunteers and that the books are donated. In years of straitened budgets, it is no longer possible to provide any service without considering the cost.

Many libraries charge the borrowing library a fee for interlibrary loan. It might be a standard transaction fee ($5 - $10), it might be

"Please reimburse postage," or it might be a per-page photocopy charge. Should the library absorb these charges, as well as its own labor and overhead, or should the person using the material pay? It is all well and good for the ALA Interlibrary Loan code to suggest that each library should absorb its own nominal charges, such as copying and postage; however, it is not always feasible to do so. since the issue is bound to come up eventually, it is well to discuss it now and set a formal policy.

Since the reference librarian is again unlikely to know which library charges how much or for what kind of services, it is dangerous to attempt to provide an estimate for the borrower. Instead, such questions should be referred to the ILL staff. There may still be ways of getting the material at low cost.

## *LENDING RESTRICTIONS*

Every library has collections that do not circulate. Often these include such materials as genealogical materials, local history or newspapers, doctoral dissertations, or masters theses. Location tools such as the *National Union Catalog* or the OCLC terminal do not indicate whether the title is in such a special collection. When verifying a title for a patron or checking for holdings, it is important that the reference librarian keep such possible restrictions in mind, though it is not necessary to explain them in full detail.

The interlibrary loan office probably has a notebook full of interlibrary loan policies for at least those libraries with whom they do a lot of business. If using the OCLC terminal to transmit and receive requests, the interlibrary loan office also has access to its online Name-Address Directory, and the up-to-date policies therein. For these reasons, it is unwise for the reference librarian (who does not have access to such information) to attempt to answer such availability questions. Even though he/she wants to appear helpful and knowledgeable to the borrower, the librarian who volunteers information that he/she does not have eventually hampers the service. A requestor whose loan is refused by another library despite what the reference librarian promised will not think as well of the library afterward. No reference librarian would dream of making up the answer to a question without checking it in an appropriate source first, but that is what you do when you promise availability too glibly for ILL requests.

Because the material may be unavailable at the first or closest library, it is important to convey to requestors a willingness to send the request to a second, or a third, or a fourth library in the hope that someone will eventually fill it, if time permits.

## DOCUMENT DELIVERY

Most people who request material are working under a time deadline (a paper due at the end of the semester, a business report due next week). Therefore, rapid document delivery is becoming increasingly important. Fourth class (library rate) mail delivery is no longer adequate for many requests. It is not unusual for a package containing ILL material to take three weeks to reach South Dakota from either coast if it is sent library rate. Such delays are difficult to absorb if the semester is only fifteen weeks long.

Because requestors are usually in a hurry for material, and because reference librarians are eager to accommodate requests, they may promise delivery within an unreasonable period of time. This is especially true if they believe that a nearby library owns the material needed. It is then left to the ILL staff to explain the delay: that the nearby library was not able to fill the request, that the package is not travelling first-class mail, that the other library may not be handling the request very quickly. It is understandable that the requestor will vent his/her fury at the only accessible link in the chain (his local ILL person). But the reference librarian also looks incompetent and unknowing in these cases. So in your own best interest, don't promise too much. It may come back to haunt you.

Commercial information brokers and document delivery specialists greatly extend the reach of the ILL office. When time is of the essence or the request cannot be easily verified, it is a boon for all to send them to the commercial broker and get on with the other, easier ones yourself. These firms really do work miracles in delivering copies of obscure material. But these services are in business as a profit-making venture, and charge for their services. It may bother some ILL requestors to pay for an outside vendor to provide service that the library provides *gratis*. But if information is a valuable good, then perhaps expectations that it can be provided at no cost to the consumer are unreasonable. Where the library once absorbed all the delivery costs, it now passes on the real consumer the extraordinary costs.

## CONFLICT RESOLUTION

There is always a conflict between the ideal reference service that we would like to provide and the external constraints imposed upon the library. Examples of these constraints are budgetary appropriations and reductions, civil service or other hiring requirements, or Board of Trustees policies. None of these will go away, whether ignored or acted upon. The first step toward better service (if that is what we all want) is simply to talk to each other and to establish some service priorities.

Interlibrary loan is itself an answer to some of the constraints and conflicts which the library faces. Since limited budgets make it impossible for any given library to have in-house all materials that its registered borrowers could ever want, some method of obtaining these esoteric materials, other than purchasing them, is necessary in order to stretch the budget dollars as far as possible. Therefore, interlibrary loan must be thought of as an extension of the reference desk, providing borrowers another method of access to information. Viewed in this light, there should not be much conflict between reference and interlibrary loan.

It is the abuse of the system that leads to conflicts and to problems. In order to minimize these abuses, I have found it helpful if the interlibrary loan librarian is a member of the reference staff, possibly serving scheduled hours at the public desk and seeing what borrowers actually know (or don't know) about interlibrary loan and libraries generally.

Several years ago we had in this library a problem of vacation schedules, with both full-time interlibrary loan people gone during the same week. One of the other reference librarians (who has a nine-month contract and would not ordinarily work in July) came in half-days for two weeks to keep a rudimentary service open. After only two weeks of coping with a random sample of interlibrary loan problems, she commented how valuable the experience had been and how she had never realized how much was involved in the interlibrary loan process. It is very easy for each of us to get so involved in our own myriad responsibilities that we dismiss as trivial problems in other departments of the library. Perhaps an occasional short-term change in assignments for the librarians, on a planned basis rather than an emergency ad hoc basis, would help rejuvenate sagging morale and provide a better perspective on the library as a whole system.

## *CONCLUSION*

Due to staff shortages and budget reductions over recent years, all library employees (professional as well as clerical) are being asked to do more than ever before, more than is possible in the standard work week. It is all too easy for each staff member to assume that he/she is the only one working so hard. Short-term job exchanges may help each person realize what the other department is doing and how it benefits the library's users. There should be no conflict between reference and interlibrary loan, as both offices provide users with the information and materials they require.

## REFERENCES

1. *Library Reproduction of Copyrighted Works (17 U.S.C. 108)* Report of the Register of Copyrights. Washington, D. C., GPO, 1983. p. 136.
2. *Ibid.* p. 94, 99, 139.
3. *South Dakota Interlibrary Loan Code.* Pierre, S. D.: South Dakota State Library [and] South Dakota Library Association, 1979. p. 5.

# Check Your Catalog Image

Marcia J. Myers

Academic institutions issue catalogs designed for use by prospective and current students which explain the facilities of the institution, its philosophy, its programs, its staff, and its organization. This article indicates there is a significant relationship between the catalog image of library services and performance on fact-type queries asked via telephone. Reference librarians can examine the information about the library contained by the institution's catalog as a simple, practical step in the evaluation of reference services. Since the catalog is a primary vehicle of information for academic students, an appropriate description of the library could help in projecting a positive image of the library's philosophy, collections, and services.

Reference work is one of the most difficult aspects of library services to evaluate; yet, librarians are faced with an increasing need to assess the effectiveness of these services. The controversial national "Developmental Guidelines" for reference/information services do not suggest minimum levels of performance.[1] Consequently, we have progressed very little since 1964, when Samuel Rothstein noted: "Evaluation presupposes measurement against a specific standard or yardstick or goal, and no area of library service has been more deficient in such standards than reference services."[2]

Studies of reference services usually indicate that patrons are well pleased; user satisfaction is frequently above 80 or 90 percent. Librarians report that they are answering better than 90 percent of all questions; however, data from unobtrusive measurement studies indicate that there is reason to suspect these findings.[3] Unobtrusive studies using contrived observations, when the subjects were not aware that their performance was being observed, provide evidence

---

Dr. Myers is the Associate Director of Libraries for Administrative Services at the University of Tennessee Library, Knoxville.

© 1985 by The Haworth Press, Inc. All rights reserved.

that only about half of the reference questions are answered correctly.

The first major test of reference/information services performance using proxies posing as patrons was conducted by Terence Crowley in 1968.[4] Crowley's methodology was to simulate actual reference conditions by using in-person and telephone fact-type queries in twelve medium-sized public libraries in New Jersey. Sixty-five of the analyzed responses, or 54 percent, were considered correct.

Most recently, in their unobtrusive study of reference services for government publications, Charles R. McClure and Peter Hernon used seventeen academic government depository libraries and twenty in-person or telephoned questions. They found a 37 percent overall rate of accuracy in answering test questions.[5]

The unobtrusive data used in this article was collected using twelve fact-type queries in forty academic libraries. There is 95 percent confidence that the population of 361 academic libraries in nine southeastern states would have given the correct responses to the twelve-query performance test 49 percent of the time ($\pm 1.5$ percent).[6]

Unobtrusive measurement studies of reference services are numerous[7] compared to studies of the image of the library as portrayed in the institution's catalog. The catalog image has been examined in the community college setting by Mari Ellen Leverence,[8] Doris Cruger Dale,[9] and Lynn C. Dennison.[10]

## *LEVERENCE STUDY*

Leverence examined the catalogs from 47 colleges listed by the Illinois Community College Board using a checklist form she developed. The rating scale used assigned one point if the library was listed in the index, one point if the library was listed on the table of contents page, and two points for a description of more than 225 words. An additional two points were given if the catalog description showed evidence of reflective thinking and included something on the philosophy of the library, services to students, the professional library staff, etc. The highest possible point score was six; a score of four points was considered a favorable image. Leverence found that only 10 of the 47 institutions, or 21.3 percent, presented a favorable image of the library according to her rating scale. Thirteen institutions, or 27.7 percent, scored zero points on the rating scale.

Among other findings Leverence discovered that a higher percentage of colleges ranking the library director with the administration rather than with the faculty did have a favorable image of the library in their institution's catalog. She did not feel that her findings were conclusive because there was a trend in all of the catalogs to list the staff in alphabetical order regardless of whether they were classified as clerical, faculty, or administration. Leverence also points out that very little literature is available dealing with catalogs and their potential uses as advertising and educational tools, or their success or failure at communicating.

Dale used a slightly revised version of Leverence's scale in her study of twenty-nine community college libraries in six states. One point was assigned if the library was listed in the index; one point if the description was under 225 words; two points if the description was over 225 words; and two points if the description included some information on services, philosophy, and/or staff. The highest possible score was six points and none of the twenty-nine libraries received this score. Three libraries were not even mentioned in the college catalog and only eight libraries, or 27.6 percent, scored four or more points. Dale felt that community college librarians failed to take advantage of the institution's catalog as a means of communicating with prospective students.

## DENNISON STUDY

Dennison studied twenty catalogs from community colleges in ten states. One point was assigned if the learning resource program was listed in the table of contents; one point if it was listed in the index; one point if the description was under 225 words; two points if the description was over 225 words; and two points if the description included information on services, philosophy, and/or staff. The highest number of points was six. Four institutions, or 20 percent, had six points; two institutions, or 10 percent, earned zero points. Twelve of the twenty institutions, or 60 percent, were given a catalog rating of four or more points.

Dennison found that those community colleges that provided a greater degree of separation of materials and card catalogs and that organized their staffs on basis of form, clientele, or geography (as opposed to function) earned lower scores (zero to three points) in the rating of information in the institution's catalog. She points out that the college catalog as currently used may not be a good indicator of the level of services provided by the learning resources program and that all the institutions visited furnished other types of materials for promoting their learning resources services.

## PROCEDURES

The population, defined as academic libraries in nine southeastern states which had more than partial data available in the 1975 Library General Information Survey (LIBGIS), was extracted by the staff at the National Center for Education Statistics using the EDSTAT II data files. The investigator placed additional constraints on this population which was limited to 361 institutions which were not specialty colleges, had at least two staff members with a graduate degree, and which did not have a predominantly black student body.

A disproportionate stratified random sample of libraries was drawn and responses from forty academic libraries to fact-type queries asked via telephone were subjected to final analysis. The twelve fact-type queries and the percentage of correct responses are presented in Appendix A.

The queries were randomized for each institution as to day of week and time of day within dates and times the institution was open for a normal academic term. The institution's catalog was obtained prior to the telephoning of the test queries to determine term beginning and ending dates, official holidays, and other events.

Half-hour intervals between 9:00 a.m. and 3:30 p.m. Mondays through Fridays were selected as the time for the initial contacts, since all types of academic libraries were likely to be open for full service during these hours. The queries were telephoned to each of the libraries at the rate of one query every other week beginning February 1977 and ending in December 1977. The queries were asked in the same order at each library during approximately the same week. While the length of the data collection period may have introduced some bias, any contaminations were probably offset by a longer period between queries. Many sample academic libraries would probably have become aware of the test situation if the queries had been asked at more frequent intervals.

Since all institutions in the sample had either a coed or female student body, only white female proxies were used. If asked, each proxy indicated that she was a student at the institution.

Only those responses received in nonreactive manner were subjected to final analysis. Twelve fact-type queries with predetermined short answers were telephoned to forty academic libraries. Each correct answer was scored as one point; no points were given for partially correct or incorrect answers. The lowest possible number of points using this method was zero; the highest possible number of points was twelve.

The catalog from each institution was examined and evaluated using a rating scale developed by the investigator. One point was assigned if the library or learning resources center was listed in the table of contents; one point if it was listed in the index; one point if the description was longer than 225 words; one point if the description mentioned reference services, reference staff, reference collections, or reference philosophy.

Four points were assigned to rank the placement of the description within the institution's catalog. Zero points were given if there was no description; one point was given if there was information on the library placed with the description of the institution's building, grounds or other physical features and facilities; two points were assigned if the library description was placed with general information on the university, college, or campus life; three points were assigned if the description on the library was placed with academic information; four points were assigned if the library information was given a separate listing. The lowest possible number of points using the rating scale was zero; the highest possible number of points was eight.

## FINDINGS

### Reference Performance Test

Table 1 details the scores from the twelve-query reference performance test. The highest score was nine correct, or 75 percent, the lowest score was three correct, or 25 percent. Twenty-seven of the forty institutions, or 67.5 percent, scored six or more points. The median reference performance score was 6.14.

As indicated in Appendix A, the queries used in this study were not particularly difficult, yet no library answered all twelve correctly. Performance was poorest on queries which could not be easily answered with the usual tools. There was also evidence that even

TABLE 1
REFERENCE PERFORMANCE SCORES

| Points Earned | Number of Institutions | Percent of Institutions |
|---|---|---|
| 9 | 2 | 5.0 |
| 8 | 5 | 12.5 |
| 7 | 9 | 22.5 |
| 6 | 11 | 27.5 |
| 5 | 5 | 12.5 |
| 4 | 6 | 15.0 |
| 3 | 2 | 5.0 |

when the library owned the appropriate scores, staff members either did not consult, did not know how to use, or misinterpreted the information given in the scores. Analysis using additional data indicated that the two independent variables which accounted for the most variation (56 percent) in the number of correct responses were the number of volumes in the reference collection and number of hours per week that reference services were offered.

### Catalog Image Rating

Table 2 details the ratings of information from the institution's catalog. Two institutions, or 2.5 percent, received zero scores. Six of the forty institutions, or 15.0 percent, scored 5 or more points; thirteen, or 32.5 percent, scored 4 or more points. One institution received a perfect score of eight. This institution was also one of the two institutions which scored nine, or 75 percent correct, on the twelve-query performance test. The median catalog image score was 2.7.

### Relationship Between Reference Performance and Catalog Image

Spearman rank-order correlations were used to test the relationship between the score on the twelve fact-type queries and the catalog image score. The results of these rank-order correlations are displayed in Table 3. The overall catalog image score (eight points) correlated with the performance score (.45) at the .04 level of significance. The component of the catalog image score which correlated the highest with the performance score (.51) was when the library or learning resources center was mentioned in the table of contents. Other good indicators of the score on the performance test

TABLE 2
CATALOG IMAGE SCORES

| Points Earned | Number of Institutions | Percent of Institutions |
|---|---|---|
| 8 | 1 | 2.5 |
| 7 | 1 | 2.5 |
| 6 | 2 | 5.0 |
| 5 | 2 | 5.0 |
| 4 | 7 | 17.5 |
| 3 | 9 | 22.5 |
| 2 | 5 | 12.5 |
| 1 | 11 | 27.5 |
| 0 | 2 | 5.0 |

TABLE 3
RANK ORDER CORRELATION MATRIX FOR THE INDIVIDUAL CATALOG IMAGE COMPONENTS
AND THE TOTAL CATALOG IMAGE SCORES

| | R.P.S. | T.C. | I. | D.L. | D. R. | D. P. | T.C.I.S. |
|---|---|---|---|---|---|---|---|
| Reference Performance Score | . . . | | | | | | |
| Table of Contents | .51* | . . . | | | | | |
| Index | .39* | -.03 | . . . | | | | |
| Description Length | .31* | .39* | .27* | . . . | | | |
| Description Mentions Reference | .01 | .00 | .17 | .44* | . . . | | |
| Description Placement | .43* | .45* | .39* | .54* | .38* | . . . | |
| Total Catalog Image Score | .45* | .44* | .58* | .79* | .57* | .87* | . . . |

* $p \leq .05$

were the description placement (.43), having the library or learning resources center listed in the index (.17), and the fact that the description was over 225 words (.31). That is, those library or learning resources centers, with a long description, were also those more likely to perform higher on the performance test.

## *IMPLICATIONS*

This study shows there is a significant relationship between the performance on fact-type queries and the image of the library or learning resources center as portrayed in the institution's catalog. It would be ludicrous to suggest that reference librarians could improve their performance by improving the image of the library or learning resources center in the catalog. However, the image should be examined since it is obviously a good proxy measure of performance. The placement and length of the library's description in the catalog and its listing in the table of contents and index may very well reflect the institutional view of the library or learning resources center.

A separate description and listing of the library or learning resources center in the institution's catalog is a desirable feature. Library or learning resources centers which are listed in the institution's catalog table of contents, index, or have a description exceeding 225 words are more likely to score higher in a performance test. You should check your catalog image and see if it is properly informing your students about your library's or learning resources center's philosophy, collections, staff and services.

## REFERENCES

1. American Library Association, Reference and Adult Services Division, Standards Committee, "A Commitment to Information Services: Developmental Guidelines," *RQ* 18 (Spring 1979):275-78.

2. Samuel Rothstein, "The Measurement and Evaluation of Reference Service," *Library Trends* 12 (January 1964):459.

3. Terry L. Weech, "Evaluation of Adult Reference Services," *Library Trends* 22 (January 1974):331.

4. Terence Crowley and Thomas Childers, *Information Service In Public Libraries: Two Studies* (Metuchen, New Jersey: Scarecrow, 1971).

5. Charles R. McClure and Peter Hernon, *Improving the Quality of Reference Service for Government Publications* (Chicago: American Library Association, 1983).

6. Marcia J. Myers and Jassim M. Jirjees, *The Accuracy of Telephone Reference/Information Services in Academic Libraries: Two Studies* (Metuchen, New Jersey: Scarecrow, 1983).

7. See for example the following studies: Crowley and Childers; McClure and Hernon; Myers and Jirjees; Geraldine B. King and Rachel Berry, *Evaluation of the University of Minnesota Libraries Reference Department Telephone Information Service: Pilot Study* (Minneapolis: University of Minnesota Library School, 1973). ERIC Document Reproduction Service, ED 077 517; David E. House, "Reference Efficiency or Reference Deficiency." *Library Association Record 76* (November 1974):222-23; Thomas A. Childers, "The Test of Reference," *Library Journal,* 105 (April 15, 1983):924-28; Terry L. Weech and Herbert Goldhor, "Obtrusive versus Unobtrusive Evaluation of Reference Service in Five Illinois Public Libraries," *Library Quarterly* 52 (October 1982):305-324.

8. Mari Ellen Leverence, "Images of Illinois Junior College Libraries as Portrayed in College Catalogs," (M.S. research report, Southern Illinois University, Carbondale, 1974).

9. Doris Cruger Dale, "Questions of Concern: Library Services to Community College Students," *Journal of Academic Librarianship* 3 (May 1977):81-84.

10. Lynn C. Dennison, "The Organization of Library and Media Services in Community Colleges," *College and Research Libraries* 39 (March 1978):123-29.

APPENDIX A

PERCENTAGE OF CORRECT RESPONSES TO TWELVE TEST QUERIES

| Percent Correct (N = 40) | Query |
| --- | --- |
| 30.0 | What is the symbol for a population mean? |
| 90.0 | What are the names of the books that make up Lawrence Durrell's Alexandrian tetralogy? |
| 25.0 | Who said something like: the naive and the beautiful have no enemy but time? |
| 7.5 | Who is the President of the American Society for Information Science? |
| 40.0 | What is the Zip Code for Behrend College in Erie, Pennsylvania? |
| 87.5 | When did China orbit its first satellite? |
| 65.0 | Is the book Albert Einstein and the Cosmic World Order by Cornelius Lanczos recommended for laymen? |
| 10.0 | What is the address of Mexico City College? |
| 72.5 | Who is the President of the American Library Association? |
| 85.0 | Who were the stars in the 1960 Broadway Production of Camelot? |
| 55.0 | Where is the nearest airport to Warren, Pennsylvania? |
| 37.5 | Who said: "There are two good things in life, freedom of thought and freedom of action"? |

# Uneven Reference Service: Approaches for Decreasing This Source of Conflict at the Reference Desk

Fred Batt

Psychological definitions of "conflict" typically connote a state of indecision which occurs when an individual is influenced simultaneously by two opposing forces of approximately equal strength. The person is motivated to engage in two or more mutually exclusive activities such as approaching or avoiding a goal.

The reference desk provides a vehicle for a variety of conflicts. In my opinion, the major stimulus for conflict is uneven reference service. It is my contention that uneven service at reference desks is a painful reality for heads of college and university reference departments as well as members of the academic communities who depend on this primary library service point. (Most unobtrusive testing research seems to point to a 50-60% accuracy rate.) It creates conflict for patron, librarian and supervisor alike.

Patrons have to decide which person to approach at the desk, if they decide to approach the desk at all. The oldest? The youngest? The one who helped before? The one who couldn't help before? The one with the smile? The one with a built-in frown? The gay one? The sexy one? The male? The female? The one using the computer? The one looking too busy to bother? The one staring into space? The one working on a crossword puzzle? Just asking a question can cause trauma for some individuals. They have to decide not only what they need to ask, but how to ask it and whom to ask. A naive freshman might not have a feel for expectations at a reference desk situation. We've all heard, "Excuse me, I'm sorry, this may sound stupid, but where can I find . . . ?" A naive professor might

---

Mr. Batt is Head of the Reference Department, Bizzell Memorial Library, University of Oklahoma, Norman, 73019.

flounder for hours in the reference collection before getting up the gumption to approach a perceived inferior and perhaps appear fallible. Without even considering that the service may be uneven or perhaps inaccurate, the reference desk is fraught with potential conflict. Reference desk personnel can experience conflict simply because they have to serve the public, often under less than ideal situations. Conflict can also stem from having to work in close proximity as well as cooperatively with others of varying effectiveness. Supervisors' conflict can arise from having to decide how to most effectively staff the public areas as well as train and motivate reference staff to provide accurate service.

## The Desk

Reference and/or information desk(s) usually mirror the library. For patrons, it is a reflection of the effectiveness of the library system. It is where you find out where information is, what services are offered, who to contact, etc. Patrons should be able to expect reliable service. What happens at this central library service point can have a great impact on patron perceptions as well as success of library programs. A sourpuss at the reference desk can be destructive. A negative image can undo much good service. Alber notes that "Nothing is more damaging to success than uncooperative or unqualified employees."[1] Anthony writes that "Competent managers become slaves to incompetent people. Ignoring incompetence does not make it go away . . . it is an issue to be faced head-on in a no-nonsense fashion." He believes that "Human behavior at work can be managed. Within limits, people can be influenced, guided, controlled and directed. Deciding exactly what steps to take to change behavior is not always easy."[2]

How can I effectively improve performance of a tenured librarian who has been at reference desks for nearly as long as I've lived, prefers not to partake in some aspect of reference services, and has already heard most of my brilliant ideas innumerable times from the previous dozen reference heads? How can I help the librarian who displays symptoms of burnout? How can I work with the new librarian who is secretly petrified at being left alone at the reference desk backed by thousands of reference sources which he/she never saw in library school. How can I cope with what Rutledge described as "Rigor mortis" in the library. She noted that "Indeed, the deadliest job on a campus is often in the library . . . The situation is this: the high cost of energy and housing together with the cutbacks occurring rapidly on college campuses have resulted in the academic truism of the 1980's—a no-movement, stable faculty." Rutledge calls them "permanent librarians."[3]

## Horizons

Some librarians have not broadened their horizons for years. Some display a knack for making easy questions difficult and difficult questions too easy. Some are "down" because of the inherent nature of their work. Many studies have demonstrated that 50-80% if not more of questions answered by reference librarians are simply directional or informational. It can get tiring over the years. For example, Kok and Pierce demonstrated at their institution that only a fifth of 14,000+ questions fell in the reference category and only 0.7% required research away from the desk by a professional librarian.[4]

Some reference desk personnel may function well with little pressure but tend to fall apart when all three phone lines ring precisely at the same time that two irate faculty members, three seniors (entering the library for the first time with a paper due yesterday), and a large dog all converge at the reference desk. Some librarians begin quaking in their shoes when a specific type of question appears, e.g., a nice juicy business question, or online access to citation indices. Some librarians lack the extra dose of motivation to learn something beyond the minimum, e.g. they can sit next to an OCLC or RLIN terminal for months at a time but never really master much beyond basic search techniques. Many other reasons for ineffective service are possible such as poorly organized reference areas, inadequate reference collections, lack of leadership, and even misuse of the reference desk, e.g. the librarian who considers himself/herself "on stage" when at the desk, or strives for great "traffic control" at the expense of helping patrons with research tools and techniques, or attempts to use the desk for social reasons.

Individual differences are a potent psychological variable. Quite simply some people do certain things better than others. Different librarians excel at different aspects of reference desk service, e.g. knowledge of sources, communication abilities, teaching abilities, stamina, situational responsiveness, reactions to stress, ability to not let personal biases influence service, etc. Also, different personality types perform better in certain environments than others. For example, Caplan and Jones believe that "employees with Type A traits would be of great value to organizations devoted to productivity and achievement." However, it is noted that this may be "at some cost to their own mental and physical health."[5]

## Effective Librarian

I'd love to see the most effective librarian at the desk during all hours that the library is open, e.g. the one who best analyzes and gets to the root of questions, is pleasant, knows when and how to refer, and efficiently selects the most correct sources to fill a request. I would never experience that horrible feeling of helplessness when I'm not certain who is doing what at the reference desk; an alarming sort of freefloating anxiety because I really have little control over the quality of the service at a given moment. With a variety of styles and levels of expertise among the variety of librarians (reference and non-reference), classified staff, graduate assistants, students and even administrators caught by patrons in the vicinity of the reference desk, there may simply be too many potential variables to effectively accomplish quality control.

This paper will provide suggestions for activities and strategies which may improve the quality of reference desk service. Some of these items may reinforce things already being done. Some might provide ideas to consider. Some may not work in specific situations. Some should be applicable to all situations. The ultimate goal is to increase the quality of reference desk service by creating the best possible physical and psychological environment. This increase in quality control should ultimately alleviate some of the conflict routinely built in to the reference desk situation for librarians, supervisors and patrons.

## Counteracting Library Frustrations

No matter how hard we try, libraries are fraught with frustration. Frustrated patrons lead to frustrated librarians and ultimately decreases in service effectiveness. Few libraries can afford added copies of everything in demand. No reference desk can completely anticipate when the mad rush will occur, e.g. a student who just waited in a long line to drop a course followed by a long line to eat a crummy lunch will start to get irritated while waiting in line to find out why a reference book which does not circulate is not on the shelf, tables or to-be-shelved areas. Reserve restrictions also can get patrons angry, e.g. the student who needs to take out a specific book but finds that the book is on reserve for a different professor and he's fifth in line just to get his hands on it. Malfunctioning copy machines can lead to anger. Mutilation and theft problems can create severe frustrations. When some lazy so-and-so razors out the desired abstract from *Psychological Abstracts,* both the patron and librarian are ready to throw hands up in despair and scream. A professor assigning 200 students to do the same assignment in the same source usually can devastate a reference service. The existence of branch libraries can usually get a patron mumbling expletives. Pity the poor night student who needs five books which are in three different libraries at three different ends of the campus. Two are closed in the evenings. Anything we can do to decrease frustrations can only improve the service we offer at the desk. We should try to anticipate when duplication of sources would make life easier for many patrons. We should be ready with alternatives when an initial strategy hits a roadblock. We should work carefully with faculty producing library assignments to avoid frustration-producing situations. We should provide free online access to remedy information that is not available, e.g. a quick, cheap search can print a ripped-out abstract. We should have logical explanations for why things are done the way they are done. If our explanations are not logical, we should strive to change the procedures.

## *Quick Fixes of Experience*

One truism that I find for reference services is that there is no substitute for experience. Reference supervisors should strive to offer a variety of inputs in order to speed up experience with resources and strategies. Each regular department meeting could have a segment which discusses "reference sources of the month/week." These can be new sources which appear particularly useful, sources in demand for particular assignments, or sources which can be used more effectively and deserve review. Inexperienced librarians should be offered extra training and enrichment by being scheduled at the desk with each other librarian so that he/she can see different styles in action and benefit from the varying subject expertise. Initial training of a new librarian should be spread about the reference staff. Other special enrichment or review sessions for all reference staff should be periodically scheduled for difficult and/or important sources, e.g. citation indices, Oscar Buros publications, online database review, etc. Also, all new reference books (except continuations) should be placed at or near the reference desk for perusal by all reference desk personnel prior to being shelved.

Ongoing training should be part of the job. Much research has demonstrated that staff performance can be improved through in-service education. If anything, this provides staff members an opportunity to interact with each other in a hopefully more relaxed situation.

## Job Enrichment

One would assume that job enrichment (i.e. making jobs more complex and challenging) would have positive effects on overall performance. Not all research completely supports this theory. Some people respond better to enrichment than others. Oldham, Hackman and Pearce demonstrated that employees with strong growth needs who are also satisfied with the work context (i.e. pay, security, supervision, etc.) respond more positively to enriched jobs than do employees with weak needs for growth and/or less satisfaction with work context.[6] Other research I've examined has demonstrated that the possible benefits of job enrichment are enormous, but there are many pitfalls. Job enrichment should be attempted with care.

## Empathy

Train librarians in empathy. Librarians should be reminded that just because they have explained the use of specific indices thousands of times doesn't mean that the next confused patron doesn't deserve as careful and considerate an explanation as their first.

## Difficult Situation Training

Special training should be considered for handling difficult situations such as extremely busy times or difficult patrons. This can include effective telephone strategies, delegation techniques, effective use of available student assistants, reference interview procedures under pressure, quick online access, etc.

## Listening and Communication Skills

Promote the development of important listening and communication skills via seminars, papers, articles or other available vehicles.

## Time Management

Promote awareness and development of time management techniques as well as general organizational skills. The weights and strains brought on by poor organizational skills can have negative impacts on reference desk effectiveness. Someone who has learned how to effectively manage time will be more apt to better manage the reference desk.

## Current Awareness

Provide library staff easy access to library science information by either routing selected journals and/or pointing out specific articles that relate to reference services. If routing is not feasible, consider routing photocopied table of contents pages on a monthly or quarterly basis or published current awareness services.

## Clarify Expectations

Everyone scheduled at the reference desk should have no doubt as to what is expected, what is not acceptable, and how to go about fulfilling expectations. This goes hand in hand with the next item.

## Reference/Information Services Policy Manual

One effective way to communicate expectations is to have an up-to-date policy manual. In my opinion, one should not get too carried away with every gory detail of every possible reference services option. Instead a well-organized short treatment of major policies and procedures should adequately convey the flavor of what is to be accomplished. Myers and Jirjees study on accuracy of telephone reference/information services in academic libraries noted that poor performances "suggest the need for reference/information service policy for academic libraries. Such a written policy would enable the reference staff members to have a clearer concept of what they are trying to do and how they are to do it."[7] This manual could include items ranging from procedures to ethical considerations.

## Updater, Card File

Recent information should be conveyed to all reference desk personnel in a looseleaf "Updater." This should be required reading for each staff member coming on duty and can include information about current assignments, new regulations or policy changes, potential problems, missing items to keep an eye out for, etc. Many "Updater" items eventually become incorporated in the "Reference Manual." A card file of frequently asked and/or difficult questions can also be maintained.

## Emergency Procedures Manual

Separate from reference policies, this manual should be close at hand and succinctly describe the responsibilities of the reference area (as well as other areas) in the event of anticipated emergencies.

## Reference Desk Online Access

OCLC and RLIN have proven to be exceedingly valuable sources for a variety of reference desk uses. I believe every library should also have a high speed printer with access to one or more of the search service vendors at the reference desk. With only a small budget, librarians can use their discretion to do short and free (to the patron) quick reference searches when warranted, e.g. garbled citations, recent terminology, obscure subjects, difficult combinations of terms, etc. This provides excellent public relations, brings guaranteed success to the reference desk, and improves and speeds up access to difficult-to-find information. This service can be separate from the library's regular search service. A special phone line or jack can be installed for this purpose rather than disrupting reference desk phone service.

## Interdepartmental Communications

It is quite frustrating for a patron to receive misinformation about library services. Accurate information about policies and procedures of all library areas should be shared and updated so that staff at public service locations do not misinform.

## User Surveys

Collecting data on effectiveness of service can often uncover problems that you aren't aware of or even provide support for changes you wish to make. Strong writes that

> Well-defined goals and objectives, a plan for data collection, analysis of the data, and the guts to change the service when the data indicate change is needed are the components that will contribute to the improvement of a library's . . . service.[8]

## Suggestion Box Program

This is another effective way of improving service library-wide as well as offering a potentially excellent public relations tool. With a comprehensive suggestions box program, patrons can be provided a vehicle for voicing their opinions, suggesting library resources, complaining or even complimenting. Well placed suggestion boxes with forms for patrons to fill out (including optional space for name, address and telephone) serve many positive functions. An ongoing display can provide selected questions and answers. Any patron signing their name can be individually answered by mail or phone by the person on the library staff in the best position to treat the problem (perhaps filtered through a public services administrator when necessary or sensitive). A periodic report of suggestions, responses, library modifications, etc. can be made to library staff, relevant library committees, etc. This kind of a system essentially says "We are accountable here." As an offshoot, it even provides the library staff with more than an occasional chuckle.

## Name and/or Position Tags

I believe that patrons have a right to know who they are dealing with; if not by name, at least by function, e.g. reference librarian, graduate assistant, classified staff, student assistant. These tags should be worn at least minimally when a person is scheduled at the desk.

## Handouts, Library Guides, Pathfinders

Many questions can be answered simply by creating a series of library guides. One possible series might include: a general guide providing an overview of major library programs, services, hours, etc.; a guide geared specifically to finding books; a guide geared specifically to finding periodical articles; and a variety of other guides each elaborating on a specific program or service, e.g. online searching, ILL, microforms, etc. Subject and function oriented guides are also useful, e.g. floor plans, using citation indices, how to find book reviews, reference sources on specific subjects, etc.

## Knowledge of Expertise

With effective referral an important aspect of any reference service, we should consider collecting and maintaining a file of people in the university community with particular expertise. A prime example is a language inventory.

## Logical Desk Schedules

Anything that can be done to place a less effective reference staff member capable of improvement in a situation where observation of effective reference desk work is possible should be attempted. If you use a variety of levels of staff members at the desk, avoid scheduling just non-professionals without at least having the available reference librarian back-up close at hand. Avoid scheduling anyone for long stretches. Attempt to plan the level of staffing to coordinate with expectations of busyness based on statistics which reflect the number and nature of interactions. Things start to go haywire when there are too many people wanting service from too few staff. Try to standardize a desk schedule for a specific time period, e.g. semester, so that librarians can organize their activities.

## Team Philosophy

Try to foster a team approach at the desk where referral is encouraged. This support structure is crucial since no one person knows everything. Asking for help and advice should be considered a positive behavior rather than a sign of weakness.

## Desk Organization

The reference area should be arranged in a logical fashion with frequently used sources in sight and often-consulted online access, e.g. internal online catalog, OCLC, etc. also close at hand. Reference desk staff should leave the desk in order, with questions in progress not lost in the shuffle, quick reference sources back into place, etc. The reference collection should be maintained by frequent student assistant reshelving and shelf-reading assignments staggered throughout the day. It should not be beyond the librarians to reshelve, pick up and straighten when things get out of hand during busy periods.

One ideal organization for a busy library: patrons and service might benefit most from a system with two clearly marked desks for specific activities so that information/directional questions are diverted to one area and reference/instructional questions are diverted to another. Clearly marked signs near each desk noting the desired types of questions would eliminate much patron confusion and unnecessary queuing.

## Delegation

Share the work and share the kudos. Delegating is crucial for a reference head to keep his/her sanity, as well as foster an environment where activities and rewards are shared. This can often be difficult when some individuals are more effective than others unless you can assign work to reflect a particular individual's assets while additional training, enrichment, etc. attack the liabilities.

## Evaluation

Some evaluation systems do more damage than good. They are worth the effort when done right. "A performance appraisal works when it helps people do their jobs with the skill and commitment needed to produce the best possible results with the lowest possible expenditure of money, time and resources—another way of defining productivity."[9] With money tight, libraries are forced to think more of productivity. Without being threatening, evaluations should be a vehicle that can point out areas where improvement is desired, provide a vehicle for this improvement, provide an opportunity for discussion and (equally important) reinforce performance which is perceived as satisfactory or better. Individuals evaluating should have an understanding of the work, performance, etc. Nothing is more frustrating to an employee than perceiving that someone who really doesn't observe his/her work performance or totally understand what he/she is doing is assigning some numerical ranking to their performance. It is a skill to both offer and take criticism.

Actually, evaluation should be an ongoing procedure. Feedback about performance should be frequent. Rewards should be at appropriate times, when deserved and contingent on performance. They shouldn't be overdone. Reinforcement is considered more effective than any approach entailing punishments or threats. A little bit of praise goes a long way. Accomplishments should be recognized. When deserved, I like to write a letter or note of thanks for a particularly excellent performance or accomplishment to the individual with a copy to the library administration. At the same time accountability is also necessary. Individuals should be held responsible for poor performance. We must be consistent. Tactful corrections or suggestions at the point of error would appear to be the most effective approach for improving performance. Beware: it is easier to shape behaviors than attitudes.

Hand in hand with evaluation is something that I've heard termed the "Pygmalion Effect." Simply put, people sometimes become what others expect them to become. The implications for managers are obvious. They should maintain a proper positive climate with effective verbal and nonverbal feedback. Under ideal circumstances such a manager would not only shape the expectations and productivity of the staff but also influence their attitudes toward their jobs and themselves. Rosenbaum offers a list of actions which motivate and enhance the employee's self esteem such as praising a specific task or job, actively listening, asking for opinions on how to solve problems, delegation, smiling, inviting someone to join you for coffee, etc.[10]

## Participative Management

I've heard the saying "No one of us is as smart as all of us." Participative management is thought by many to improve job performance. Schlesinger has noted the "belief that greater worker participation will lead to increased worker satisfaction and improved productivity."[11] Marchant recently wrote that "People prefer to be trusted and allowed to contribute. They like their jobs better under those conditions, particularly if they choose the nature and magnitude of involvement." He believes that "service is better in libraries that involve the staff in their management than in libraries run by authoritarian methods." He does concede, however, that "Participative management alone does not assure success. Other requirements must also be met. The staff must be competent or capable of becoming competent." Marchant believes that management must replace those who will not respond to an environment of trust if the library is to improve.[12]

## Effective Discipline

Not everyone meets every standard all the time. Broadwell notes that "We simply can't run an organization in which people continually fail to meet the standards set by those in position to know what a good standard is. Nothing lowers morale more quickly or destroys our effectiveness as a supervisor more completely than allowing someone to constantly break the organization's rules." He recommends taking a positive attitude towards a disciplinary interview and believes that "No matter how much we dread the confrontation, it won't get any easier if we put it off. Second, this kind of interview rarely is as bad as we expect it to be."[13]

## Handling Burnout

I feel burnt out about reading and hearing about burnout, yet I am convinced that it is a very real phenomenon and deserves careful attention. I've certainly seen it in operation throughout libraries and particularly at reference desks. As Potter noted, "Anyone, in any profession, at any level can become a candidate for job burnout."[14] According to Vash, Burnout appears to be a function of the distance between expectation and actuality . . . supersane maintain a narrow gap between the two."[15] Supervisors should be aware of the symptoms such as fatigue, inefficiency, boredom, apathy, sadness, anger, instability, frustration, forgetfulness, disappointment, despondency, self-destructive behavior, appetite problems, paranoia, physical complaints, frequent clock-watching, high absenteeism, etc. Massive lists are available throughout the literature of strategies for preventing burnout including staff development activities, determining priorities, changing jobs and role structures, management development, organizational problem-solving and decision-making, self-awareness, reducing work load, realistic goals, vacations, flexible working hours, expressing feelings, exercise, learning to say "no," lowering standards, doing something "silly," incentive programs, etc. According to Cherniss, any factor that contributes to helplessness, unpredictability, and/or failure will produce considerable stress that may result in burnout.[16] Burnout at the reference desk was recently treated by Ferriero and Powers. Their recommendations parallel the items mentioned in most burnout literature and can apply far beyond reference desks or even librarians to keep staffs happier and more productive.[17]

## Conclusion

I hope that the right combination of these suggestions may lead to improved reference quality control. A reference and/or information desk where a patron stands a good chance of receiving effective service will alleviate much of the conflict inherent in the system and result in many positive ramifications throughout the library.

## REFERENCES

1. Antone F. Alber, "How (and How Not) to Approach Job Enrichment," *Personnel Journal* 58:837-841,867(Dec. 1979).
2. William P. Anthony, *Managing Incompetence* (N.Y.:AMACOM,1981).
3. Diane B. Rutledge, "Job Permanancy: the Academic Librarian's Dilemma is the Administrators Challenge for the 1980's," *Journal of Academic Librarianship* 7:29,41 (March 1981).
4. Victoria T. Kok and Anton R. Pierce, "The Reference Desk Survey: A Management Tool in an Academic Library," *RQ* 22:181-187(Winter 1982).
5. Robert D. Caplan and Kenneth W. Jones, "Effect of Work Load, Role Ambiguity, and Type A Personality on Anxiety, Depression and Heart Rate," *Journal of Applied Psychology* 60:713-719(1975).
6. Greg R. Oldham, J. Richard Hackman and Jone L. Pearce, "Conditions Under Which Employees Respond Positively to Enriched Work," *Journal of Applied Psychology* 61:395-403(Aug.1976).
7. Marcia J. Myers and Jassim M. Jirjees, *The Accuracy of Telephone Reference/Information Services in Academic Libraries: Two Studies* (Metuchen, N.J.:Scarecrow Press, 1983).
8. Gary E. Strong, "Evaluating the Reference Product," *RQ* 19:367-372 (Sum 1980).
9. V.R. Buzzotta and Robert E. Lefton, "Performance Appraisal: Is it Worth It?" *Industrial Engineering* 11:20-24(Jan.1979).
10. Bernard L. Rosenbaum, *How to Motivate Today's Workers: Motivational Models for Managers and Supervisors* (N.Y.: McGraw Hill, 1982).
11. Leonard A. Schlesinger, *Quality of Work Life and the Supervisor* (N.Y.:Praeger, 1982.)
12. Maurice P. Marchant, "Participative Management, Job Satisfaction, and Service," *Library Journal* 107:782-784(April 15, 1982).

13. Martin M. Broadwell, *The New Supervisor* (Reading,Mass.:Addison-Wesley, 1979.)
14. Beverly A. Potter, *Beating Job Burnout* (San Francisco:Harbor,1980).
15. Carolyn L. Vash, *The Burnt-Out Administrator* (NY.:Springer,1980).
16. Cary Cherniss, *Staff Burnout: Job Stress in the Human Services* (Beverly Hills,Cal.: Sage, 1980).
17. David S. Ferriero and Kathleen A. Powers, "Burnout at the Reference Desk," *RQ* 21:274-279(Spring 1982).

# Yours, Mine and Ours: Reference Service and the Non-Affiliated User

Debbie Masters
Gail Flatness

As reference librarians, we are schooled in the philosophy that information should be freely available to all. Equal access to information is an important component of a democratic society, and a value we are taught to embrace. How then do we confront the conflict presented in a centrally located, private university in an urban setting in which our own users, the University's faculty and students, are indistinguishable from a sea of non-affiliated users, all needing "information," but competing for our resources, both staff and materials? These conflicts may be more obvious at our particular Reference desks, but our situations are not that unique. Reference librarians everywhere are forced to make decisions daily about whom to serve and how much service to provide.

In keeping with the general philosophy of free information most university libraries, whether public or private, retain open access for use of their collections on-site. At George Washington University(GW) and Georgetown University(GU) access to the buildings and main collections are unrestricted. George Washington, for security reasons, does check user identification at the door, but almost no one is denied admittance. Restrictions apply to such services as circulation, use of reserve and media resources, but these are relatively easily controlled since presentation of a University or otherwise authorized identification card is necessary to complete a transaction.

Reference service is another matter, especially extensive reference service. Neither library feels that it has the human resources to

---

Ms. Masters is Head of Reference, Gelman Library, George Washington University, Washington, DC 20052. Ms. Flatness is Head of Reference at the Lauinger Library, Georgetown University, Washington, DC.

© 1985 by The Haworth Press, Inc. All rights reserved.

provide this level of assistance to the general public. We do, however, have a certain obligation to users to whom we have extended borrowing privileges and to the students and faculty of the members of the Consortium of Universities of the Washington, D.C. area. But even then, unless the question relates to unique or exceptionally strong parts of our collections, we do not provide them with extensive assistance. Although both reference departments maintain a desk collection and exchange books from that collection for an I.D. card, our intention is not to deny access to anyone, but to keep some heavily used materials secure and accessible for all. Aside from this small area, there is no easy way to distinguish our own patrons from those of other area schools, or from business people, employees of government agencies, etc. GW is especially vulnerable. It is in the middle of a downtown area, an easy walk from a subway stop and from many area businesses and government offices. The conflict for us is really two-fold. We are expected not to cross a certain line with non-affiliated users and give "too" much service. This runs counter to a very basic tenet of our profession, to help all users to the fullest extent we can, and it is difficult for Reference librarians to offer less. On the other hand our desks are so busy that we often feel frustrated because our own primary users are not getting the extra assistance they could use because they are competing for our services with non-affiliated users.

## *HIGHER REFERENCE USE*

One phenomenon that we have observed, but not documented with actual statistics, is that a higher percentage of non-affiliated users approach the reference desk than our entry tallies would indicate. This pattern is especially evident on weekends when more non-affiliated users come to our libraries. GW counts a fairly consistent 10% non-GW user traffic by requiring identification at the door and documenting outside users. Unlike our own faculty and students, however, outside users are not familiar with our building, collections, or such access tools as serials lists or online systems available for public use. They have not been exposed to the basic level bibliographic instruction that we try to provide for our own undergraduate students, or to the more sophisticated introductions to the reference sources in a discipline that we offer for upper division undergraduates and graduate students. As a result, we feel that a higher percentage of outside users approach the desk, and that they tend to require more assistance in using our libraries than our own users. This same phenomenon was discussed by Anne Piternick in her article on resource sharing where she observed that at the University of British Columbia, "while only 16% of the questions were from external users, they required about 25% of the total time expended in answering questions" due to the complexity of the questions and the knowledge of the users.[1]

Another aspect of the problem is represented by the high volume of phone questions we both receive, many of which center on card catalog or serials holdings checks, or questions about building access and circulation policies. While we have clear policies to serve in-person patrons as a priority over phone requests, and we limit the amount of work we do over the phone (e.g., only three titles will be checked at a time), we still have a dilemma. How do we make sure we are serving *our own* users first? What if the phone call that is on "hold" is a faculty member at our own institution and the in-person traffic at the desk consists of a local consultant, a student from another area school and a lawyer on her lunch hour looking for a journal article? We sometimes feel we are forcing our users to come into the building because it is so hard to get through to us by phone.

At Lehigh University Library an analysis of transactions from the reference divisions showed that 15-20% of the daily, non-interlibrary loan inquiries came from the outside community.[2] Like GW and GU, Lehigh serves a metropolitan area with a large population of alumni and technically-oriented professionals. In response to the increasing demands for library service by the non-University community, Lehigh established a fee-based information service. In considering staffing at the reference desk, both GW and GU have considered the times when non-affiliated users constitute a majority of our clientele and adjusted staffing accordingly. For example, neither library currently provides staffing on Friday evening when our own users are not the primary clientele for our services.

## *LITTLE GUIDANCE*

The literature offers little guidance in facing these dilemmas. The document prepared by the Standards Committee of the Reference and Adult Services Division of A.L.A., "A Commitment to Information Services: Developmental Guidelines", acknowledges that reference or information services will vary with "the user the institution is designed to serve," and that "eligibility of users will be determined by the role, scope, and mission of individual institutions."[3] These guidelines, however, do not really help reference librarians distinguish between those users the institution is designed to serve, and those non-affiliated users who have equal access to the building and the reference desk. The *Reference and Online Services Handbook* documents the reference service policies of a number of academic libraries.[4] Most document a policy of open access to library buildings and collections, although not borrowing privileges, for non-affiliated users. For those that distinguish among users for purposes of reference service, most answer quick reference questions for all users. Some have a fee-based service for extended reference to non-affiliated users, although it is a judgment call as to when that distinction is made. Others suggest that when an inquiry becomes an extended reference transaction, user affiliation may be requested and distinctions made. Several libraries also recommend referral of the outside user to his or her own library or to the public library to pursue time-consuming inquiries unless the question involves the use of materials uniquely available at that library. Tax-supported institutions, especially when they are the largest library in an area, generally feel an obligation to respond to the needs of the community provided that such service does not interfere with the primary goal of service to the university.

At the meeting of the ACRL Fee-Based Information Service Centers in Libraries Discussion Group at ALA Midwinter in January, 1984, there was some discussion of the issues such a service presents at the Reference Desk. Generally, "ready reference" inquiries of up to fifteen minutes were done for anyone without charge. After that, the fee-based service was suggested. One library indicated that desk inquiries were monitored, with no charge the first few times. If a pattern was perceived, the fee-based service was suggested and librarians avoided continuing to answer questions free. Such services encounter the problem of the reference desk giving away services that are included in the fee-based service (e.g., providing verification, identifying local locations, etc.). One suggestion was to routinely ask for presentation of an I.D. card at the Reference Desk when a question is asked. The problem of establishing priorities when the same staff is used for both free and fee-based service was also addressed. Academic users are given priority, but another conflict emerges when faculty members request reference service in connection with a consulting job for a corporation for which they themselves will be paid. At Georgia Institute of Technology, such clientele are included in the fee-based service.[5]

## *LIMITATION POLICIES*

At both George Washington University and at Georgetown University, some policies on limitation of reference service have emerged. Reference librarians at our desks very quickly learn that, when a question extends beyond a certain point in time, they are expected to find out if the patron is a member of our primary clientele. We try not to be overt, but will subtly withdraw from the question or refer the person elsewhere if they turn out to be a non-affiliated user. Both of our institutions limit computerized literature searches to our own users. In an area like Washington, D.C. where information brokers and other for-fee services are widely available, and where there are a number of other public and private universities willing to provide the service, we feel no obligation to use staff time and university equipment to provide searches to outsiders, even with a surcharge. We also limit checks for other area holdings on OCLC to our own clients on the premise that the user's own library or the public library should be using OCLC or other sources to identify local holdings. Since OCLC charges for holdings displays, this is a fairly easy policy to justify, although it sometimes requires an explicit question to determine user status at the point that we have verified a needed title and determined that we do not own it. Having to limit service and enforce these rules, however, can be difficult for Reference librarians trained to use all available information sources.

We have several proposals for how libraries facing these kinds of conflicts can address them:

1) Probably the best thing any library can do is to have a written statement describing its policies relative to non-affiliated users. In a recent survey, the Association of Research Libraries polled its members and found that "61 out of 64 had written formal policies for external user access and services."[6] Many such policies relate more to borrowing and building access but several, including Georgetown's do attempt to address reference service policies as well. Although a policy won't solve all the conflicts, if nothing else it will help raise the consciousness of the staff and provide more consistency in handling requests.

2) Fee-based services offer a real alternative, particularly if they are handled by a separate staff that can respond to the requests in a timely fashion, and on a cost-recovery basis. Problems can develop when this service is handled by the same staff as that serving regular daily reference questions. For one thing, it is difficult to distinguish free from for-fee service, and to determine when to draw the line. Another consideration is the timeliness with which fee-based requests can be processed when they are competing for the same staff time that must respond to the seasonal demands of the reference desk, bibliographic instruction, etc. Do fee-based requests always go to the end of the queue? If so, how effectively can such a service be marketed given the business community's need for timely information?

3) Access policies could be restricted. For those libraries that monitor the entrance and require identification at the door, certain outside users could be excluded except under exceptional, preauthorized circumstances. We would need to continue to offer access to students from the Consortium and honor other reciprocal agreements to insure similar access for our own students and faculty at those institutions, but could limit access for individuals working for corporations, etc. We would still encounter some conflicts at the reference desk, but they would at least be among academic users, not between academics and for-profit groups. If a library does not want to go to an across-the-board limitation on access it might want to consider limiting access at particularly busy times, such as during term paper season or exams. For example, the medical library at GW limits access by non-medical center clientele during evening and weekend hours, and GU's law and medical libraries restrict access during final exams.

4) To help identify our own users on the phone, the phone number listed in campus directories for the Reference Desk could be different from the publicly listed one. Another possibility for holdings checks would be for libraries in a region to institute a central number that could take calls for checks on all area holdings. Given the wide participation by local libraries in OCLC, and a union list of serials, many such questions could be answered in an central location with the cost of the service shared by the participating libraries.

5) For those users to whom borrowing privileges are extended, a library orientation of some kind could be required to secure a borrower's card. Patrons might be required to take a Self-Guided Tour, view a videotape or slide-tape program, or undergo some other ori-

entation program not requiring an investment of staff time in order to insure their basic orientation to the building and its collections. At the very least, a library should make sure that a basic guide to its building and services is given with each card. The library's sign system could be examined and improved to reduce directional questions and make the building easier for the occasional user to understand without assistance.

The Reference Desk will probably remain one area of library service where distinctions in level and type of service offered to different categories of users will be difficult to define and enforce. For libraries facing these conflicts, however, perhaps these suggestions will offer some help in dealing with the necessary setting of priorities in these days of tightening library resources and increasing staff demands.

## NOTES

1. Anne Piternick, "Problems of Resource Sharing with the Community: A Case Study," *Journal of Academic Librarianship* 5 (July, 1979): 157.

2. Berry G. Richards and Susan A. Cady, "A New Fee-Based Information Service in an Academic Library," *Fee-Based Research in College and University Libraries*. Proceedings of the Conference on Fee-Based Research in College and University Libraries, June 17-18, 1982. (Greenvale, N.Y.: Center for Business Research, B. Davis Schwartz Memorial Library, C.W. Post Center, Long Island University, 1983), p. 131.

3. "A Commitment to Information Services: Developmental Guidelines," *RQ* 18 (Spring, 1979): 275-278.

4. *Reference and Online Services Handbook: Guidelines, Policies, and Procedures for Libraries*, ed. Bill Katz and Anne Clifford (New York: Neal-Schuman, 1982).

5. Ibid, p. 53.

6. Association of Research Libraries. Office of Management Services. Systems and Procedures Exchange Center, *External User Services*. SPEC Kit 73. (Washington, D.C.: A.R.L., April 1981), unpaged.

# Conflicts in Reference Service: A Personal View

George R. Bauer

When it comes to conflict, surely the basic one in libraries generally is the tension between providing information to everyone who demonstrates a need and keeping intact the sources of that information so that it is continuously available to the collective whole who pay for it through their taxes, tuition, fees, and other forms of support. On this rest all of the laws and the prophets.

But ancillary to this are many smaller problems and conflicts (challenges may be the more just and upbeat word), and it is to some of these highly practical considerations that the author of this paper will address himself. This will be, for the most part, a strongly personal and pragmatic viewpoint, reflecting fourteen years experience in a moderately sized university library, which opened its doors just fourteen years ago. Needless to say, not all of the situations described will be familiar to all types and sizes of libraries or to the same degree. Some of the points may seem mundane, even petty, but in an age of shrinking budgets and increasing expectations they often attain a poignancy out of proportion to their outward show.

As a late-vocation librarian, it came as a surprise to me at first that librarianship is often classified as a stressful occupation. In my early innocence I thought that living intimately, day after day, with thousands of books had to be the most delightful, relaxed, and satisfying occupation one could choose. But even the venerable *Occupational Outlook Handbook* warns that "[l]ibraries generally are busy, demanding, even stressful places to work. Contact with people, which is often a major part of the job, can be taxing. Physically, the job may require much standing, stooping, bending and reaching."[1]

And lately the grim spectre of burnout has reared its ugly head.

---

Mr. Bauer is Head, Reference and Instructional Services, at the University of Wisconsin Library at Green Bay, WI 54302.

© 1985 by The Haworth Press, Inc. All rights reserved.

Recently Smith and Nelson warned that increasing pressures on librarians and members of other helping professions can lead to "exhaustion, boredom, disappointment, stagnation, frustration, or apathy. An employee can become so overwhelmed that service to the public becomes ineffectual and indifferent."[2]

Regardless of one's personal reaction to the idea of burnout (and I confess to a certain amount of impatience with the concept), the constant tug of conflicting demands and dwindling time and energy can take its toll. A reasonable resolution of some of these small day-to-day problems can help immeasurably to restore perspective and sharpen functioning.

## *HOW TO FILL THE SLACK TIME AT THE REFERENCE DESK AND STILL BE ALERT TO NEEDS*

Ideally the demands on the reference desk librarian's time would be paced so that questions come one at a time in measured order so that each can be given optimum attention. But of course this ideal situation never (or hardly ever) prevails. Either you are bombarded with simultaneous questions and hard put to retain your wits, or there are long fallow periods when your main problem is to appear as if you are really earning your salary and still be aware enough to respond to a query.

In addition to "being available," I have at various times: 1) checked filing in the card catalog nearby; 2) worked on flyers and pathfinders; 3) replaced paper in or made minor adjustments to ailing copy machines; 4) worked on ideas for that new display on the history of printing; 5) prepared bibliographies for faculty members developing new courses; or 6) planned strategy for a computer search. But my favorite fill-in is reading: from professional literature to books, magazines, or newspapers of every stripe. I cannot regard any time spent on reading by a librarian, regardless of the topic, as wasted or frivolous. Many times a tidbit dredged up from the memory deposit of my recent reading has enabled me to provide a quick and satisfying solution to a reader's request. Such things do not happen by mere chance, which, we are assured, favors a prepared mind. Why, then, do I feel so guilty when eyed askance or when a passing faculty member (on his way to the newspaper reading room, no doubt) remarks: "You obviously don't have enough to do in your job."

But it is impossible to escape the conclusion that for the reference desk attendant, the first and foremost consideration is the client, with his immediate needs, and this includes the need to make a special effort to engage the shy or diffident one who stands silently, shifting his weight from one foot to another, or wanders about the card catalog in an obvious fog. Alternative tasks must necessarily be the kind that require little or no concentration or sustained attention, lest the client in need be overlooked.

## *FOR WHOM THE BELL TOLLS: JUGGLING IN-PERSON AND TELEPHONE QUESTIONS*

Related to this overall conflict is the question of how to handle telephone questions when austerity forbids the luxury of two reference librarians on duty at once. It would seem axiomatic that the person who makes his request on the spot should take precedence over the caller who at his leisure at home or office idly lifts his phone to his ear. But most of us cannot ignore a jangling telephone and it must at least be acknowledged. The most that should be required in such a situation is to take the number and promise to call back. But there is always the chance that the question can be answered in no more than the time it takes to ascertain name and number, and before you know it you may be mired in a knotty search. Surely by this time it is proper to defer the service to a later time when in-house demand has slackened.

This is not always so easy. Sometimes the person calling will be away from his phone shortly and the call back never is completed. This is likely to result in an unhappy patron. Even worse is when a lengthy search that has produced happy results is never delivered to the person who originally requested it—more waste and frustration.

Probably the best approach is to establish as policy that telephone calls during busy periods should be jotted down in a log with a promise to pursue the question or call back for more details as soon as practicable. After all, the current insistence on instant gratification must bow now and then to plain necessity.

Perhaps the catch-as-catch can nature of much of telephone reference leads to the low rate of satisfactory answers as reported in a recent book by Myers and Jirjees, who found that only a modest 282 out of 560 questions in their survey were adequately answered.[3] If these figures accurately reflect the state of telephone reference, they are indeed sobering.

But telephone reference has its light side as well. A long-time teacher of reference in one of our universities passed on to me this story, which he insisted actually happened. The telephone at a busy college reference desk rang, and the caller asked: "Can you tell me the gestation period of a lemming?" "Just a minute," said the librarian, turning toward the biology reference books. "Thank you," said the caller brightly and hung up.

## THE REFERENCE LIBRARIAN AS FACTOTUM

Consider this scenario: The circulation librarian is home with the flu. The reserve librarian is still trying to get out of a snowbank. All of the student assistants who were assigned for the morning have called in "sick" (it is mid-semester exam time). Your reference desk is part of a complex that includes circulation, reserves, and some aspects of interlibrary loan. In this no-man's land you are the only trooper, for the time being at least. You sigh with relief when one student assistant shows up, and dispatch him/her to the security desk at a remote point. The rest is up to you!

These, surely, are the times that try librarians' souls. There is nothing to do except grapple with things as they come, establish priorities ("So your typewriter isn't working? Here's your refund. Try another.") And pray.

Even when the staffing machinery is functioning smoothly, you can bet that the machinery machinery is not; and it is the nature of machinery to choose the worst possible time for malfunctioning. Being only human, the copy machine always needs paper or gets its coin mechanism jammed when the lines are six deep. Or didn't they tell you when you were an innocent in library school that much of your library time would be spent wet nursing machines? You mean you passed up that dandy elective *Microfilm Readers 102?*

## FURTHER ANIMADVERSIONS ON THE CONCEPT OF MAXI-SERVICE/MINI-STAFF

The 1976 statement, "A Commitment to Information Services," states flatly that "A professional librarian/information specialist should be available to users during all hours the library is open."[4] This is plainly impractical in our situation. Our library is open ninety-two and a half hours per week during regular semesters. There are three reference librarians. One works at the reference desk for only eight hours per week, having as her principal task the business of coordinating (and doing much of the teaching of) library instruction. The other two are at the reference desk for 21 and 22 hours each week respectively. All have a number of other responsibilities.

Obviously the only way to reconcile over ninety hours per week of service with forty hour work weeks is to take turns coming in late and staying late, drawing back somewhat from the hundred per cent hours concept, and pressing technical service staff into public service for at least a few hours of the time. At best, this is cutting off one end of the loaf to add to the other end, and often sacrifices staff at the busiest time of the library day. Our compromise is to provide reference service until nine o'clock at night on most week-days, and for four hours each on Saturdays and Sundays. This gives community people and evening class students with daytime jobs at least a few hours a week to confer with experienced reference staff people.

Aside from the frustrations of overmuch concentration on the same activities for hour after hour, such scheduling has other disadvantages. It leaves to a minimum the time available for research, writing, on-the-job training, and such other tasks as loom so gratifyingly large in annual evaluations and have so much influence on the likelihood of advancement. Though you are immersed day after day in the only activity that really matters to most library users, immediate satisfactions are rare. The sincere "thank you" and (better yet) the letter of appreciation with a copy to your supervisor are rarities. Of course, technical service librarians, with their less regimented schedule and relatively greater freedom are likely to have their correlative complaint: lack of contact with the ultimate benefactor of all their efforts can be equally frustrating.

After awhile the commitment to reference service becomes so strong that you find yourself avoiding even those state and local meetings that once proved so helpful to you in keeping up with advances in the field and refreshing your outlook by bringing you in contact with librarians from outside your constricted circle (attendance at the annual ALA Conference or the Mid-Winter has obviously long ago gone by the boards).

## *THE OVER-DEMANDING PATRON— WHERE DO YOU DRAW THE LINE?*

In most undergraduate libraries in this country, it is usually taken for granted that the ability to do independent research in a library is as valuable as any other skill learned during one's college career, and that the librarian is doing no good service to do all or much of the student's work for him. Of course the librarian must be more than willing to take the beginner by the hand, show the way, and be available whenever snags develop, as they surely will. But to develop lengthy bibliographies, plan papers, or proofread them is beyond the call of duty, not to mention impossible with potentially hundreds of students clamoring for help. Most professors are aware of this and expect their students to develop independence; and most students recognize the need for adding this dimension to their growth in scholarship. There will always be those few, however, that attempt to waltz through college with as little effort as possible.

In the case of international students, a growing presence in many of our colleges and universities, as pointed out in a recent article by Sally Wayman,[5] the situation may be exacerbated. She suggests that most foreign students represent the more affluent segments of their countries' population, by the very fact that they can afford to attend American schools, and in some cases are used to a certain amount of servility from librarians.[6] If this tendency surfaces, the student should be politely but firmly steered in the proper direction.

Wayman's article, by the way, can be recommended as an eminently practical and helpful guide for the librarian whose student population is leavened with the enriching presence of students from other lands and cultures.

## *JARGONRY AND ACROMANIA*

Sometimes it seems that no other profession is so given to the creation of ear-jarring neologisms and acronyms, and to take it for granted that its public is in full command of this language as librarianship. The average library user is hard put to keep afloat in this alphabet soup. OCLC (not to mention LC), ISBN, ISSN, SDI, BRS, PTLA, BIP, PAIS, PDR, AV, NUC, CBI, the list is endless. Add to these the short titles so familiar and dear to librarians, and you'll find that to the average student using libraries, in the words of Oscar Hammerstein's King of Siam, "*is* a puzzlement."

What, after all, do "Ulrich's," and "Ayer's" mean to the uninitiated student? "Microfiche" is bad enough, but with the shortened form already rampant, you may find yourself fiching in troubled waters. Sometimes the problem is as simple as the confusion of "bibliography" for "biography" or "reference" for "reserves" (presumably because they both start with "r").

A good rule in reference work is not necessarily to avoid the familiar shortened forms but to follow their appearance with a brief explanation of what they signify. This is especially important in library instruction but is also recommended in one-on-one reference assistance. Throughout their college careers and beyond, students will be stubbing their toes on these nasty excrescences. Best to clear them up early in the game.

The problem is compounded in the case of printed forms such as interlibrary loan applications, where, to save space, there is a natural tendency to abbreviate.

And of course the best regulated card catalogs can fall prey to blind references and circular references, not to mention the subject terms that are meaningful only to the catalogers at the Library of Congress. But a whole paper could be written on the latter topic and enough has been said elsewhere.

Some library users seem destined to persist in their first wooly misconception, regardless of all your efforts. At our library, recently, this charming exchange was noted:

> Patron (matronly type): "I've been told that you have old issues of magazines on microwave film in your library."
> Librarian: "Yes, we do have *microfilm* backfiles for many of our magazines and newspapers. Do you have a particular issue in mind?"
> Patron: "I have it written down here. Will you come with me to the microwave area and show me how to use it?"
> After going to the periodicals floor, the librarian gets the appropriate roll of microfilm and proceeds to mount it in the machine, all the while carefully explaining how the machine works and slightly emphasizing the word *microfilm* every time it occurs, hoping thus to gently correct the patron.
> Librarian: "There, I will leave you to read your article. You should have no problems with the microfilm."
> Patron: "This is just marvelous. Thank you. To think that there is a whole year of magazine issues on one roll of microwave film."
> Librarian leaves. To one patron, at least, it will always be microwave film.

## MUSCLING UP FOR THE FUTURE

In the face of the growing disparity between user expectations and the size of the library staff, what can the small to medium sized library do as it faces the future? Can it continue to provide the same level of personalized services? It is probably overly sanguine to expect budgets to improve greatly; and if more funds are forthcoming, they are likely to be diverted to purchases of high tech storage and retrieval systems and other automated marvels. Here are some suggestions.

Make better use of time and personnel available. Now, if ever, it is imperative to do a thorough time management study. Make sure regular staff are achieving the proper balance between meetings and other activities and their principal activity: rendering service to the students, faculty, and other library users.

Are support personnel being utilized to their full capabilities? Every crop of new student assistants has one or two that stand out, that show a real aptitude for library matters and in addition have genuine enthusiasm for the work. With a little grooming such students can be given greater responsibilities and can function as reference assistants, especially during the graveyard hours when regular staff are not available. They can always refer to regular staff any questions that go beyond their experience or competence.

Utilize new technology and remember that the machine is a servant, not a master. If new systems do not result in greater efficiency as well as accuracy, then they are failing their purpose and should be seriously questioned. But technology in its turn makes great demands, and librarians who for years followed the same hallowed routines with their file cards and checkout slips will have to shed their timidity and master a whole new set of skills, procedures, and even language. There is also some encouragement in the thought that it is likely that new generations of equipment will become increasingly more "user friendly."

## PEDAL POINT AND CODA

Recently I assisted a student in locating and using the *New York Times* microfilm in a commonly assigned exercise to find the front page for one's birthdate. Never having performed this for myself, I decided to try it, and was considerably chagrined to note that the first headline on my birthdate was: "Velvet Breeches Shunned by Dawes at Royal Court." This has little or no significance except perhaps as a variation on Calpurnia's line in Shakespeare's *Julius Caesar* that "When beggars die there are no comets seen," and is one more chastening observation in an occupation that is not noted for grand effects. But it may well be that better times are coming.

A number of recent observers have noted that this nation has already made the transition from an industrial society to an information society. In fact John Naisbitt has pinpointed the approximate turning point of this phenomenon as occurring sometime during 1956 or 1957, adding "It is now clear that the post-industrial society is the information society."[7] If this is the case, and there is every reason to believe it is, librarians surely have cause for celebration. After all, libraries and librarians have been in the information business since Ashurbanipol and before; the information society should seem like familiar ground. True, there will be vastly more refined methods of storing and retrieving the floods of information spewing out in geometrically increasing amounts, and librarians will be severely challenged to master these methods. But what other profession has such a long tradition to build on and such a record of success? What other profession has the confidence of so many satisfied searchers after truth (or at least facts). And what other profession knows that, in spite of bytes and chips and floppy disks, the provision of information must operate in a human and humane fashion. If this is held as an ideal, let 1984 bring on its worst. The brave new world really will be a Brave New World.

## NOTES

1. *Occupational Outlook Handbook 1982-83*. Washington, U. S. Department of Labor Statistics, 1982, p. 139.
2. Smith, Nathan M., and Nelson, Veneese C. "Burnout: a Survey of Academic Reference Librarians," *College & Research Libraries*, May, 1983, p. 245.
3. Myers, Marcia J., and Jirjees, J. M. *The Accuracy of Telephone Reference/Information Services in Academic Libraries*. Metuchen, N.J., Scarecrow, 1983, p. 55, 56.
4. "A Commitment to Information Services: Developmental Guidelines," *RQ*, Summer, 1976, p. 329.
5. Wayman, Sally G. "The International Students in the Academic Library," *The Journal of Academic Librarianship*, January, 1984, p. 336-341.
6. *Ibid.*, p. 339.
7. Naisbitt, John. *Megatrends: Ten New Directions Transforming Our Lives*. New York, Warner Books, 1984, p. 4.

# Reference Philosophy vs Service Reality

Larry D. Benson
H. Julene Butler

It is 12:30 p.m. at the Reference Desk. The mid-semester library assignments are due and the students are getting serious about writing research papers. An inventor, totally unfamiliar with libraries, wants to find patents; a telephone patron needs to know schools offering home study courses in nursing; a student wants the figure on the total number of people who have lived on earth; a political science student is having trouble finding a government document; someone else asks for an explanation on how to use the *Social Science Citation Index*. None of these are unreasonable requests, but all come within a fifteen-minute period! To top it all off, an unattended child pulls too many drawers from a cabinet which then falls on him. You reach for the reference librarian's "crisis line", but no one is answering. Colleagues are either in committee meetings or attending to other duties. The secretary is at lunch. There is no money in the budget for student assistant backup. You must handle these requests solo!

This represents a true but very undesirable situation in which reference librarians often find themselves. In such a situation even the most experienced and conscientious librarian must temporarily suppress his or her commitment to maximum service. Considerable conflict arises between one's personal reference philosophy and the realities of the service one is able to provide.

The intensity of that conflict depends on each librarian's attitude toward service. Those content to give patrons a brief explanation, hand them a source, and send them off to struggle on their own, or those who are not bothered by the patron who gives up and goes away will not feel guilty. However, if one's philosophy is that of

---

Mr. Benson is Social Sciences Librarian, Harold B. Lee Library, Brigham Young University, Provo, UT 84602. Ms. Butler is General Reference Librarian at the same institution.

© 1985 by The Haworth Press, Inc. All rights reserved.

caring enough to give the best assistance possible, considerable compromise must take place. One must either be content to live with these frustrations or be willing to aggressively seek solutions. This paper discusses some reasons for the conflicts and suggests several ways to resolve them.

## CAUSES OF THE DILEMMA

Most conflicts experienced by reference librarians relate to time. Time is needed to conduct adequate negotiations, assess verbal and non-verbal clues, and encourage patrons to discuss their research problems so that proper strategies can be outlined and implemented. The pressure of two or three additional patrons listening in and sending non-verbal cues to handle the first patron with dispatch, usually forces the librarian to abort proper negotiation, make quick assumptions, and hurriedly direct the patron to what may not be the best source or solution. Jack King believes that bad reference situations such as this not only make it difficult for the librarian to establish priorities among users, but also result in a 50% failure rate.[1]

Seasoned library researchers are not dissuaded by such inadequate service. They are usually assertive enough to persist until their needs are met. However, when the librarian is unable to spend time developing the trust and confidence of the novice, this patron becomes frustrated and leaves with the assumption that limited help is all that can be expected.

Conscientious librarians also feel frustration when they are finally free to offer additional assistance, but cannot locate the patron. They complain, "Why do the patrons give up so easily? I wish they would hang in there until I can get back to them!" But experience teaches the user that the library does not care enough about patron service to provide the personnel required to meet the demand. The library's credibility is compromised, as is the librarian's philosophy of reference service.

One reason reference librarians are placed in this compromising situation may relate to traditional priorities. Every administrator wants his or her library to achieve recognition and acceptance among peers by qualifying for membership in prestigious consortiums, by obtaining large collections, or by computerizing services. Though all this has an indirect positive influence on reference service, adequate support for up-front patron assistance is often lacking. The piece of the budget pie given to support the dissemination of information in libraries is often out of proportion with the percent committed to the acquisition and processing of materials. "Many academic libraries . . . continue to use a structure that reinforces a materials orientation, where priorities are placed on preservation, acquisition, and storage of materials."[2] Such a structure may neglect adequate funding for ongoing personnel demands necessary to relieve the harried reference librarian who wishes to raise the quality of service above the 50% mark.

Reference service may be viewed as a low priority due to the dearth of quantitative data in this field. Because it is difficult to set measurable standards for quality service, reference departments do not have the data needed to convince administrators. The number of questions answered can be tabulated, but how can one measure caring, in-depth negotiation or appropriate research strategy formulation? These skills require time from the librarian who is "usually uncomfortably aware that the more time spent with one user, the less is available to deal with another."[3] In addition, it is impossible to predict crisis moments at the reference desk. Librarians are seldom forewarned of class assignments. They cannot anticipate how many patrons will be motivated to come to the library at any given hour. General trends can be noted, but one day between 12:00 and 1:00 p.m. five patrons may request assistance, whereas the next day, during the same hour, twenty-five may appear. Administrators need to seriously consider these variables as they evaluate library manpower needs.

Report deadlines, committee involvement, collection development demands, and other responsibilities can also conflict with the dedication needed for good service. These extraneous pressures may cause librarians to bring other work to the desk which requires concentration and results in either conscious or unconscious negative attitudes toward patron "interruptions". The backlogs and deadlines attendant to these non-reference duties tempt even the most dedicated librarians to neglect good reference practices and go against their philosophy of service.

One librarian caught in this conflict of priorities was heard to say, "I sure could get a lot done if it weren't for the patrons!" Too often patrons are blamed for the emotional strain of reference work when the librarians themselves cause the anxieties by trying to accomplish too much unrelated work at the same time they assist patrons.

Each person develops his or her own philosophy of what comprises appropriate service. When a variety of philosophies exist within a department, several levels of assistance are provided. Friction may arise when librarians with opposing attitudes are required to work side by side at the reference desk. Interpersonal relations can be strained when one person perceives the reference load is unequally distributed. Conflicts may become even more pronounced when one librarian attempts to increase a colleague's commitment to service. Librarians can be trained in the skills of good reference principles, but each must internalize those principles before attitudes will change.

The desire to forget self in the service of others is an innate part of some personalities. For these people the conflict lies in being unable to do enough for the patron. Those who prefer to devote time to the tasks the patron is interrupting display considerable conflict of interest. Perhaps these librarians should not be in public services.

Many personal concerns may also cause reference librarians to compromise their philosophy. Emotional strain, physical problems, and non-library related commitments can seriously affect the attitude with which a person responds to patrons. Aching feet can keep one from leaving the desk to go with a patron just as much as preoccupation with other duties.

## *SOLUTIONS*

Though at times these conflicts seem overwhelming and insurmountable, specific attitudes and approaches can be adopted which may close the gap between one's philosophy of maximum service and the daily realities of mediocre service. We offer the following "solutions" which if implemented, will significantly improve reference service.

### *Sell the Importance of Service*

Library administrators, who ultimately determine the size of each division's budget, need to be convinced that a gap exists between reference philosophy and service reality. Data should be presented to them that represents more than just numbers. In some way it must measure the patron's assessment of the quality of service. Feedback should be sought to determine whether users feel the librarian devoted sufficient time and attention to their needs, whether sincere interest in their project was demonstrated, or whether the librarian was too busy or too preoccupied to appropriately deal with their requests. Librarians should report specific situations where they felt they could have offered more service had circumstances allowed. Concrete evidence may be heeded when complaints are not. Administrators must be sold on the fact that patron service is actually suffering. When this fact is accepted they will be more likely to find the budget for increasing reference staff support.

### Formalize Service Expectations

Many libraries are realizing the inadequacy of the informal policy to do only "as much for as many people as staff and time . . . permit".[4] Such an informal standard assumes that "everyone knows what the policies are."[5] However, if the requirements are ambiguous to reference personnel, an evaluation of needs will be difficult to make. Supervisors must have criteria against which to measure manpower and performance.

Written expectations remove doubt about the level of acceptable service and provide justification for support if those standards are not met. An effort should be made to involve administrators in the formulation of these documents so they will feel more loyalty to them. Guidelines may have more clout if developed by an entire library system or state. In 1979, the ALA Reference and Adult Services Division adopted "Developmental Guidelines"[6] which could be used as a basis for reference standards. These standards could be enhanced to include the quality of service rendered. Once the expectations of the library are known and endorsed by all concerned parties there is a stronger argument for support.

### Encourage Interdepartmental Assistance

At the heart of the dilemma is the fact that the reference desk is understaffed. A partial solution may lie in gaining assistance from librarians in other departments or divisions. Bibliographers, catalogers, and administrators have expertise that can strengthen reference service. These librarians can also benefit from direct involvement with the patron. Increased knowledge of services and sources patrons are requesting, and awareness of avenues for providing them, enhances the librarian's effectiveness in his or her primary job assignment.

### Seek Volunteer Assistance

Another source of reference support is the pool of individuals willing to offer volunteer service. With today's economic trends, many highly qualified people are willing to contribute time in exchange for experience in a library setting. M.L.S. graduates unable to land professional positions are often anxious to make themselves more marketable by gaining reference experience on a volunteer basis. Librarians who have dropped out of the work force may be willing to devote several hours per week to reference services simply for the benefit of keeping up on their skills. This solution brings relief at the desk and requires no commitment from the library beyond the training time provided by the supervisor/trainer.

### Recruit Quality Staff

Employers tend to give more credence to an applicant's academic background or experience than to that person's orientation to service principles. Interview questions should invite potential employees to explain their philosophy of service. Considerable insight can also be gained by asking an applicant to describe his or her own personality. If questions are left open-ended, the interviewee will usually disclose relevant information without revealing private matters. It is important to determine how applicants have dealt with the public in previous work settings. How did they cope with tense and harried situations? How did they handle irate patrons? Questions should elicit comments describing the applicant's ability to work with people in a positive, understanding and caring way. The same information should be solicited from former employers during one-on-one conversations if possible. Hiring people with service-oriented personalities will do more toward achieving positive results than will countless hours of trying to instill appropriate attitudes.

### Train for Efficiency

Many of the pressures at a reference desk can be eased with in-depth training. All public service librarians can remember their first months at a busy reference desk when they struggled with patrons' questions. They will also recall how, on many occasions, an experienced librarian came to their aid. With a few relevant questions the patron's problem was quickly narrowed to the real need, and the source for the appropriate answer was supplied. There is no substitute for thorough knowledge of negotiation skills and reference sources. A well-trained librarian can satisfactorily handle many more patrons each hour than can one less skilled. If additional support is not forthcoming, departments must maximize the efforts of the current staff through well-organized training programs.

## *Bolster Motivation*

Members of the reference team can be motivated to increase their service through discussion groups in which librarians share ideas for improvement. Formal departmental or divisional meetings which focus on service quality may provide motivation. Brown-bag luncheons or informal conversations where colleagues react to articles on reference service may stimulate thought and influence attitudes toward responsibility. Success stories stressing the positive approaches taken by one librarian or department could be shared with all library staff through an in-house newsletter. Positive feedback received from patrons could be publicized. Discussion groups involving wider library systems or larger geographic areas could be beneficial since experiences from other libraries may suggest new approaches. The object of such activities is to help unmotivated librarians realize that there are alternatives to the "sit and point" method of reference assistance. Focusing on the positive can build esprit de corps and lift all members of the team to new levels of service.

## *Foster a Team Effort*

It is vital that all reference personnel share the commitment to rendering maximum service. With such commitment each individual in the department will be willing to assist at the desk more frequently than during assigned desk hours. Clerical personnel may answer telephone requests so the person at the desk can focus on needs of walk-in patrons. Colleagues may accept assigned "on-call" hours, remaining in their offices ready to help at the desk if it becomes necessary. This commitment may also involve a willingness to temporarily drop other duties and provide assistance whenever one observes that help is needed. Rallying such dedication from coworkers in the department may be difficult initially, but if each librarian begins with himself or herself, progress will be made.

### Eliminate Distractions

The habit of bringing non-reference-related work to the desk fragments the librarian's concentration and leads to reduced attention to patrons. When a person writes a report or an article, that person usually closes the office door, posts a "DO NOT DISTURB" sign, and cancels all calls. Librarians may even sneak into the stacks, as the authors have done, in order to eliminate distractions and achieve maximum levels of concentration. When the same effort is made to eliminate distractions to reference service, by leaving non-reference work in the office, the mind is left free to focus on reference questions. Budget calculations, annual report drafts, committee assignments and collection development projects are essential aspects of the librarian's responsibility, but should not pull attention away from the patron.

If every moment of desk time is devoted to reference service and awareness of patron concerns, the quality of service is bound to improve. Snatches of time between inquiries should be used to seek out patrons who appear to be confused or who may not be finding what they need. The authors have found that the practice of leaving the desk to walk around the reference area offering assistance has increased the number of reference assists by 25%. Slack periods could also be used to become familiar with the collection so proper sources can be quickly identified. With a mind uncluttered by distracting thoughts or self-imposed priorities, it is easier to meet patron demands more efficiently.

Concentration is vital if the librarian is to handle the situation described in the opening paragraph. Charles Bunge said that "as librarians, we should respond to the patron with our whole being, letting him know that he and his question or need is the most important thing in our lives at that moment."[7]

### Show the Patron That You Care

Finally, it is important to create an atmosphere where each patron recognizes that the librarian cares about his or her specific need. It is possible to emphathize and show sincere concern even in a setting where requests come so rapidly that the librarian is tugged in many directions.

At the doctor's office the patient seldom receives the doctor's undivided attention for an extended period of time. Other patients await his time and instructions. Likewise, in a reference setting, the librarian can seldom settle in for a lengthy consultation. Rather "one must be adept at juggling the needs of several people simultaneously, starting a person out on the first step of a complicated research strategy, answering two or three 'quick' questions for others, starting someone else out on a lengthy search, and still returning to the first person in time to direct him or her in the second step of the investigation."[8]

Through this cycle the librarian can and should maintain an attitude of empathy, warmth, and respect. By offering encouragement to return for more help if information is not found, and by stressing that the patron should not give up, the librarian sends out signals that he or she cares about the patron. A quick reassurance that the librarian will return as soon as possible, goes far toward instilling a feeling of confidence and trust.

Ultimately, it is this concern and warmth that bridges the gap between the idealistic service one would hope to offer and the realistic service one is often forced to give. When efforts fail to increase staff support at the desk, or fail to improve the willingness of colleagues to offer better service, the solution to the conflict falls on the shoulders of the librarian committed to excellence. Even when staffing is adequate to meet the demands of most hours, and members of the reference department are willing to work together as a team dedicated to high quality service, there will be moments when patron demand exceeds librarian supply. In such moments, the librarian who creatively strives to increase efficiency and who communicates a willingness to do everything possible to meet the patron's need, will be less apt to compromise his or her reference philosophy.

## REFERENCES

1. Jack King, "Put a Prussian Spy in Your Library," *RQ* 18(Fall 1978):33.
2. Sandra H. Neville, "Job Stress and Burnout: Occupational Hazards for Service Staff," *College and Research Libraries* 42(May 1981):243.
3. Donald Davinson, *Reference Service* (London: Clive Bingley, 1980), p. 22.
4. Mary Jo Lynch, "Academic Library Reference Policy Statements," *RQ* 11(Spring 1972):224.
5. Ibid., p. 225.
6. Standards Committee, Reference and Adult Services Division, American Library Association, "A Committment to Information Services: Developmental Guidelines," *RQ* 18(Spring 1979):275-278.
7. Charles A. Bunge, "Seekers vs. Barriers; Getting Information to People: Your Role," *Wisconsin Library Bulletin* 70(March/April 1974):77.
8. Ann T. Hinckley, "The Reference Librarian," *College and Research Libraries News* 41(March 1980):63.

# FEES AND CHARGES

## Fee vs Free in Historical Perspective

Margaret F. Stieg

To charge or not to charge the user for access to expensive machine-readable databases is the source of the sharpest conflict in reference service today, but only coincidentally is it a question of paying for reference service. The real issue is that of paying for information, a question with ramifications far beyond the reference department. Librarians have examined the question from a variety of viewpoints, economic, political, and ethical, and almost invariably the discussion has been cast in terms of *pro* or *con*. It is clear that librarians are caught between their inadequate resources and their professional values. They find it difficult to reconcile their need with their beliefs, and a certain uneasiness is latent in the debate.[1]

What, then, are the professional values, also known as the library faith, which produce such disquiet? To a considerable extent they are those of public librarianship with roots in nineteenth century American democratic traditions, clarified by a century of professional activity and discussion. Public libraries have been the libraries which have shaped the American definition of a library and public librarians have led in defining the profession. Much of the debate over fee vs. free has been in terms of the public library and

---

Professor Stieg is a Professor at the Graduate School of Library Service at the University of Alabama, University, AL 35486.

even when it has not, the values of public librarianship have permeated it.

American public libraries are a creation of the second half of the nineteenth century. Between 1852, the date of the foundation of the Boston Public Library and the conventional beginning point of the public library movement, and the end of the century every town with pretensions to civic respectability equipped itself with one. James Wyer remarked in 1911, "No one seriously questions the propriety, the desirability, nor the civic and social necessity of publicly supported libraries."[2]

Wyer was right, by 1911 a public library was taken for granted as a civic service; it had, moreover, as a movement never encountered any serious opposition. A generation earlier William Frederick Poole had had to turn to England to find examples of objections to public libraries for his article "Some Popular Objections to Public Libraries."[3] In the United States, by defining libraries as educational institutions, the supporters of public libraries had been able to take advantage of the already-won battle for publicly supported education. They had benefitted from favorable timing; in the latter part of the nineteenth century a general expansion of governmental responsibilities and services was taking place. In that period of individual philanthropy, a philanthropist's gift would often provide the needed stimulus to a city government. In a very real sense, the case for public libraries was never tried in the court of public opinion. The public remained largely indifferent and the case for libraries was argued by professional librarians.

Supporters advocated public libraries on educational, cultural, economic, moral, and political grounds.[5] Educationally speaking, the library was promoted as a means both to provide an opportunity for further education for children who had left school early and were now earning their living and to offer adults a substitute for the opportunity they had never had. Its potential cultural contribution was less defined. American librarians failed to advance the argument, found in other public library movements, that the public library was an important preserver of culture and contributed directly to the development of culture through its influence on individuals. They did see, however, especially in New England, an important cultural role for the public library in supporting the scholars working to preserve the historical records of a growing nation.[6] And they did assert that the library would be exposing its users to mankind's cultural heritage.

## ECONOMIC ARGUMENT

The economic argument was quite straightforward:

> [The public library] is needed to furnish books and periodicals for the technical instruction and information of mechanics, artisans, manufacturers, engineers, and all others whose work requires technical knowledge—of all those persons upon whom depends the industrial progress of the city.[7]

Improved real estate values were also promised.

Librarians aligned the public library movement with the powerful forces of moral improvement and temperance. By its mere existence, a public library would minimize the reading of vicious literature. More importantly, it offered an alternative to the barroom. The English economist, Stanley Jevons, gave this argument even greater appeal when he concluded that free libraries, however expensive, would still be less costly than the prisons, poor-houses and other institutions maintained at public expense and the gin-palaces, music halls, and theaters maintained by private.[8]

Librarians posited a political function for the public library. It would act as a unifying force in the community. It would improve civic quality, attracting men of letters to its city. A source of pride, it could give a particular city an advantage over its rivals in the never-ending competition for pride of place.

A different kind of political purpose derived from its educational role. Welland has with justice described the public library as one of the most characteristic institutions of Western democracy.[9] Librarians believed that the public library had a unique contribution to make to the future of democracy, particularly to the American version of democracy with its emphasis upon equality, through developing informed citizens.

These advocates of libraries took themselves and libraries with high seriousness. Public libraries serve *serious* political, social, economic, and cultural purposes, purposes which are *important* to the community. In effect, they equated library service with the provision of information. Only very occasionally would recognition that the public library served recreational purposes creep in. The tone of the discussion conveys a strong sense of condescension. Historians have recognized for a long time that public libraries were imposed upon "The People" by humanitarians and philanthropists, not demanded by them. At least one librarian spoke of "the masses" and doubtless many more thought in those terms. Middle-class professionals defined values and stated what ought to be for the lower classes. The public library could not escape a tinge of charity.

## ASSUMPTIONS

The assumptions behind these arguments for public libraries and the conclusions deduced from them, almost more than the arguments for public libraries themselves, have determined the context of the conflict over charging. Offering database searches, which to date are for informational rather than recreational purposes, flatters our sense of the library as a serious institution. Through database searches we are serving educational and/or economic ends, and indirectly cultural and political. Because the librarian has final say over whether or not a search is to be performed and because the librarian, or initiate into the mystique of computer searching, must perform the search, the role of the librarian as authority on other people's information needs is strengthened. But in the last analysis to charge or not to charge is a matter of money and it is the financial implications of these arguments that are most relevant.

The financial resources of the public library depend upon the democratic political process and are not, therefore, purely a fiscal or economic matter. Central to all the arguments advanced in favor of the public library was the unstated assumption that the promised educational, cultural, economic, and political benefits served the common interest. The purpose of a particular line of reasoning was to prove that a library was educational, not that education was in the public interest. That had already been established, as it has been that culture was in the public interest, and a more productive economy, and a more informed electorate. This lack of dissension over fundamentals rendered the debate over public libraries no true debate and imparted to the discussions an arid quality. But it is these fundamental assumptions that are at issue in the current debate over charging.

During the late nineteenth century there was some discussion over whether or not the library should be tax-supported and open to all without the then-prevalent subscription fee, but it was very limited. Poole's 1876 article acknowledges that there had been objections to taxation to support a library, but that they had appeared primarily in conversation rather than at any more formal level of communication. He identified a resistance to increased taxation, but resistance to taxation has been a recurring theme in American history from our days as a British colony to the most recent presidential election. Poole perceived more theoretical objections; the major theme of these was that those who benefitted from libraries did not support them in proportion to that benefit. And he described the opposition to the public library that stemmed from the kind and quality of the books it circulated, notably fiction.[10]

## TAX SUPPORT

Those who favored tax-supported libraries stressed that it was economical to do so. One librarian delivered an address on the theme of the library as a paying investment, presenting the educational, cultural and economic arguments in terms of tax support. Another claimed that no other tax returned so much for so little, and several that it would save individuals money since every reader in a town could secure one hundred to one thousand times the amount of reading matter he could secure by acting individually.[11]

Although much of this discussion was simplistic, it did raise the fundamental issue of whether or not the library was a public good and answered the question affirmatively.[12] It established that a library and the educational, cultural, economic, and political benefits it produced was worth supporting. Tax support would be sensible, enabling the library to plan constructively since it was a more reliable source of income than private donations. By eliminating the necessity for charges, tax support would open the library to all, regardless of ability to pay,[13] thereby serving the American ideal of equality of opportunity. Tax support would transform a charity into an institution that was the property of all, thereby conferring increased dignity upon it. There was some recognition that taxation fell more heavily upon some than upon others, and that some would benefit more than others,[14] but the intellectual context remained that of traditional America: a relatively small and homogeneous community without great social and economic inequalities, in which all citizens participated in government, paid taxes, and derived benefits in approximately equal share. Advocates of tax support did not intend that the library should be free; they saw the library as providing services for which users paid by paying taxes.

Many of the elements in this late nineteenth-early twentieth century discussion have been recapitulated in terms of the fee vs. free controversy. The same arguments earlier fees called forth are being used again. Opponents of fees emphasize that denying an individual information (i.e., a database search) contradicts the American democratic tradition of equality of opportunity. The White House Conference on Library and Information Services, a group representing all shades of professional and lay opinion, held information to be a basic right of the individual in a free society and unequivocally declared, " . . . BE IT RESOLVED, that the White House Conference on Library and Information Services hereby affirms that all persons should have free access, without charge or fee to the individual, to information in public and publicly supported libraries."[15] Opponents of fees reassert the oft-used educational and economic lines of argument when they claim that benefits accrue to the community when an individual's information need is met. With their constant reiteration that fees prevent the poor from obtaining needed information, they recall the never completely superseded image of the public library as a form of charity, designed primarily to serve the information needs of the lower classes.

## *FAVOR FEES*

Those who favor fees counter the equality of opportunity argument by pointing out that it is equally in the American tradition for those who have succeeded to benefit from their exertions. They echo the position of the Social Darwinists: that it is inappropriate to subsidize some individuals at the expense of others. In treating user fees as a welcome source of income, they add one more source to the numerous sources proposed in the many articles on how to raise money for your library. Their assertion that user fees prevent frivolous use of services raises the question of whether the public library should not indeed serve frivolous purposes if that is what the tax-paying public wishes. The assertion that paying for information heightens an appreciation of it is an ironic variation of the earlier argument that tax support increases respect for the library.

Ultimately, of course, all these propositions can be reduced to one question: is or is not information a public good? And if it is, is it enough of a public good for the public to be willing to support it out of common resources? There are many services taxpayers judge worthwhile that they are unwilling to provide.

The conflict over charging for information is not, however, purely a disagreement over philosophical abstractions. Disputants cannot help being influenced in their views by realities of public library service as well as its ideals. They, and we, are very much aware that, however clear and generally accepted have been the goals of the public library—and that in itself is a matter of some dispute[16]—practice has often conflicted with and compromised these goals.

The most important influence has been the evident fact that the library does not serve all the people nor is it used primarily for serious informational purposes. From the beginning the large claims of educational, economic, moral, and political benefits were inconsistent with the allocation of effort. Public libraries are used and always have been used by a relatively small minority of the population, a minority which is largely middle class. Library users have, moreover, predominantly sought entertainment rather than enlightenment, fiction rather than information.

These inconvenient facts were recognized very early and much subsequent debate on the public library has focussed on the place of fiction in it. As early as 1876 some educated people were objecting to the widespread practice of libraries offering fiction in quantity. Fiction was called corrupting: in 1889 an article appeared attempting to demonstrate that libraries, established to improve moral tone by breaking the pernicious habit of too much novel reading, were encouraging immorality by making available trashy fiction.[17] Purchasing fiction was the misuse of public funds: by offering fiction the library was inequitably subsidizing the preferred entertainment of one group, the readers, while sports enthusiasts, theatergoers, and music lovers had to pay for their own out of resources that had been diminished to support the library.[18]

## *FICTION DEBATE*

But the fiction debate also raises questions that have present significance. Is the public library indeed an educational institution? Can the library really improve taste and raise the level of culture on either the individual or collective level? Does being democratic require it to give users what they request? How an individual answers these questions clearly affects whether he considers the public library a public good and whether or not he believes it should be supported from common resources. In terms of fee vs. free, the recreational, middle class character of the public library has to cast doubt upon just how important information is to library users and whether they cannot quite easily afford to pay for their information needs.

That tax-supported public libraries have not always offered all services completely free is another inconvenient historical fact. Although fees and charges[19] have not bulked large in librarians' thinking or practice,[20] they have often been levied. A recent survey shows how common and varied they are.[21]

Their fees and charges have been very heterogeneous, some have been charges for information, some for different types of services, and some for library use. Over time, the most frequently imposed has been that for use of a book in a rental collection, primarily for current popular fiction. There have also been charges for extraordinary reference service to business and industry, charges for interlibrary loans, and charges for the use of films, records, typewriters, and meeting rooms. Users have paid to have duplicate library cards issued and to use the library of a jurisdiction in which they do not pay taxes. And now there are often fees for database searches.[22] In a historical discussion of charging for services in traditionally free American libraries, Haynes McMullen described six general characteristics of charges: libraries have charged for a variety of services for a long time; libraries have not been consistent, for the same service some have charged, others have not; charges have always been controversial; charges have often been for services with which the librarian or board of trustees had little sympathy; the most serious questions about the practice have been in free public libraries; and charges have been more frequent when libraries have needed money most.[23]

## *MEASURES*

The fees libraries have collected have also displayed many of the features which characterize public sector fees in economists' terms: they have been discrete and measureable and related to benefits received; the beneficiary of a service has been readily identifiable and at least some of what has been received could be considered as solely in his private interest—the term user-specific is often encountered; and fees were easy to collect. Users found them relatively palatable because they were usually collected for new services and because they were either lower than or comparable to what charges were for the same service on the private market. They have, however, failed to satisfy one important characteristic of a public service user fee; they have not unquestionably been in agreement with the larger social objectives of the library. The distributional consequences of these fees have not been completely acceptable,[24] that is, charging fees excludes those who cannot pay them from services. Fees are particularly unacceptable when it is a fee for a database search because a database search serves the most sacred informational objectives of the public library. They are even less tolerable than earlier fees because a substitution is not available. With fiction, if a user was willing to wait, a copy of the desired title would eventually be available in the circulating collection; with photocopying, a user could write it out by hand. But databases are no longer merely machine versions of printed indexes; they do things that cannot be done with print resources, even assuming that all appropriate print resources are available in the particular library.

The arguments in the conflict over charging have been selective, as arguments in any conflict tend to be, and further discussion of the topic is only going to be fruitful if it begins to consider the real issues. We need to recognize that it is the underlying assumptions of the library faith that are at issue and clarify our terms. Are education, culture, a healthy economy, and an informed polity really public goods for which the public is willing to pay? Does the library in fact deliver education, culture, and the other rewards it promises? Is it not possible that the library instead provides other, equally worthwhile services, equally public goods?

Librarianship has changed from what it was in the late nineteenth century when the library faith was born. The existence and strength of such groups as the Association of Research Libraries, the American Association of School Librarians, and the Special Libraries Association, remind us that librarianship is no longer one profession, if indeed it ever was. The debates on professionalism have clarified that a library functions in a larger institutional environment, and that it is in that larger environment that priorities are determined. The issue of fee vs. free must be considered in many different situations.

So, too, is the present world of libraries a vastly different one from that of the late nineteenth century. To what extent do nineteenth century values continue to apply? The gigantic presence of television and radio, the growth of the information industry, the development of mass market paperbacks have significantly altered the library's environment. In this technological age it is entirely possible that the costs of database searching may diminish to a point where libraries can easily provide them free of charges. It is also possible that the funding of libraries may increase sufficiently to enable them to eliminate fees and render the entire debate irrelevant.

## REFERENCES

1. An excellent bibliographical essay summarizing the literature to its date of publication is Thomas J. Waldhart and Trudi Bellardo, "User Fees in Publicly Funded Libraries." *Advances in Librarianship* 9(1979): 31-61.
2. James I. Wyer, "What the Community Owes the Library," *Library Journal* 36(July 1911): 326.
3. *Library Journal* 1(October 30, 1876): 45-51.
4. James Howard Welland, *The Public Library Comes of Age* (London: Grafton, 1940), p. 3.
5. The next four paragraphs draw upon C.H. Cramer, *Open Shelves and Open Minds: A History of the Cleveland Public Library* (Cleveland and London: The Press of Case Western Reserve University, 1972); Phyllis Dain, *The New York Public Library: A History of Its Founding and Early Years* (New York Public Library, 1972); Sidney Ditzion, *Arsenals of a Democratic Culture* (Chicago: American Library Association, 1947); Philip Arthur Kalisch, *The Enoch Pratt Free Library: A Social History* (Metuchen, NJ: Scarecrow, 1969); A. W., "What a Library Does for a Town," *New York Libraries* 1(July 1908): 120-21; F. M. Crunden, "The Value of a Free Library," *Library Journal* 15(March 1890): 79-81; and F. M. Crunden, "What Is the Public Library for?" *Library Journal* 26(March 1901): 141.
6. Dain, p. 30.
7. Crunden, "The Value of a Free Library," p. 80.
8. W. Stanley Jevons, "The Rationale of Free Public Libraries," *Contemporary Review* (March 1881): 387, quoted in Ditzion, p. 104.
9. Welland, p. 3.
10. Poole, pp. 47-49.
11. Carl B. Roden, "The Library as a Paying Investment, *Wisconsin Library Bulletin* 8(February 1912): 5-8; A.W., "What a Library Does for a Town"; "Why the Library Should Be Supported by Public Tax," *New York Libraries* 2(April 1911): 244.
12. For an excellent discussion of the concept of public good in modern terms, see Miriam Braverman, "From Adam Smith to Ronald Reagan: Public Libraries As a Public Good," *Library Journal* 107(February 15, 1982): 397-401.
13. "Why [a] Library Should Be Free," *New York Libraries* 1(January 1908): 34-35 cites the example of the Olean Public Library as evidence that the removal of fees greatly increases membership.
14. M. D. O'Brien, "Free Libraries," in Thomas Mackay, ed. *A Plea for Liberty* (New York: D. Appleton, 1891), pp. 329-49 presents the argument most succinctly and draws the conclusion that public libraries should not, therefore, be tax supported.
15. White House Conference on Library and Information Services. *Information for the 1980's. Final Report* (Washington: Government Printing Office, n.d.), p. 46.
16. Welland, pp. 10-12.
17. Poole, pp. 48-51; James M. Hubbard, "Are Public Libraries Public Blessings?" *Library Journal* 14(October 1889): 407-409, reprinted from the September 1889 *North American Review*.
18. O'Brien, p. 344.

19. The definitions of fees, charges, and fines remain unresolved. In this article the terms fee and charge are used generally, to indicate cases in which the user pays the library for some good or service; a fine is a financial penalty.

20. Writings on public library finance and public library administration mention fees only in passing, if at all. Duncan Grey, *Public Library Finance* (London: George Allen and Unwin, 1938); *Wheeler and Goldhor's Practical Administration of Public Libraries,* revised by Carlton Rochell (New York: Harper and Row, 1981); Malcolm Getz, *Public Libraries: An Economic View* (Baltimore and London: Johns Hopkins University Press, 1980); *Alternatives for Financing the Public Library* (Prepared for the National Commission on Libraries and Information Science, 1974).

21. Mary Jo Lynch, "Confusion Twice Compounded: Report of a PLA Survey on Fees Currently Charged in Public Libraries," *Public Libraries* 17(1978): 11-13.

22. Mary Jo Lynch, *Financing Online Search Services in Publicly Supported Libraries: The Report of an ALA Survey* (Chicago: American Library Association, 1981) indicates how prevalent the practice is and analyzes the nature of the fees.

23. Haynes McMullen, "The History of Charging for Services in American Libraries that Have Traditionally Been Free," in Peter G. Watson, ed., *Charging for Computer-Based Reference Services,* (Chicago: American Library Association, 1978), pp. 3-16.

24. Nancy Van House De Wath, "Demand for Public Library Services: A Time Allocation and Public Finance Approach to User Fees," University of California, Berkeley, Ph.D., 1979, pp. 157-58.

# Fee or Free:
# The Data Base Access Controversy

## Dean Burgess

A checklist of the arguments for and against charging a fee for on-line reference searches is overdue. This article will review these arguments with their counter arguments from the point of view of the goals fees would serve, the general theory of fees and library access and as a financial question. It will then draw a conclusion.

Those who use data bases regularly can skip to "Goals." What exactly are we talking about charging for? First, we are not talking about general manual reference searches, or manual searches of computer generated COM (Computer output microform): or a printout from a computer data base purchased by a library in "hard copy" (that is printed on paper) or for access to the building and collection. What we are talking about is an on-line search (that is with our local computer tied into another computer with a large memory) and/or the subsequent printing of the results of that search if a "hard copy" is required.

Any reference department without this capability today is rather like a library without *Books in Print,* an encyclopedia and the *Readers Guide* twenty years ago: that is, a very small time operation.

Access to these data bases can be through dedicated telephone lines, computers which talk to computers, or simply a home computer with a modem (a device which allows computer data to be sent from one computer to another over regular telephone lines by calling a number in a distant city).

Everyone knows about Compu Serve, Orbit, DIALOGS, BRS,

---

Mr. Burgess is Director of the Portsmouth Public Library, 601 Court St., Portsmouth, VA 23704.

New York Times Data Base, Systems Development Corporation, Medline, ERIC, and the "Source" giving general information much as a ready reference shelf would to your computer over the phone, but you have to think for a moment to realize that the computerized ordering services like LIBRIS, the state library network union catalog, and the cataloging data base national utilities like OCLC are also of this same large family. In fact, there are more than 3,500 data bases in hundreds of disciplines in such specialized subjects as "photography" for example![1] These data bases do such varied jobs as help locate jobs for freelancers, give technical advice, make travel reservations, search specialized literature, give investment advice and dozens of other services. A good basic guide to them is Alfred Glossbrenner's, *The Complete Handbook of Personal Computer Communication* (St. Martins 1983, $14.95). Another useful guide: *OMNI Online Database Directory* (Macmillan, 1983) which is a directory of over 1,000 data bases accessible through a personal computer.

What makes these so different from the *Encyclopedia Britannica* that some reference librarians get the evil idea of charging for their use? The only real difference is that once the library has been charged the usual entry fee (rather like a membership initiation fee) you have a per use, per hour charge on most of them (rather like a long distance telephone call) and, of course, the added administrative costs in staff time (if the library insists on not opening the equipment to direct public use), space, equipment rental (or purchase) and the materials for "off line" prints of the material found "on line."

## *GOALS*

Let us now start our checklist of reasons for charging for the service with what the goals of such a charge might be:

1. To defray the unpredictable cost of use by the hour: this may be as low as $6.00 an hour or as high as $300 for a search. A patron on a very simple search could quickly bankrupt a library at the latter rate without the library being aware of it. A way to deal with this without charging a fee is to set a total number of hours the data base can be used in a budget line item and then cut off access when that figure is reached. This can be done by month or semester adjusted for the popularity of the particular data base and the projected sea-

sonal use. This guarantees that there is no longer an "open ended" and unpredictable cost and it can now be budgeted. Emergency use by a patron unwilling to wait for the free open access time of the month could still be charged for it, or the use deducted from the next open period. This would make access to the data base rather like access to the library itself: only limited by the times it can afford to be open.

2. To defray the total cost of the equipment, staff, marketing and materials (called cost recovery). On the other hand, if we do not do this with our regular service, which is often more costly in staff time and in books why should we do it for reference questions answered through data base searches?

We presume we need "marketing" only because we are unaware that the general public knows perfectly well that data bases exist and the data base owners are "marketing" them every day.

Do we charge staff, equipment and shelving space costs on our other services? Why single out this one service to pay for itself?

Some reference departments charge as much as $30 an hour for professional help and $16 for non-professionals (sounds a little like first class and tourist on the airlines) and even sell private memberships. The members are buying the time of government employees who I presume serve members first. Cost recovery makes these government employees feel they are in a private business and not subject to the library's choice of a primary clientele because private money has gone into the general fund to cover their salaries.

3. To make a profit for the library. Library service can always be sold. I will deal with the ethics of this later.

4. To make a profit for the parent institution. Some cities have learned that this is a hidden tax the public will accept in other areas (i.e. water, garbage collection, inspections, sewage and others) so why not libraries? Because the jurisdiction is doing this rather than face the public with a request for a new needed tax. It is a hidden tax, and such hidden taxes are basically dishonest and an example of political cowardice. If the public will not pay taxes for a service they don't want it! However, as D. A. Hicks points out "non-utility user charges . . . amounted to a full 14 percent" of municipal revenue in 1977.[2]

5. To raise money to upgrade the system in future without a budget defense. On the other hand, if a service would fail a budget defense is it really a service you should offer? What can you say to the

funding authority if you are caught collecting an unauthorized tax to avoid the budget cycle?

6. To discourage "entertainment" and "frivolous" use. This is, on the other hand, dangerously elitist. Is the librarian prepared to decide what is frivolous in someone else's field? Was Dr. Rubic's research on puzzles frivolous?

7. To prioritize use based on "need," "seriousness," the predetermined primary users the library is designed to serve, or some other criteria. This can only be answered by a study of the goals of the institution, but these divisions are often not clear. Are the tests you would have to introduce to fairly administer this cost effective? Are the presumptions of your "proper" audience and what is "proper" use correct? Will charging for the service really change the way the collection is used, or needs to be used? What are the public relations liabilities? Is this discriminatory?

8. To encourage the user to learn how to use the other less costly resources of the library before going "on line." This seems valid to an old reference librarian like myself on the surface, but it actually grows from an antitechnology bias. This is based on the presumption that there is some intrinsic good in knowing how to use hand methods in a reference search. In fact, in this electronic age such methods may no longer be a primary reference skill. The first place to go now may be the "on line" data base, then proceed to the hard copy it guides you to. There is also a great and growing body of information only available "on line" and never likely to come out in print. On line material is also often much more "up to date" than the material in printed form. There is also a question as to whether "on line" data is more costly than a hand reference search. A study by Stanley Elman indicated the average cost for an on line search with DIALOG is $47.00 while the average cost for the same hard copy search when staff time is factored in is—$250.00.[3]

9. To increase respect for the service among the public. The marketplace values a service or product in direct proportion to what they must pay for it, and so let's charge them and win their respect. I do not believe this even though I have heard it often and do not doubt a study could be designed to prove it (for example in studies of the most respected professions doctors, who certainly are expensive, get the most respect). If this were a valid goal we would want to see what the marketplace charges for information and charge more.

On the other hand, is our purpose to distribute information as widely as we can or to win the public's respect for ourselves and our products? I do not think frequently, with a glow of respect, about the person who wove the fabric of my three piece suit but without him I would be naked. Respect is overrated.

## *THE RIGHTS OF ACCESS*

But why are we even arguing this question? Isn't the right to use a library a freedom protected in law in America? The answer is no! The British have a clause in the "Public Libraries and Museums Act of 1964" which says: "no charge shall be made by a library authority,"[4] but we have no such law. In fact, the precedent for completely free access to libraries is not all that clear: hence the need for the resolution of the White House Conference on Libraries and Information Services advocating "full" access[5] and the 1977 American Library Association resolution on the subject[6] saying in part: "charging of fees and levies for information services, including those services using the latest information technology is discriminatory in publicly supported institutions providing libraries . . ."

Ironically ACRL has a discussion group on "Fee Based Information Centers in Academic Libraries. . ." and the ALA had a conference program presuming such a charge.[7] It had also defeated an earlier effort to make this point.[8] Any argument that such free access is guaranteed by the First Amendment is untested in the courts and, considering precedents, dubious.

A decision against fees was rendered by the Attorney General of California but that involved only the contract for service with non-residents who pay for service if an added fee is charged. It also is based on a California law guaranteeing "Free Access to the resources of libraries" as an adjunct to the free education system.[9] The library in Royal Oak, Michigan in the 1970's charged rental for the use of modern fiction (their funding authority didn't want to use tax dollars for this dubious purpose), and many libraries did this in the 1950's. Most older libraries grew from "rental collections" (some still have them) and James Rettig adds, fees for: ". . . reserving circulating books, replacing lost library cards, photocopies, interlibrary loans, genealogical searches, use of meeting rooms, . . . even, Haynes McMullan discovered, for using a dictionary for more than 15 minutes . . ."[10] Overdue fines which make a borrower ineligible are also a limit on "free access" through a fee.

I joined in the WHCLIS debate on the "free access" resolution as an alternate delegate when it lost in panel debate. It lost again on the floor where the word "free" was deleted from the resolution and replaced with "full." Free access to any of our services is not guaranteed. If we believe in it we must "fight on the beaches . . . Fight on the landing grounds . . . Fight in the fields and in the streets . . . Fight in the hills" and "never surrender."

## *DISCRIMINATION*

Isn't what we are talking about discrimination? As James Rettig so clearly outlines in the article cited above—if everyone must pay the fee (faculty, graduate students, undergraduates, non-students, children, librarians) a fee in itself is not legally discriminatory. It is a class of people, not the individual, who is protected. What is discriminatory is tagging the fee to certain user groups. On the other hand, those who oppose fees argue that the fee itself discriminates against those who cannot afford to pay the fee as a class and our libraries simply ". . . make themselves necessary to those in positions of influence. . ."[11] Our tax base they argue is disproportionately paid for by the poor and our services disproportionately go to the middle class.[12] This is exacerbated by adding fees, they believe. On the other hand, it can be argued that a service fee for everyone is actually fairer as it does not charge those who do not use the service while taxes charge every one.

An intriguing sidelight to the discrimination issue is provided by William Heinlen. He points out that the "trade off" California State College, Stanislaus used to make free on line data base access possible was to defray the cost by discontinuing some expensive "hard copy" indexes. He argues that, as data base searches require the intervention of a librarian at that college in using the terminal and the hard copy indexes do not, going exclusively to such technology is as discriminatory as keeping books in a locked cage. He poses the question: is it "better to restrict access to these materials so they may be offered for free?"[13] To be fair Heinlen was responded to by California State, Stanislaus, librarians saying that the librarians were simply "facilitators" and did not obstruct access and that the hard copy index cancellations in their case were only coincidentally at the same time the data base became available. No matter, Heinlen has a good point: access is access.

These data bases are designed by their vendors to be marketed directly to individuals or industries not requiring the intervention of a priest/librarian between the user and the data base. We must learn to let the public put its hands on our data base access terminals without supervision. The future requires that they know how to use them as well as they know how to read a book or use a dictionary.

To prove that fees by their nature are discriminatory against some particular class of people is at best difficult even though common sense tells us they are.

## FINANCIAL QUESTIONS

James Rice argues[14] that there is a rapid rise of "information brokerages" using data bases in the private sector and that in New York City the "clearing house" for these is not the New York Public Library but the Chase Manhattan Bank. He argues that libraries will be eclipsed by the private sector in one of our primary products (information) because we cannot afford to compete as a result "of declining budgets." He continues that if we attempted "cost recovery" on a "not for profit basis . . ." libraries "would not only undercut the profiteers but . . ." libraries " . . . might also improve their image."

He cites as his precedent for "cost recovery" the "books by mail" services which are now popular and points out that most libraries do collect for postage and handling in this service.

He says that not providing data base services for financial reasons is in itself "restricting access." He says if paying a fee is required to get what the public needs then let's charge a fee.

Hicks adds to this the point that public libraries are primarily funded by the property tax and that it is not an equitable tax. Libraries ". . . distribute their products at zero price while financing them through coercive, unequal taxes." He concludes that a user charge is "a worthwhile partial remedy to overcome the dependence on local property taxation."

What if we prove, for financial reasons, less able than the commercial "information industry" to survive? What will that hurt? F. M. Blake points out that private industry would only provide the information that sells for a profit.[15] This way lies a mandate that we charge for our service in order to keep alive and be able to compete with a broader spectrum of information to assure greater equity than a purely private sector information service would offer.

A financial argument for factoring the cost of data base searches into the total budget and then offering the service free of charge that does not appear in the literature is that, as demonstrated by Stanley Elman (and referred to earlier in this article), it is actually cheaper to do a literature search on most data bases than it is to do it by hand. I suspect this is ignored because the only way this economy will offset the cost is by reducing the personnel in the reference service, or by using less trained and thus less expensive, personnel. No librarian wants to face that although it is the most logical way to defray the cost of introducing data bases without charging a fee.

While we are talking about financial matters there are two financial arguments against charging fees often presented. They do not seem to fit anywhere else so let's put them here. Both, I think, are very weak.

First, there is the argument that fees require us to pay twice for the service: once through taxes and once through the fee. Unfortunately this is so general in all other government services that it doesn't hold much water. We pay highway tolls, sales taxes, garbage collection fees, water bills and dozens of license fees to the taxing agency as additional hidden taxes.

Second is the argument that if we opened the door to "cost recovery" our funding agency would realize we can pay for ourselves and discontinue its subsidies. Government officials are not fools. They know that the whole cost of a library system could not be raised through fees. They are occasional users of the system and generally know its value. They know that libraries are popular with the taxpayers and when libraries want to we can raise a very strong lobby. It continues to amaze me how librarians underestimate their strong political position: no one hates us, most people love us, everyone admits we have a worthwhile job to do, 60% of the people in most cities are registered borrowers (more than for most city services) and our supporters are well read and articulate. This argument is a red herring.

Even from a practical point of view library cuts have little impact on the financial stability of governments no matter how hard pressed they are. John Smith points out that we represent only 1½ percent of government's costs.[16] Hardly an attractive area in which to resolve a government deficit.

Finally, there is the question of whether a fee will reduce the use of a service. No hard statistics on this are in the literature for data base use, but in the case of general circulation D. A. Hicks finds instituting "out of town fees" does reduce circulation. This, he points out, also reduces the efficiency of the system, but most libraries he admits are not judged by efficiency.

## REALITIES

A study of California libraries in 1979 indicated that 70 percent of the libraries responding to the survey offered data base search capability. Of those 60 percent charge "at least some users at some time." If this is a nationally valid statistic it is twice the "less than one third" Mary Jo Lynch estimated charged for this service in 1977.[17] Among public libraries, 52 percent offered service without charging, while in community college libraries some 60 percent charge for searches. Among public college and university libraries 79 percent of those offering data base searches charge for them, and 88 percent of the private colleges and universities charge for search."[18]

Data base use is certainly widespread and charging for it, though uncertain in the public library, is a fact of life in the academic library. Milo Nelson actually argues that public library users are ready for charges and ". . . it might be the very best time . ." to hit them with it.[19]

## CONCLUSION

Data base searching tools and the data bases themselves are not different in any essential way from a book on our reference shelf except that they contain more, do not require new editions, are better indexed, may be searched with a multipart formula of words rather than a single word and are paid for only when they are used and then only to the extent they are used.

Our impression that we are dealing with a totally different creation is false. It is based on a misunderstanding of what a data base does: either a fear of the technology, or an unwarranted respect for it.

The data base is nothing more than a newer and better *Reader's Guide,* directory or encyclopedia. If your library could not afford a particularly expensive encyclopedia would you decide to buy it anyway, keep it behind the desk and charge for anyone to use it?

That is exactly what we are doing with data base access when we charge a fee. The idea to charge for its use is the opportunistic inspiration of those who have throughout believed that information should be a commodity of commercial trade and not a right of the citizens of a democracy. We must, like J. K. Chesterton's "Freethinker," "Face the curate bold and free and never sit upon his knee."

If we think that public library service is the essential underpinning for free enterprise guaranteeing each of us access to the information to compete in the free marketplace, the kingpost of our republic set in place by Thomas Jefferson himself and the centerpiece of egalitarianism then we must keep all public library services free and not single out one part to charge for because it is particularly popular, new, or efficacious. The same is true for school and college library services. If we believe the library central to the learning process, in fact, the service around which the institution was built all its services must be free to all students and faculty on an equal basis.

All library services should be free. If you believe this and cannot afford the data base then admit the planning tool of the budget has not proved the need and don't buy it.

On the other hand, if we believe that the library is a reasonable revenue generating source for our hard pressed public and private funding agencies and this out ranks the public's general informational needs, let us frankly say that and charge for the whole library service and not use newness as an excuse to charge for any one selected part as we add to it or expand it, or set up an adjunct false "private" business in the academic library to salve our conscience.

If we understand what "free research" is (the one thing which has raised us above those unimaginative, plodding, ordered societies which "direct" research) we must not prejudge the value, or seriousness of a student's enquiry and charge him for something because we do not understand its value. We must not set up a requirement of the availability of cash as an obstacle. The library's services must be free. There is no law which says this but there is a clear benefit to our nation in free service and a clear tradition and a moral imperative for us to supply it. The arguments in the literature for charging fees seem, to me, to sound suspiciously like the justifications "after the fact" of administrators forced into a course of action they know is not desirable. If what we want is some respect for the service and the profession, that posture is not one which will gain it.

## REFERENCE NOTES

1. Sealfon, Peggy. "Telecomputing"—*Peterson's Photographic* 12: 28-9. February 1984.
2. Hicks, D. A. "Diversifying fiscal support by pricing public library service." *Library Quarterly* 50: 453-74 October 1980.
3. Elman, Stanley A. "Cost comparisons of manual and on line computerized literature searching." *Special Libraries* 66: 12-18 January 1975.
4. "Charges by fair means or foul." *Library Association Record* 85: 133, April 1983.
5. White House Conference on Libraries and Information Services. *Resolution.* WHCLIS, Washington, D. C. 1979.
6. "ALA policy manual" in the *ALA Handbook of Organizations 1983-84.* ALA, Chicago. 1983 (page 205).
7. *Fee or Free* (2 audio tapes) ALA, Chicago 1983. (Note: This title is misleading. The program started with the presumption that every one charges fees. It simply advises how those fees should be assessed.)
8. Berry, John. "The fee dilemma." *Library Journal* 102: 651 March 15, 1977.
9. "California nixes fees for basic library service.: *Library Journal* 104: 451-2 February 15, 1979.
10. Rettig, James "Rights, resolutions, fees and reality." *Library Journal* 106: 301-4 February 1, 1981.
11. Rice, J. G. "To fee or not to fee." *Wilson Library Bulletin* 53: 658-9 May 1979.
12. Weaver, Frederick Stirton "For public libraries the poor pay more." *Library Journal* 104:352-7, February 1, 1979.
13. Heinlen, William F. "Letter" *Library Journal* 104: 498-9, August 1979.
14. Rice, James R. Jr. "Overdue" *Wilson Library Bulletin* 53: 658-9 May 1979.
15. Blake, F. M. "The selling of the library." *Drexel Library Quarterly* 12: 149-58 January to April 1976.
16. Smith, John "A conflict of values—charges in the publicly funded library." *The Journal of Librarianship* 13: 1-8 January 1981.
17. Plotnik, A. "The issues revisited." *American Libraries* 9: 432 July - August 1978.
18. DeWath, Nancy "Letters" *Library Journal* 104: 1292 June 15, 1979 (a follow up in clearer terms of an earlier article by her)
19. Nelson, Milo "Editorial" *Wilson Library Bulletin* 53:676 June 1979.

## BIBLIOGRAPHY

"A library and information science research agenda for the 1980's: Summary report: *Library Research* Fall 1983.
Watson, Peter G. *Charging for Computer Based Reference Services.* American Library Association: Chicago, 1978.
Mananjian, L. "Fee based information service." *Bowker Annual of Library and Book Trade Information* 1980. R. R. Bowker, New York, 1980.
Amerian Society for Information Science *Proceedings* (Volume 16 and 17) The Society, Minneapolis, 1979.
Ferguson, D. "Cost of charging for information service" in *On line Bibliographic Services: Where We Are Where We Are Going.* American Library Association: Reference and Adult Services Division, Chicago, 1977.

## ABOUT INSTRUCTION

# Conflicts Between Reference Librarians and Faculty Concerning Bibliographic Instruction

David Isaacson

Who was Perkin Warbeck? Who is the current Nizam of Hyderabad? Name a book written by Smelfungus. Who said "I'll lug the guts into the neighbor room"?

These are some typical reference questions from an assignment to a Freshman expository writing class which our reference department tries to help students answer each semester. Some of the questions have been difficult for our staff to answer, so it is not surprising that the students in this class are usually bewildered by them. Since at least twenty students a semester are given this assignment, this is, from the point of view of our staff, an ideal opportunity to suggest to the professor a session in library instruction. But our point of view is not the only one which must be considered. The professor objects to his students being helped with this assignment. Our staff doesn't want to defy the professor, but we sympathize with the students' frustration with this assignment.

This situation can be considered a typical example of a conflict between reference librarians and faculty. My attempt to make some

---

Mr. Isaacson is Assistant Head of Reference and Humanities Librarian in the Dwight B. Waldo library at Western Michigan University, Kalamazoo, MI 49001.

© 1985 by The Haworth Press, Inc. All rights reserved.

sense out of the conflict I have with professors who give assignments like these—and who refuse offers of library instruction—has been the catalyst for this essay.

This conflict is particularly distressing because I made the mistake of taking it personally. I called up the professor (whom I had not met before) to suggest that his students might benefit from a session of library instruction. I thought I was being tactful, but his immediate, angry response was something like:"you run the library, mister, and I'll teach my own class."

It has taken me some time to realize that however deferential I thought I was in making this suggestion, the professor clearly interpreted it as an unwarranted intrusion on his pedagogical "turf." I was angry for being treated unfairly. Upon reflection, however, I can view his objection more objectively. I must have given the impression that I was questioning the professor's authority or competence as a teacher. Perhaps I helped to set up the conflict by implying that the library "belongs" to librarians, rather than teachers and students.

Because of this confrontation not only was an opportunity for collegial exchange lost, but, more importantly, I think the students involved lost an opportunity to learn something of value. This professor apparently believes, as many do, that students should learn how to use a library by trial and error. He may believe, since he provides no assistance to the students himself, and since he does not want librarians to assist them, that instruction in library use will prevent students from learning on their own. He may believe that the main point of such an assignment is to separate the able from the less able students. The assignment appears to be unfocused. I'm not sure there is discussion of it in class. I am sure that some of the students copy answers from one another. It is very difficult for our staff to provide each student with assistance in the location of types of reference sources that will help them with this assignment without giving them the exact sources of answers to these questions.

The professor hasn't placed a context around these questions. For example, Hyderabad is a state in India that was ruled by a Nizam—at the time the professor first gave the assignment. But this is no longer true. The correct answer to this question now, as of 1983, is that there is *no* current Nizam of Hyderabad. Similarly, the students have no clue that "I'll lug the guts into the neighbor room" is a quote from *Hamlet*. How can they be expected to know they need a concordance to Shakespeare unless they first know what a concordance is and then that a character from one of Shakespeare's plays makes this statement?

## *WORKING TOGETHER*

I agree with this professor that students ought to learn how to work independently, but as an academic reference librarian I believe I have a responsibility to assist students, formally or informally, directly or indirectly, to gain confidence in their use of the library. I hope my motive in offering library instruction is to help students, rather than to make things easier for our staff or to challenge a professor's library assignment.

Under ideal circumstances reference librarians and faculty would cooperate in teaching what each knows best; the content of a subject would be closely integrated, or at least related, to library instruction so that each reinforced the other. Under the best of circumstances there would be no conflict of pedagogical territoriality. Students would, presumably, enjoy finding out that there is no current Nizam of Hyderabad because they have some appreciation for the process of political change *and* for the process of selecting reference sources to document such changes. Some appreciation for the variety of Shakepeare's language might make "I'll lug the guts into the neighbor room" not simply an idle chore of identifying a quotation. For all the innocent student knows, Mickey Spillane might have written this line. Hamlet says this to his mother just after he has killed Polonius. Why does he choose such seemingly brutal words? Did these words have the same connotations for Shakespeare as they do for us today? A professor and a librarian who trusted one another might create a library assignment in which such questions were the real focus—not simply the identification of a quotation. Such an assignment might provide students with the opportunity to take pleasure out of finding a sense of order in the library.

Such a partnership does sometimes exist, especially at small liberal arts colleges like Earlham, where a tradition of collegiality between reference librarians and faculty has developed. But even there, and during the experiment conducted by Patricia Knapp at Montieth College, less than ideal relationships between librarians and faculty have been acknowledged.

Most conflicts between the two groups are usually not as overt or as extreme as the one I have described. My intention here is to identify the major reasons for conflicts between reference librarians and faculty concerning the function and significance of bibliographic instruction. I would like to distinguish between conflicts which may be a source of constructive interchange, and those which are probably not worth trying to resolve. Some of the conflicts about bibliographic instruction are due to the differences in role and status of the faculty member and the reference librarian. There is a need to acknowledge some of the often unstated and sometimes unconscious conflicts between these two groups if there is reason to hope the conflicts can either be resolved or result in better understanding of respective differences. There is considerable benefit in transforming what is at first perceived to be a conflict into what is later understood to be simply a difference that need not threaten the self worth of either group.

## *STATUS CONFLICTS*

When the conflicts between faculty and reference librarians concern only a struggle over status, they can be regarded as unfortunate. But when we consider our fundamental shared responsibility—to help students learn—these conflicts must be regarded as trivial. When such conflicts prevent or hinder students from learning, a bond of trust between teachers and students, or between librarians and students, has been violated. The relatively inconsequential conflicts about role and status may not have to be either fully understood or resolved, but we should try to understand and resolve those conflicts which interfere with students' education.

One of the most basic sources of conflict between faculty and reference librarians is that many faculty simply don't regard the library as a place where useful teaching can or should be done. As Patricia Knapp said: "Most college instructors, however much value they set upon problem-solving skills as an objective of liberal arts education, do not think of the library as an instrument to be used in the solution of problems. They think of it as a place to get books. And perhaps too many librarians, familiar as they are with the complexity of the organization they maintain, think the library functions to its fullest capacity when it merely supplies books."[1]

If faculty members cannot conceive of the library as anything but a repository of books, the librarian may have a difficult job convincing them otherwise. These faculty are, however, simply innocent about the use of the library as a means of teaching; they are not necessarily hostile to the notion. If they only think the library is a place to get books, it is not likely that they will devise library assignments for their students, and therefore no open conflict is likely to develop with the reference librarians.

But many faculty do in fact have a more sophisticated view of the library, although it is still a perspective quite different from that of most bibliographic instructors. When these faculty acknowledge that their students could benefit from library instruction, they often have only the mechanics of decoding citations in mind. Patricia Knapp, in another publication, describes these faculty as follows: "Most college faculty see library instruction as dealing with bits of information, undeniably useful, but fragmented, not related to any single framework, not calling for problem-solving behavior, for critical thinking, for imagination. Most college students see it as sheer high school busy work."[2]

These faculty, unlike the first group, apparently do see the library as more than simply a storehouse, but they don't appreciate that effective use of the library involves anything more than elementary skills. And since the students often have an even more negative image of what library instruction can do for them, it is not surprising that librarians often have a difficult job convincing both students and faculty that library instruction can be something more than an exercise in boring and obvious finding techniques.

## *THIRD GROUP*

There is a third group of faculty with whom the reference librarian would presumably feel more at ease. These faculty want their students to understand much more than the basic mechanics of using the card catalog and *Reader's Guide*; they want their students to become adept researchers. But very often these faculty, quite understandably from their point of view, conceive of library research only as something they already know how to do, not as something a librarian can help them—or their students—do better. Once again, Patricia Knapp has described this group well and the potential for conflict between them and some reference librarians: "We conceive of the library as a highly complicated system, or better, a network of interrelated systems, which organizes and controls all kinds of communication. A few instructors understand this conception, but we believe that more conceive of sophisticated library understanding and competence as 'command of the literature of a field of study.' This is what they, themselves, have acquired in their years of training and experience, and this is what they hope to stimulate their students to acquire."[3]

This group would presumably be easier for the librarian to work with than faculty members who can't conceive of the library as a teaching instrument, or who view library instruction as teaching only decoding techniques. But this third group may be just as reluctant to cooperate with bibliographic instructors because they may believe, with rather understandable professional pride, that research skills can't or shouldn't be separated from knowledge of a discipline. They have a point of course, but it is a point which need not put them in conflict with reference librarians.

## *FOURTH GROUP*

A fourth group of faculty may be more easily persuaded to admit that the library is a place larger than their subject specialty, and they may also understand that librarians are uniquely qualified to teach them and their students how best to exploit the library's resources. But this group may still come into conflict with reference librarians because they may resent the fact of the library's resources presenting a challenge to their point of view. They may then also resent the librarian as an extension of the threat represented by the library's collection. Evan Farber describes this source of conflict as follows: "Many teachers have fragile egos, and because someone wants to work with their students—someone who can point out materials and methods with which they may be unfamiliar—it is easy for them to infer that others think them inadequate."[4]

These faculty present the most unfortunate conflicts with reference librarians because, on the one hand, they acknowledge our expertise and seem to recognize, however begrudgingly, that we could help their students, but, on the other hand, they appear to think of librarians as rivals rather than colleagues.

A fifth group of faculty likely to come into conflict with reference librarians may share some of the characteristics of the other groups, but their major characteristic is, or appears to be, laziness. This group can't be bothered to discuss a library assignment with the librarian before the bibliographic instruction session. They may agree with all the suggestions a librarian makes about the objectives of the instruction—as long as there is no assignment they have to grade after the session. Typically, these faculty schedule the library class on days when they will be out of town, or they have something they regard as more important to do.

## GOOD ADVICE

It is usually advisable for the professor to be present during bibliographic instruction in order to underscore the significance of this instruction. Interaction between the professor and the librarian should help to establish the relevance of the instruction to specific library assignments. It is possible, however, that a professor does not want to be present during the library instruction because he believes that his presence would undermine the librarian's authority. If the professor and librarian do not wish to share their teaching responsibilities, it is possible that the professor's presence in the library may even inhibit the librarian from establishing an effective teaching relationship with students.

So far I have been describing conflicts that exist because faculty don't sufficiently understand what bibliographic instruction is or what bibliographic instructors can do for them and their students. But librarians also contribute to these conflicts with their own preconceptions concerning the faculty.

Some conflicts between faculty and reference librarians have little to do with role conflict, but may result from a failure to understand what the professor intends the bibliographic instruction to accomplish. Librarians may intend to provide sophisticated instruction when the faculty only want library orientation, or we may provide only orientation when they expect instruction. We may, in fact, not deliver what we seem to have promised. A professor who expects his students to know the major resources in history may not understand the librarian's suggestion that instruction in the intricacies of Library of Congress subject headings ought to precede instruction in the use of *Historical Abstracts*. Unless the librarian discusses the assignment with the professor, and, indeed, makes sure that *some* library assignment is to be related, or better, integrated with the library instruction, the bibliographic session may be irrelevant to the objectives of the course. Some librarians may go so far as to believe the opposite: the objectives of the course are irrelevant to the objectives of bibliographic instruction. It takes diplomacy to persuade many faculty that we know things about the library that they don't know. If the professor and the librarian don't understand one another, the librarian runs the risk of alienating both the professor and the students by presenting information that may be too simple or too complex for their needs.

Another source of conflict may result from the typically bureaucratic organization of most reference departments versus the typically collegial organization of most faculty departments. Most librarians who teach do so in addition to other duties. With notable exceptions like Sagamon State University, most bibliographic instructors are reference librarians who have numerous other responsibilities besides teaching. Although it is true that faculty often have research as well as teaching responsibilities, if they are conscientious about teaching they are accustomed to spending considerable time preparing for lectures, grading assignments, advising students, and so on. The typical bibliographic instructor, on the other hand, may not have as much time to devote to preparation for teaching. But it is also true that, with the exception of semester courses in library use, most bibliographic instruction takes place in an hour or two. Teaching is a primary activity for the faculty; it is usually a secondary activity for reference librarians.

It should be obvious then, that most bibliographic instructors are not nearly as responsible as conventional faculty for the intellectual development of students. For librarians to claim that short bibliographic instruction sessions are equivalent to a semester of teaching by the faculty would be absurd. Nevertheless, some librarians, without devoting nearly as much time to instruction as faculty, want to claim a teacher's prerogatives.

## *INTERNAL DISPUTES*

Another source of conflict about bibliographic instruction does not concern conventional teachers at all, except as they may be the indirect victims of it. This conflict centers around internal disputes that sometimes arise between bibliographic instructors and other librarians about priorities. Some bibliographic instructors may neglect other duties in order to have time to prepare for instruction. Other reference librarians who don't teach may resent those who do. And, of course, if the reference department hasn't settled the perennial dispute about how much of the work of the department should be devoted to instruction and how much to conventional reference service, there is bound to be a conflict. Even if the reference department has settled this question for itself, various members of technical services may not appreciate, and may in fact resent, the more public visibility of the librarian who teaches. Many advocates of bibliographic instruction are quite idealistic and sometimes give the impression of being self-righteous reformers and elitists. Some bibliographic instructors are quite proud of being members of what increasingly is coming to be regarded as a revolutionary, or at least a highly political movement within librarianship. Reactions to the sometimes strident rhetoric and the dogmatic pronouncements of some members of this movement are, therefore, to be expected. It is not surprising, either, that some of the reactions to this movement are themselves dogmatic, generating more heat than light.[5]

But even when there is no serious conflict between bibliographic instructors and other librarians, and even when reasonably clear communication exists between bibliographic instructors and faculty, there is still another possible source of conflict. This conflict may arise when the librarian chooses to covertly or overtly challenge the authority of the teacher. I hope such a conflict does not often occur, but the potential for it exists every time bibliographic instructors allow themselves to react defensively when they are treated by faculty as subordinates, rather than as colleagues.

It is easy to bristle somewhat when faculty appear to make no effort to understand the difference between an orientation tour and the loftier ambitions many of us have for bibliographic instruction. We should not expect many faculty to understand the difference between orientation, instruction in the mechanics of using basic sources, and more sophisticated and specialized bibliographic instruction. Evan Farber, among others, suggests that we should prove to faculty that we are interested in their research before suggesting library instruction. He also suggests that we establish a reputation with them for being able to run the library well—what, after all, they expect us to do—before we suggest an innovation like bibliographic instruction.[6]

But for all of our best efforts, some faculty are going to persist in viewing library instruction differently from reference librarians. Some reference librarians, seeming not to understand the difference between serving the faculty and acting servilely, may be tempted to subvert them. Joseph P. Natoli, for instance, has argued that the traditional academic structure in which professors are the only teachers prevents students from learning anything outside the "institutionalization of learning" through prescribed courses and the professor's apparent monopolization of knowledge. As he says:

> As a librarian, I think the fundamental issue here is a dichotomy between a librarian within an academic institution but not institutionalized, not dependent at core upon the academic structure, and a professor totally dependent and totally supportive of the academic structure. And that academic structure, according to a vast amount of evidence, is not conducive to learning but generally confuses efficient teaching with sufficient learning. I call this a dichotomy on an intellectual level but in practice what it amounts to is conflict. When I resign myself to tending to academic structure I know is destructive not only of learning but of people, students, faculty and librarians, I give up my true function as a librarian and play a role assigned to me.[7]

Natoli is correct in arguing that teachers, because of the rigidities of academic structure, sometimes actually prevent students from meaningful learning. But he believes this occurs most of the time, whereas I think this is an occasional phenomenon. But even if his analysis is essentially correct, I can't agree with Natoli's revolutionary role for reference librarians acting against the institutionalization of learning. Until there is no difference between a professor who professes to teach and a librarian who professes to teach, I think librarians should be content to support, not supplant, the teaching efforts of the faculty. The student ought to be the primary concern of both the reference librarian and the faculty member. If librarians believe that teachers are not, in fact, meeting their pedagogical responsibilities, it is usually better to ignore those with whom we can't agree, rather than to defy them. I see no justification for overt rivalry between bibliographic instructors and faculty.

## *JUSTIFICATION*

There is justification for reference librarians to assist students on library assignments for which the professor has not expressly forbidden our assistance. We may "subvert" a student's expectations about the library without ever coming into conflict with a faculty member. Sometimes, of course, learning is not directly related to what a teacher says; a teacher may be more effective as a guide than as a lecturer. Some librarians can be quite effective in their informal teaching role at the reference desk; this role is sometimes more significant than formal bibliographic instruction.

Conflicts between faculty and librarians are likely to continue concerning bibliographic instruction. Some of these conflicts may be resolved by a mutual willingness to understand each other's prerogatives and preconceptions. Other conflicts need not be resolved if they do not deter each group from doing its work. The most fortunate aspect of some of these conflicts is the opportunity they provide for two groups with many differences to see that they nevertheless have other things in common. The most unfortunate aspect of some of these conflicts, however, is that they may prevent students from learning valuable connections between library use and mastery of a subject. The student's loss is far more significant, finally, than any threat to the prestige or status of a librarian or a faculty member.

Bibliographic instruction should not be an end in itself, but neither should the teaching of a conventional subject. Perhaps the most important goal of both the faculty and bibliographic instructors is not to teach a given body of knowledge but how to "frame" questions. As Paul Lacey has said: "I speak of framing rather than asking questions, for obviously all inquiry begins with simply asking something. What I am trying to get at is the process by which one examines a body of material, or an event, or a phenomenon, and at the same time examines the tools or the means by which a further examination of that event or phenomenon can be best made."[8]

Lacey is describing a particularly harmonious relationship between himself as a professor and reference librarians who have helped him think more clearly about both his research and the library assignments he gives to students. It may be a mistake for bibliographic instructors to assume that our primary teaching responsibility is to provide information, or instruction about how to locate information. Surely it is more correct to say that we provide *sources* of information, and that beyond demonstrating how to use various library sources, we have an opportunity to help both students and faculty to frame questions, or to see relationships between questions and the process of using library resources to explore those questions.

Of course, if patrons don't want our assistance in this endeavor, we shouldn't force it upon them. Sometimes we have no direct teaching responsibility. But, to the extent that reference librarians can help students think more clearly, as well as showing them how library resources "work," we share a fundamental responsibility with faculty. Though our expertise is often quite different from the faculty, librarians and faculty ought to see their differences as complementary ways of helping students, not as divisive conflicts between themselves.

## REFERENCES

1. Patricia Knapp. "College Teaching and the Library" *Illinois Libraries* 40:833. December, 1958.
2. Patricia Knapp. *The Montieth College Library Experiment.* New York: Scarecrow Press, 1966. p. 27.
3. *Ibid.,* p. 40.
4. Evan Farber. "Librarian-Faculty Communication Techniques" in *Proceedings of the Southeastern Conference on Approaches to Bibliographic Instruction.* Edited by Cerise Oberman-Soroka. Charleston, South Carolina: College of Charleston, 1978. p. 72.
5. See, for instance, the results of recommendations made by the ACRL Think Tank on Bibliographic Instruction in *College and Research Libraries News* pp. 394-98. December 1981 and "Reactions to the Think Tank Recommendations" *Journal of Academic Librarianship* 9: 4-14. March, 1983.
6. Farber, p. 74.
7. Joseph P. Natoli. "Toward an Existential Future" *The Reference Librarian* 1/2: 109-10. Fall/Winter, 1981.
8. Paul A. Lacey. "The Role of the Librarian in Faculty Development: A Professor's Point of View" in *Library Instruction and Faculty Development: Growth Opportunities in the Academic Community.* Edited by Nyal Z. Williams and Jack T. Tsukamoto. Ann Arbor, Michigan: Pierian Press, 1980. p. 19.

# Help Your Administration Support Bibliographic Instruction

Robert E. Brundin

Any library contemplating offering a comprehensive program of library instruction must begin by asking three questions: will the program meet student needs, will the goals and objectives be realistic, and will the program be cost effective?[1] The last question is probably the most difficult to answer, yet it is a question which must certainly be answered if administrators are to be convinced of the need to support and commit funds to programs of library instruction.

The problem of convincing administrators in an academic institution of the cost-effectiveness of library instruction is certainly not a new one, but one which has been with us for as long as such programs have existed, which, according to one researcher, has been for more than one hundred years.[2] Over the years academic librarians in reference departments responsible for programs of bibliographic instruction have no doubt employed many and varied methods to convince administrators to support such programs; I would like to concentrate on a few which I have found, through experience, to be most workable.

I remember at least fifteen years ago having to work very hard to convince the administration of a community college of the need to institute a course on "how to use the library." In the end I was able to get the course approved as it was organized on a self-study basis, thus attracting large numbers of students and bringing increased revenues to the institution. In short, the course actually made money for the college, and this turned out to be by far the best means of gaining administrative approval!

Now, however, with the economy down across North America

---

Dr. Brundin is Professor, Faculty of Library Science, University of Alberta, Edmonton, Alberta. He was for many years director of a large community college library in California.

© 1985 by The Haworth Press, Inc. All rights reserved.

and library budgets being cut in many institutions, the problem of convincing administration of the need to finance programs of library instruction has become more difficult than ever before. As librarians, we must be able to demonstrate conclusively that library instruction represents a vital element, probably one of the *most* vital elements, in the program of any academic library.

Institutional administrative support is critical to ensure the success of any program of library instruction. Such programs often involve obtaining released time from regular functions for existing staff; the securing of additional staff; funds to create or purchase instructional materials of various sorts; printing costs for workbooks; support for staff travel to conferences or workshops or for in-service training; the obtaining of facilities in which the instruction can be held; and often funds to support such activities as use of the computer or of various types of audiovisual equipment. If instruction is course-integrated, significant amounts of time must be spent in working with faculty to develop instructional units, and time means money for salaries.[3]

No program of library instruction can be offered at absolutely no cost, nor is it right that the costs of such a program be absorbed in a library budget not designed to accommodate them. Thus support of administration becomes crucial if the program is to be viable and effective.

As has been pointed out frequently, academic administrators are under many pressures in the 1980's, faced on the one hand with decreasing resources and on the other with inflation, increasing enrollments, and demands for new programs.[4] As part of this administrative group, academic library administrators are subject to many of the same pressures; in fact, with respect to the factor of inflation, they are probably under more pressure than are other administrators.[5]

## *PRESSURES*

In the face of these various pressures, the degree to which administrators view the role of the library as essential to the work of the institution can affect the task of obtaining support for a program of library instruction. It should go without saying that if the program does not enjoy the support of the library administration itself, the task will be quite impossible.

Some college and university administrators hold a quite limited view of the role of the library in the institution, one that in some cases, unfortunately, has not changed much since the nineteenth century. In short, these administrators persist in viewing the library primarily as a *storehouse* for materials, rather than as a *workshop* in which these materials are explained and used, to employ two favorite analogies.

This limited view of the role of the library is, I believe, often the result of two factors: (1) busy administrators tend not to make great use of libraries in general, either professionally or for recreational purposes; and (2) they tend not to enter their own campus libraries very often, at least not for periods long enough to enable them to get a real picture of what is going on inside. Likewise, the tendency is sometimes to view the graduate and special collections as resources for the faculty and doctoral students only, and the undergraduate facilities as mainly study areas.[6] Library instruction, in this context, becomes a very non-essential activity.

What can be done to change this picture? What can you, as a bibliographic instruction librarian, do to show administrators not only the value of the library within the institution but the value of library instruction itself?

First, you can make efforts to get them inside the library to see what is taking place there. (Obviously, this will be a much easier task in the small college than in the large university.) Invite administrators to join any instructional sessions you are scheduling for new students or faculty; more importantly, give them roles in introducing such sessions, so that they *have* to be present! I found this worked to some degree.

Frankly, I think if you can through some means *involve* administrators in a library instruction session, this is the best method of all, since you "kill two birds with one stone," as it were. They are introduced to the many contributions the library makes to the educational process, and to the program of library instruction at the same time. This might be a difficult task, though in my own experience at the college level we made such sessions mandatory not only for new faculty members coming to the institution but also for new administrators. This might not be an unworkable idea even at the university level.

I also found that scheduling certain meetings in the library which involved the presence of administrators also brought them in contact with library operations, though they often had little time for observation. Some librarians have had success with holding "open houses" to which all faculty and administration are invited.

## *FULLY INFORMED*

Second, I feel you should make an effort to keep administration fully informed with respect to all of your activities. Write annual reports which are brief, to-the-point, and well-illustrated; your graphics staff can help you with this. Few administrators, or others, for that matter, have the time to read through a 50-page annual report of the library, but most do have time to examine a five-page brochure nicely illustrated with photographs, and with statistics prominently displayed by means of graphs and charts.

Bring to the attention of administrators important statistics with relation to your bibliographic instruction program. Such statistics might include the results of pre-tests and post-tests with respect to an instruction session; increases in materials circulation figures; activities of information services librarians; etc.

A number of studies cited in the literature show a positive correlation between a student's scholastic grade point average and his or her ability to use the library.[7] If you have figures which show an increase in the level of academic performance of a class as a result of a program of library instruction, make certain the appropriate administrators are informed.

Good statistical record-keeping, and informing the right persons with respect to these statistics, can be of great help in creating an effective library instruction program.[8] A major function of colleges and universities is to instruct students, and if this instruction is helped through specific programs of the library, it is to everyone's advantage to support such programs. Instructional time saved is money saved for other portions of the budget.

## *ENLIST SUPPORT*

Third, enlist the support of your faculty, for they can often have great influence on administration. The increased ability of a class to make use of the library might result in the production of better assignments and research papers, which should please instructors who have to mark such work. If your faculty are enthusiastic about your library instruction programs, they will support your efforts to achieve increased administrative support.

In my own experience, I enlisted the aid of college instructors in biology to gain funding for a library-centered auto-tutorial program in their subject. I also benefitted from the help of a number of faculty in getting administration to fund a position for a graphic artist who would help them design materials to be used in the program.

At the university level, it is most certainly of benefit to the institution as a whole to have faculty and graduate students who are able to make efficient and effective use of library materials, as the quantity and quality of research is improved thereby. With budget reductions occurring in universities over North America, research assistants are no longer so readily available, and it is more necessary than ever that faculty be able to handle effectively all of the details of their own research projects.

Do not forget to call upon your library committee for support. Faculty members on a library committee can be a source of problems if the committee is poorly structured and its mission unclear. However, operating within proper guidelines, faculty members on a library committee can be a source of strength and help when budget time is at hand, or a new program, such as that of bibliographic instruction, is being proposed.

Fourth, enlist student support. This can sometimes be of even greater benefit than the support of the faculty. Some librarians have found it useful to hold a coffee, lunch, or some other social affair at the end of a program of library instruction, to which administrators are invited. Students are able to relate their experiences in the instruction program, and voice their feelings about an expanded program to reach more students.[9]

Most college and university courses are now subject to some type of formal evaluation by students on conclusion. Assuming student evaluations of a program of library instruction are favorable, copies of such evaluations might be sent to administrators, particularly to those who control funding of such programs.

## *PROGRAM INFORMATION*

Fifth, when a specific program of library instruction must receive administrative approval, make certain all the needed information about the program is provided. The proposal for the program should include the target group at which the instruction is to be aimed, the teaching methodologies to be employed, an outline of the subjects to be covered, listings of needed materials and equipment, the timing of the instruction, and planned methods of evaluation. Include in your proposal background information on the concept of bibliographic instruction, and be certain to provide an estimate of the budgetary implications of offering the program.

It might be wise to append to your proposal any relevant standards or guidelines which might cover various aspects of the program you are proposing. The "Guidelines for Bibliographic Instruction in Academic Libraries," adopted by the Association of College and Research Libraries of the American Library Association in 1977, make mention of many of the essential requisites for an effective program.[10]

Finally, and above all, keep communications going—a good program of library instruction requires a great deal of public relations efforts to get it initiated and to keep it running efficiently and effectively. Hopefully, if you follow the courses of action outlined, you will be able to gain administrative support for library user education despite the fact we are presently in times of economic restraint.

## REFERENCES

1. Vogel, J. T. "A Critical Overview of the Value of Library Instruction," *Drexel Library Quarterly*, 8, 3, July 1972, 315.
2. Hopkins, F.L. "A Century of Bibliographic Instruction: the Historical Claim to Professional and Academic Legitimacy," *College & Research Libraries*, 43, 3, May 1982. 192-198.
3. For a concise overview of the costs of offering programs of bibliographic instruction, see "Costs of a Bibliographic Instruction Program," in Beaubien, A. K., S. A. Hogan, and M. W. George, *Learning the Library: Concepts and Methods for Effective Bibliographic Instruction*, New York, Bowker, 1982. p. 243-248.
4. Boissê, J. A. "Selling Library Instruction," *Southeastern Librarian*, 29, 2, Summer 1979, 81-82.
5. *Ibid.*, p. 82.
6. Boissê, J. A. "Library Instruction and the Administration," in Kirkendall, C. A., ed., *Putting Library Instruction in Its Place: in the Library and in the Library School*, Ann Arbor, MI, Pierian Press, 1978, p. 5.
7. For some citations, see Cassata, M. B., *Library Instruction Program Proposal*, Buffalo, State University of New York, 1973.
8. This was one conclusion of a study by Hannelore B. Rader, published as *An Assessment of Ten Academic Library Instruction Programs in the United States and Canada* by the Council on Library Resources, Washington, D.C., in 1976.
9. Rice, J., Jr., *Teaching Library Use: a Guide for Library Instruction*, Westport, CT, Greenwood Press (1981), p. 29.
10. Published in *College & Research Libraries News*, no. 4, April 1977, p. 92.

# Promoting a Positive Image: Hints for the New Reference Librarian in Dealing With Faculty

## Eric W. Johnson

Beginning reference librarians in an academic library are often in the same situation as a new fish introduced into a fish tank. Not only must they quickly familiarize themselves with their new surroundings and associates but also determine their position in the local hierarchy.

Reference librarians in the academic community are often in a class by themselves. Those librarians whose positions afford them faculty status have the advantage of identification with a particular college group. Those without faculty status are usually included in a diversified professional or administrative body, thus further divorcing the role of the librarian from the educational role exemplified by the faculty.

The new librarian, then, must sometimes fight for professional respect, especially from the faculty. Faculty members come in all types and temperaments, as do librarians. They bring to the library their own attitudes and prejudices, and view reference librarians in different ways. How reference librarians are perceived depends largely on how they perceive themselves. They must develop an image that reflects their abilities and self-worth, and actively impress that image on the academic community.

Although much has been written concerning the status of the academic librarian, very little of it deals with faculty perceptions. Two studies, conducted roughly ten years apart, questioned faculty

---

Mr. Johnson is Associate Librarian, Public Services, University of New Haven, West Haven, CT 06516.

© 1985 by The Haworth Press, Inc. All rights reserved.

members as to whether librarians should be given faculty rank. The results of these studies shed an interesting sidelight on how the librarians were viewed.

Patricia Knapp directed her questions to the faculty of Knox College, Galesburg, Illinois in the mid-1950s, and determined that the faculty were not in favor of any librarians except the head librarian holding faculty status.[1] Florence Holbrook canvassed the English Department at the University of Kentucky, and reported in 1968 that 5 out of 7 faculty members approved of faculty status as long as the librarian's qualifications and research warranted the ranking.[2] A third study undertaken by M. Kathy Cook at Southern Illinois University in 1981 showed faculty in favor of faculty rank for librarians, again suggesting that the librarians conduct research.[3]

Each of these studies exhibited differing faculty perceptions of the role of the librarian. Knapp's faculty were ready to embrace the head librarian as a brother because he already had faculty status, had taught English, and had served on administrative committees. Holbrook's respondents judged the librarians on the basis of scholarship and professional activities, and ignored the inherent differences between the two groups. Cook's faculty regarded the most important function of the librarians to be service, but added that librarians should also be involved in research.

## *PERCEPTIONS*

The different perceptions of the librarians and their roles by the faculty groups underscore the fact that many faculty members are simply not aware of what the professional reference position entails. Those instructors who do use the library may be aware that an important part of the reference position is the providing of information, but as reference librarians know, this is only one of the tasks they may be called upon to perform. It is the duty of the reference librarians themselves to educate the faculty as to the multifaceted and crucial roles they play in the university environment.

Before discussing what reference librarians can do to foster a better image of themselves, it will be helpful to examine the roles they should avoid, even though these may be the images that the term "librarian" connotes to the faculty member.

1) Faculty servant. The new librarian is often at a loss in dealing with the first request to photocopy an article or check a multi-page

bibliography against the card catalog. Where does one draw the line between providing reference service and doing work that could be performed by a library clerk or, better yet, the professor's secretary? The library should have a policy, preferably in print, setting forth the tasks that librarians are expected to do and those that they can refuse to do. There is a world of difference between service and servitude.

2) Research assistant. Many faculty members (or at least departments) employ a graduate student who is paid to assist in gathering material and performing general research. Those instructors without a research assistant may try unofficially to ensnare the reference librarian into this position. Be wary. If you provide a bibliography on demand for one professor, you must be prepared for a barrage of similar requests. Again, a written policy would be helpful.

3) Baby-sitter. Some instructors have discovered that the library instruction class provides a handy alternative to one or more regular classroom sessions. They can arrange for their students to meet at the library and leave them in the care of the librarian. There is no question that library instruction is a necessary and beneficial part of library service. However, it should be geared toward the needs of the students with the assistance and input of the instructor, and not viewed as merely an hour's respite from the classroom. In addition, students in a one- or two-session orientation tend to take more of an interest in what is being presented when their regular instructor is present. One way to ensure an attentive audience is to require that the instructor attend the orientation. (This is usually to the instructor's benefit, since he or she will invariably learn something new about the library.)

4) Guardian of the books. As antithesis of the three previous roles, this is perhaps the worst manner in which librarians can be perceived, since it calls to mind the stereotype of the librarian that the profession would like to eliminate. Librarians should never present themselves, consciously or unconsciously, as wielding their M.L.S. as a weapon and seeing themselves as being above everyone else in their divinely-chosen role as Gatherers and Retrievers of the World's Knowledge, misanthropes who would undoubtedly be happier if there were no patrons, only books. Librarians must remember that the reason for their existence is to provide service to the public, and that the total concept of the library is incomplete without a public to be served. An attitude of superiority or aloofness does not result in a good faculty-librarian relations.

## *GOOD IMAGE*

A positive image is essential. As professionals, librarians should consider themselves on a par with the faculty, since they share some of the same duties and responsibilities and are working toward similar educational goals. The reference librarian, by assisting students and explaining the use of reference tools, formally or informally, is continually teaching, and may be considered an extension of the professor. Librarians and instructors both perform administrative duties and can be involved in research. There are differences, of course, but the point is that the gap between the two groups is not so wide as many think.

New reference librarians can make their presence known in many ways. They will, of course, be judged by the assistance they provide to both students and faculty. Are the librarians approachable? Are they knowledgable? Are they thorough? If the library does not contain the needed information, do they refer the patron to another library or source of information?

Beyond basic service, however, there are other ways to promote a positive image to the faculty. The following suggestions should help the new librarian in achieving this goal.

1) Make the effort to keep in contact with the faculty. Get to know as many of the instructors as you can. Faculty members who take an interest in the library can be of inestimable assistance in obtaining materials and supplies, and can have a positive effect on the library's budget. One of the best ways to become acquainted with the faculty is to frequent the school dining facility, especially if there is a separate faculty dining area to which librarians have access. Contact with the faculty will make the new librarian's presence and capabilities known, which will in turn spur the faculty into using the library more.

2) Work with the faculty members. Consult with them on their students' assignments. Determine to what extent the instructor expects the librarian to assist his students. If the students seem to be lacking library skills, arrange an orientation session. Show the instructor that you are interested in his coursework.

One beneficial side effect may be the instructor's informing the library of upcoming class assignments. Material can then be put aside before it disappears, and information guides can be created. A quick explanation of pertinent reference tools can be planned, eliminating the unnecessary repetition of individual queries.

3) Instruct the faculty. Few faculty members have the time or means to keep up with the latest reference services and materials. The reference librarian can easily send to interested faculty copies of advertisements and notices of library acquisitions in their areas of specialization. Faculty may not be as familiar as they should with the library's holdings and possibilities. Offer tours or mini-orientation presentations, highlighting subject areas or services provided. Demonstrate database searching. Well-informed instructors will make better use of the library, and will urge their students to do the same.

4) Involve the faculty in library events. A series of cultural gatherings—lectures, films, readings, concerts—can be planned in conjunction with the faculty. Faculty members themselves may perform, or may suggest colleagues and acquaintances. Library displays which feature faculty publications or favorite books can be mounted. If the library publishes a newsletter, faculty might be contacted for articles and ideas.

5) Involve yourself in university affairs. Don't isolate yourself from the rest of the campus. Join committees. Working side-by-side with faculty members on university business will help point out the equal importance of librarians and instructors to the institution, and will also prompt those who are not regular library users to see what they have been missing.

New reference librarians should remember that, as representatives of the library, they have a hand in determining whether that library will be viewed merely as a repository of books or as the vital and intrinsic part of the university that it should be. The reference librarians' active promotion of its use through working with the faculty as closely as possible can only serve to strengthen the library's role on campus and, at the same time, generate the respect that is due them by the faculty as fellow professionals.

## REFERENCES

1. Patricia Knapp, *College Teaching and the College Library,* ACRL Monograph No. 23 (Chicago: American Library Association, 1959), pp. 82-86.

2. Florence Holbrook, "The Faculty Image of the Academic Librarian," *Southeastern Librarian,* 18 (Fall 1968), 174-193.

3. Cook, M. Kathy, "Rank, Status, and Contribution of Academic Librarians as Perceived by the Teaching Faculty at Southern Illinois University, Carbondale," *College & Research Libraries,* 42 (May 1981), 214-223.

# A Collection of Books: The College Professor vs the Reference Librarian

## Melissa Watson

The "olive grove of Academe" is rarely the peaceful haven of scholarly pursuit and reasoned debate that the term "ivory tower" somehow implies. The average campus teems with a heady mixture of intrigue and scandal that is worthy of the worst afternoon soap opera. It is not surprising, then, that those who would seem to be the most natural of allies, the professor and the librarian, sometimes come to be locked in mortal combat, brewing up tempests to rattle the lid of the academic teapot.

Every academic librarian who has had the opportunity to preside over the reference desk has had an encounter somewhat similar to the following:

Professor Q storms up to the reference desk, eyes flashing with righteous indignation. He has been sending his students to the reference area for an assignment and they haven't been able to find the book they need. As he had described the book to them in some detail, giving the specific author and title, he cannot understand the librarian's inability to help his students. Is the library staffed by total incompetents? Don't they even know the contents of their own reference shelves?

The librarian, who has begun to feel an all too familiar ache around the temples, attempts to soothe the professor's ruffled feathers. True, his students had been coming to the reference desk with great regularity, asking for Hinton's *History of English Litera-*

---

Melissa Watson is Reference Librarian, St. Petersburg Junior College, Clearwater Campus, Clearwater, Florida.

*ture*, the 6th edition. Unfortunately, the library does not happen to own a copy of the work in question, and a check of the *Cumulative Book Index* for the last 30 years does not reveal a title remotely similar to it. Naturally, the librarian had tried to offer his students one of the many fine reference books on English literature that the library *did* own, but they, being well indoctrinated by their instructor, wanted Hinton or nothing at all.

Professor Q is little placated by this tale of woe. He knows the library has that book—HE has used it! With that, he steps smartly over to the English Lit section and with a flourish pulls out his book: *A Critical Survey of British Writers*, 5th edition, edited by Hunter. Only somewhat chagrined by this discrepancy of titles, Professor Q retreats, tossing the remark over his shoulder that the librarian should have *known* that was what he had meant in the first place.

## *NO WIN*

In such a case as this (which is only slightly exaggerated), the librarian cannot win, which often seems to be the case in any dispute with the faculty. This stems from a problem which seems to lie at the base of the librarian/faculty conflict, many members of the teaching faculty haven't the slightest idea what librarians *do*. While most do not object to the library as such, some professors seem to view it more as an educational status symbol than the intellectual heart of the campus. Some faculty members (non-users for the most part) view the reference librarian as a somewhat overpaid keeper of a collection of books, someone who reads all day and occasionally blows the dust off an old encyclopedia to answer some trivial question. As far as they're concerned, the library might be a nice place to visit (if it's raining outside and one has nothing better to do), but it is hardly anything which needs much attention, and certainly should not demand a very large share of the general budget!

Another viewpoint is found among those faculty members who use the library and the reference collection with great regularity. To them, libraries are an essential part of the education process and reference librarians are wonderful creatures who can answer their every question even before it is asked. They wax lyrical in their praise of reference librarians, seeing them as possessors of arcane knowledge, shamans of the abstruse, astute manipulators of the mysteries of card catalog, index and online search. Flattering as this viewpoint is, it is not without its difficulties. Such unswerving faith do these people have in their reference librarian that they come to expect the impossible, and woe betide the hapless librarian who fails to prove equal to the task. It matters not that the required information is available only in a book owned by the British Museum and cannot be obtained on loan. It is of no avail that he wants in five minutes a reference that would take three hours to trace. Is this not a *library*? Are you not LIBRARIANS? For holders of this viewpoint, human frailty is not an excuse; the librarian had better be a wizard, or else.

As with all things, there are those who vacillate between the aforementioned extremes. These faculty members are largely indifferent to the library and its lowly caretakers until they find themselves in need of a piece of information. Then, through the chemical process of their need, the librarian is transformed from a keeper of a musty collection to a magician of valuable resources. The transformation will hold until the faculty member's need has been met, then, as far as he or she is concerned, the librarian turns back into a pumpkin until the next time of need.

## *ANOTHER AREA*

Another area of faculty/librarian conflict centers on that most basic of educational components, the student. Students are notorious for arriving in the library with incomplete or incorrect information about their assignments, which is hardly the fault of their instructors. However, problems do arise when the information that the instructors have given to their students is faulty, as in the case of Professor Q. Yet even more insidious is the instructor who knows EVERYTHING about the library. He checked out a book once, maybe he even took a library science course, whatever, he is convinced that he knows everything there is to know. What is more, he informs the reference librarian that his students should not require any assistance at all, he has told them all *they* need to know. So, his students arrive—misinformed, invincible in their instructor-inspired ignorance. As they flounder about, the reference librarian is faced with an ethical dilemma: should the librarian interfere, and run the risk of showing up the instructor as an idiot? Or should he or she let the students struggle on, perhaps never finding what they want and winding up with a library inferiority complex for life?

This touchy situation is more common than one would desire, and can result in a great deal of ill will between the faculty members and librarians in question. Of course, there are many faculty members who make regular use of the library and are quite well-informed about its intricacies and are more than capable of passing this information along to their students. These stellar individuals regularly have their praises sung throughout the hushed environs of the library and their students are a joy to assist. The main difference between these instructors and he who knows EVERYTHING about the library is one of attitude. The instructors who use the library on a regular basis are aware of their limitations and look to the librarians for assistance when they reach a dead end. They respect the librarians' abilities and expertise, and just as they would not expect the librarian to presume to teach *their* subjects, they defer to the librarian in his or her own realm. The know-it-all lacks this sensitivity and it is his students who ultimately suffer, although the librarian may get another headache in the bargain. It is no easy thing to tell someone who thinks he knows it all that he is wrong, and even more difficult to convince him of the fact. Because egos are involved, the reference librarian will have a difficult time in resolving this particular conflict. Perhaps the best solution is to aid the students as much as possible without making it painfully obvious that their instructor has given them incorrect information. The person who can do this would surely qualify to be named the Kissinger of the academic library world.

## *THE ISSUE*

Diplomacy is an issue in yet another faculty/librarian conflict, that being the one over the maintenance of the reference collection. Every reference librarian is aware of the need to keep his or her collection as current as possible, and he or she is also aware of the need to get faculty input regarding what is held in the collection. Faculty members who are regularly consulted about their subject areas are far more likely to see that their students make use of those areas, so in a sense, the librarian's continued viability resides in maintaining a good relationship with his or her faculty in this regard. However, professors are busy with many matters, and occasionally they may lose track of recent publications in their field. One hopes that the reference librarian has seen to it that they have been receiving information on the newer publications, yet even such conscientiousness on the part of the librarian does not guarantee that the faculty member will be ready to discard the old standby.

For many people, particularly those who have sweat over their own theses and dissertations, there is something sacred about a book. No matter how outdated, unused or tacky it may be, it is simply *heresy* to even consider throwing it away. When the reference librarian ventures the opinion that it might be time to retire a volume or two, cries of anguish echo from the circulation desk to the periodicals room. The book was written by experts in the field! It has just the information her students need! It doesn't matter that this professor hasn't made an assignment that requires library research in 15 years, someday she just might. The librarian can only sigh and risk provoking the professor's wrath when discarding becomes a dire necessity. This same professor would be angered if the librarian didn't keep her subject area up to date, so professional discretion is called for on the librarian's part . . . and sometimes a large bottle of headache pills.

Faculty/librarian relationships are rendered even more complex when the question of personal research arises. Any reference librarian is more than willing to help a faculty member with normal reference questions and with class-related bibliographies and research projects. Yet when one approaches the area of personal research, the issue is no longer so clear cut. How much should the reference librarian be expected to do when the research required is for a class the instructor is taking? The instructors would take great exception to a librarian doing all of one of their student's research work, yet sometimes will expect the librarian to do that very thing for them when they are taking a class. Sometimes the credit received for one of these classes will result in a pay raise for the instructor; is this equitable if the reference librarian is the one who did all the research? Ethics generally preclude charging for services that are essentially part of one's job description, but is personal research for a faculty member part of the basic services reference librarians should provide? If one decides that one can help the instructor up to a point, what is that point? Doing a little research is like getting a little pregnant, it's all or nothing. There is once again no simple solution to this dilemma, each reference librarian must face this situation and make his or her peace with it. Whatever decision is reached, there will be a faculty member somewhere who isn't satisfied with it.

## RELATIONSHIPS

It is easy to see that the faculty/librarian relationship is a delicate matter, subject to many a whim and twist of fate. Yet all the previous areas of conflict pale beside those which arise when budgetary problems come to pass; this is an area of darkness which no amount of levity can appreciably brighten. There are few academic institutions in the country that have not felt the sting of financial exigency in the past decade, and, as the eighties progress, the frequency and severity of budgetary crises will only increase. These will be times to try librarians' souls, because when a budget crunch hits, the library is always the first to get cut. Expenditures are curtailed, hours are cut, personnel are laid off, and often the reference librarian will have to fight to keep just the basic reference collection updated. It's sad to say, but times of financial crisis are also times when the faculty/library relationship often reaches its nadir.

Professors are human, and it's not surprising that when a crisis occurs that they should look to their own jobs first. The first rule of survival is to protect oneself, yet it is a sad state of affairs when self-protection is translated into active attacks on everyone else. Department will cast aspersions on department, questioning the other's necessity and viability while touting its own. It is also distressing when faculty members will lead the attack to slash the library first. Even the dedicated library user is not immune to speculation about the amount of money appropriated for the library. Surely it is not necessary for the library to purchase that many new books, after all, they have so many already. And don't they seem to have an awful lot of people working over there, couldn't they do without a few of them?

## CONFLICTS

Even this dark conflict is not without the ambiguity that marks other areas of the faculty/librarian relationship. Faculty members will call for limits to the amount of money spent in the library, so long as *their* area is not neglected. An instructor will mention to the librarian that it would certainly be nice to see this set of books purchased for the reference collection, since it contains the latest information for her area. When she is reminded of the current budgetary crisis, she replies that if she had been given the amount of money the library had spent on books for the last several years she could have gold-plated her office three times over. The message is, go ahead and cut the library's budget, but don't cut the services I expect from it.

The situation is further complicated when the librarians themselves are classified as faculty. Members of the teaching faculty are highly distrustful of librarians and counselors being put in the same classification as themselves. It doesn't matter that the reference librarian may have equal academic credentials and be actively engaged in the instruction process in the library every day, the teaching faculty does not want to accept the librarians as being on the same level. If concessions are required of the instructors, such as teaching larger class loads without an increase in pay, those instructors will immediately demand to know what is being required of the librarians. Again, it does not matter that librarians are usually held to a much stricter time schedule than teaching faculty and that they already have been required to curtail some of their activities due to the lack of funds. The instructors want to see the librarians cut and they want to see the blood.

Budgetary crisis or not, conflicts will continue to arise between instructors and librarians as long as academic institutions continue to exist. Despite the headaches that accompany many sorties with recalcitrant faculty members, most reference librarians are philosophical about their lot. After all, conflicts could not exist in a vacuum, and their very presence indicates that the library is still a viable part of its institution. The academic library that sails placidly on with nary a professor troubling the waters is probably moribund—no one complains because no one uses it. It's far better to endure the occasional tempest than to risk stagnation.

# ABOUT THE ROLE OF THE PROFESSIONAL

## Nonprofessionals on Reference Desks in Academic Libraries

Nancy J. Emmick

Probably the first impression a new librarian gets of reference desk duty involves the wide variation in types of questions addressed. Topics range from obscure basic research to the trivial and commonplace. When working a busy desk, the new librarian also becomes aware of the high frequency of nonreference questions, such as "Where is the bathroom?" or "Where are the copy machines?" Such questions hardly stimulate creative talents. Nearly every reference librarian dreams of some easy way to eliminate these questions, particularly during peak periods. But even a cursory look into the literature shows that the obvious ways are steeped in controversy. For example, two librarians write that 80% of the questions fielded at the reference desk could be handled as efficiently by nonprofessionals and librarians should attend only to the difficult questions.[1] At the other extreme, a chairperson of a reference department holds that it is best to have a professional make the first contact at the reference desk because of the delicacy of the reference interview. To do otherwise, she avers, is to deny patrons the benefits of a thorough exposure and development of their information needs.[2]

---

Nancy Emmick is Reference Librarian, San Jose State University, Clark Library, San Jose, CA 95192.

In recent years, many changes have taken place at the typical academic library that exacerbate this controversy. First, declining student populations have caused restrictions in library budgets. Second, the recent economic downturn further restricted budgets at tax-supported schools, forcing a loss in book and periodical budgets and policies against replacement of staff lost through attrition. Third, advances in technolgy have removed the walls of libraries. Huge, nationwide database systems are now accessible at most libraries through online search services, interlibrary loans, and the like. These advances have increased the continuing education and professional development obligations of librarians. Fourth, librarianship has made considerable progress toward its goal of professionalism. Faculty status has been attained at many colleges and universities, bringing an additional work load to each librarian. Aluri and St. Clair point out, "As librarians move toward the goal of full faculty status . . . they will have to accept many academic responsibilities and obligations." These include "research and publishing . . . memberships in academic groups and committees as well as visible community and university service."[3] Librarians, hard pressed to cope with the increased work loads, cannot afford to overlook the possibility of using nonprofessionals wherever it is cost-effective. Staffing the reference desk is part of this scrutiny.

This paper is written to clarify the duties of the typical reference librarian as determined by a 1981 reference survey of 367 academic U.S. and Canadian libraries,[4] to discuss ways nonprofessionals are used at the reference desk, to examine the controversial consequences of using nonprofessionals at the reference desk, to present related information from the author's 1981 survey of academic libraries, and finally to formalize some conclusions and offer some observations.

## *DEFINITION OF TERMS*

The professional reference librarian today is typically a graduate of an accredited library school with a master's degree (MLS) in librarianship who specializes in and performs reference services. The duties of a typical reference librarian are more diversified than laymen may suspect. The 1981 survey depicts[5] those duties as usually consisting of reference desk duty (about 40% of the workweek); collection development (10-15%); library instructional lectures—

tours, descriptions of basic library resources, and in-depth descriptions of sources in specific subject areas (up to 10%); online literature searching (up to 10%); student counseling, particularly on term paper writing (up to 5%); and professional development—workshops, seminars, professional meetings, and research and writing for publication (up to 10%). In addition, the reference librarian participates in various library committees, performs special library studies and many administrative functions. Committee participation may include campus meetings and other faculty activities. At many libraries the reference librarian might also handle such functions as interlibrary loans, government documents, serial acquisitions, cataloging, media, and staff supervision. Reference librarians do not simply sit at the reference desk waiting for questions.

Most libraries employ nonprofessional staff—employees without a master's degree in library science—in the reference area to perform clerical functions. This nonprofessional staff usually includes a permanent cadre of library assistants and clerks, and a number of temporary student assistants, who together provide the housekeeping services of the library. Their tasks include reshelving materials, shelfreading, check-in and checkout of reference materials, filing, and typing. Sometimes they answer simple patron questions and show them where materials are located. In some libraries nonprofessional make the first contact with reference desk patrons.

## *REFERENCE DESK STAFFING ALTERNATIVES*

It is not easy to minimize the impact on reference services once a decision has been made to reduce professional desk hours. Basically only three options are open to administration: 1) reduce the number of hours the reference desk is open (this can be the same as reducing the number of hours the library is open), 2) reduce the number of reference librarians at the desk at any one time, or 3) transfer some reference functions to nonprofessional staff. Reducing the number of hours a day that reference services are provided does not reduce patron service demand, it simply forces patrons to come to the library at more restricted times. Even worse, when they do arrive they join others in suffering increased waiting times in the queues. Often this forces them to take time from work, or to stay in the queue and miss or be late to classes, or any of a number of consequences that increase the cost—to the patron—of using the library.

Reducing the number of librarians at the desk also increases the length of the service queues and the cost and frustration levels of the patrons.

The third alternative, to use nonprofessionals at the reference desk, seems more attractive in that a large percentage of the queries are simple. The argument is that professionals should treat only complex research/reference questions. Most research indicates that the percentage of routine questions lies between 50% and 85% of the total. Several sources suggest the higher level. Boyer and Theimer cite a Canadian administrator as believing that "There is no doubt at all in the minds of most Canadian academic library administrators that 85% . . . of questions at public service desks can be answered by nonprofessional staff."[6] St. Clair and Aluri determined the percentage as 80.[7] Heinlen noted that 70% of questions concerned library operations.[8] Although the percentage is disputed, it seems clear that the true number is significant. If nonprofessional time can be substituted for librarians' time, worthwhile savings might result. Young has established that "for the professional [the time saved] amounted to an average of 13 of the 15 hours per week the student worked."[9] Kok and Pierce "estimate a 35% savings in equivalent staff 'costs' could be achieved if support staff were employed to handle the more-routine questions."[10] Reports of such savings indicate that the substitution would be economically desirable.

A fourth alternative is sometimes postulated, suggesting that each librarian's desk duty hours be increased proportionately to absorb the hours served by those who terminate, thus maintaining status quo at the reference desk. One need only refer to the typical workload of a reference librarian, as described earlier in this paper, to realize that the remaining librarians would have to absorb not only the desk hours but all of the other functions of the former librarian as well. This so-called option is not feasible and will not be considered here.

Of the three feasible options, the use of nonprofessionals seems the most practicable in that it promises to minimize the penalties to the library patron. Young noted that "Since one of the essential characteristics of a profession is the identification and differentiation of job tasks and the training of personnel to accomplish them, it would seem imperative that the routine duties of the reference function be separated from the professional ones and allocated to nonprofessionals."[11]

## THE CONSEQUENCES OF USING NONPROFESSIONALS AT THE REFERENCE DESK

Choosing to use nonprofessionals in the reference area is neither all good nor all bad, as is true for most management decisions. The actual balance between good and bad depends on conditions at each library.

The primary argument against using nonprofessionals on the reference desk is that they lack the education and experience to conduct a reference interview. Because of these limitations, they cannot recognize when a patron's question might be incorrect, faulty, or indirect in nature.[12] Often patrons are unable to describe their needs with precision, have only vague impressions about their topic and potential sources, and thus ask simple directional questions about reference sources they are familiar with. Pastine, in her response to Aluri and St. Clair, commented, "It is difficult for paraprofessionals (and sometimes even professionals) to define the depth and extent of an initial inquiry. The question negotation process, then, is one of the most important facets of reference desk work, and one that seemingly can best be handled by the expert reference librarian."[13] If the nonprofessionals do not recognize a need for further professional help, their answers may be incorrect or incomplete. Nonprofessionals can be trained to refer true reference or problem questions to the reference librarian and avoid this problem. In spite of such training, however, the nonprofessional has a tendency to become over-zealous in his/her desire to be useful. Bunge commented, "Untrained staff typically attempted to answer all types of questions as they came up, referring only those which they could not answer . . . to professional staff, if and when the latter were available."[14] Halldorsson and Murfin noted that the "concept of their basic role as 'teaching about how to use reference materials' [caused them to be] eager to explain the use of catalogs, indexes, and reference books without probing further." They defined the core problem to be the "nonprofessional failure to utilize referral and consultation to the fullest."[15]

It seems that the decision to use nonprofessionals requires careful planning if patrons who need a reference interview are to receive one. When nonprofessionals make initial contacts, they must do so as employees who are well trained, not in the reference skills but rather in recognizing the types of questions that may indicate the need for a full reference interview. The reference department must take the time to define "safe" question types which the nonprofessional can answer, supply standard answers for the referral process (even when the patron is unaware of the need), design a training seminar or manual, conduct the training of the nonprofessionals, and monitor the effectiveness of their training by observing performance at the desk. In effect, a new specialty is created. To do less is to guarantee that patrons will ultimately be deprived of the benefits of the reference interview.

Research indicates that a number of benefits accrue from the use of nonprofessionals at the reference desk. The most obvious benefit is derived from lifting the burden of numerous simple, routine questions from the professional. The time saved may make it possible for a smaller number of librarians, answering only the more difficult reference questions, to conduct the in-depth reference interviews that are needed. As Dickinson and Pempe stated, "While these [routine questions] are essential to the user's orientation in the library, they detract in terms of time and attention from the ability of the reference librarian to respond to more complex reference questions that require concentrated searches and user instruction."[16] A corollary of this benefit is the possibility that the desk hours of librarians might be reduced to permit them to accomplish more of their other professional duties efficiently.

A significant improvement in the morale of the librarians can be achieved by using nonprofessionals. Librarians have been educated and trained to respond to reference questions; doing so stimulates their creative abilities and raises their estimation of themselves as professionals when they are successful. There is no question that when lines are long, librarians are unable to take the time required to respond effectively and adequately to each patron's question. In Heinlen's words, "Our students—carefully trained and supervised—allow us to help our people and to modulate better the assistance provided."[17]

It is also argued that the use of nonprofessionals can reduce the sense of harassment and anxiety that is prevalent in some libraries at peak times. If the waiting lines can be shortened by having nonprofessionals, it seems clear that the librarians, who are now free of having to keep an "anxious eye" on the waiting line, can devote more time to the reference/research questions. It seems futile to argue that "librarians [are] disturbed at the notion of allowing students to answer simple reference questions"[18] when there is a "lack of time to conduct proper interviews and examine reference sources to obtain correct information"[19] anyway.

Differentiation of function, which is also called specialization, can be valuable to the library patron, who often feels that his/her question does not justify the time of a professional and is reluctant to approach the desk. When an alternate nonprofessional information source is available and properly designated, the patron has the opportunity to select between a professional reference source and simpler assistance. But to make such an opportunity available, it is essential that information sources of different types be clearly distinguishable by the patron by the use of badges, signs, physical separation, and any other useful means. Young has noted that patrons "did not hesitate to approach the reference assistant, and some students were able to relate more effectively to a peer than to a professional."[20] In the same vein, Peele opined that "All the friendly smiles we can muster may not be enough to overcome the fact that it is easier to go to another student to say 'help me' than to go to an authority figure."[21]

Research clearly shows that there are both benefits and penalties in using nonprofessionals at the reference desk. In deciding whether to do so, management must assess the balance between the two for its own situation and then choose its course.

## ACADEMIC LIBRARY REFERENCE SERVICE PRACTICES

In the spring of 1981, the author, working with Luella [Hemingway] Davis of Emory University, conducted an extensive survey of academic library reference service practices.[22] A questionnaire was sent to 500 undergraduate libraries at campuses in the U.S. and Canada; 367 of the libraries responded. The following is a selection of questions and responses related to alternative staffing of the reference desk.

To the question "Does your library have a separate information or directional assistance desk?" 21.8% of the libraries responded "yes" while 70.8% answered "no." The remaining percentage answered in some other way.

A second question asked, "On the average, how many questions are answered by a reference librarian per hour?" The range of the most frequent responses was 5-10 questions per hour per librarian.

The survey also asked, "What percentage of the questions require searching or instruction?" The most frequent response (67% of the libraries) was in the range of 41-60%. About as many libraries fell above that range as fell below it. When, as a check on the validity of the responses, we asked, "Is your response based on records or an estimate?" 44.4% said that they were estimates, while 38.7% said they had records to support their answer. It appears reasonable to conclude that about half of the questions are true reference questions and that about half might be answered by a nonprofessional.

Another question asked by the survey was, "Does a reference librarian staff the reference desk during all the hours the library is open?" and "If not, who does?" The following responses were specified:

| | |
|---|---|
| Only reference librarians | 13.2% |

The responses for "If not, who does?" were:

| | |
|---|---|
| No reference service given | 28.5% |
| Support staff and/or student assistants | 41.4% |
| Circulation staff | 4.8% |
| Other librarians | 4.2% |

It is reasonable to conclude that about as many schools use nonprofessionals as use only professionals at the reference desk.

Cross-tabulations were prepared to see whether the characteristics of the schools had any effect on the frequency with which nonprofessionals were used. The geographic location of the school was found to have such an effect. The following areas ranked highest in using nonprofessionals on the desk when reference librarians were not there: South Atlantic (48.2%), South Central (52.1%), and Mountain (53.0%). The following regions were more likely to close the reference desk completely: Canada (58.8%), New England (57.1%), and Pacific (53.3%).

Cross-tabulations of the size of the school (FTE student body) show that the smaller schools, (fewer than 1,000 students), with 48.6%, and the larger ones (15,000-20,000 students), with 50.5%, used student assistants and support staff more than the medium-sized schools (34.1% avg.). The largest schools (over 20,000 students) were close to a majority (47%) as well. Those schools with 5,000-10,000 students were least likely to use nonprofessionals (49.4%). This pattern agrees with the survey done by Boyer and Theimer, who established that "The libraries at the middle-sized colleges use significantly fewer students than the libraries of either the smaller or larger schools."[23]

Cross-tabulations by terminal degree showed that the schools offering BA/BS (50%) or master's programs (57.6%) were more likely to use student assistants or nonprofessionals than were schools offering Ph.D.s (43.9%).

The size of library holdings again showed that the smaller schools (with libraries of fewer than 200,000 volumes) were more likely to use student assistants and nonprofessionals than the middle-sized libraries (200,001-500,000 volumes). Libraries with 600,001-999,000 volumes were the least likely to use nonprofessionals.

## CONCLUSIONS AND OBSERVATIONS

A careful review of the survey results leads to the following conclusions and observations about the use of nonprofessionals at the reference desk. First, there exists a rising level of interest in the use of nonprofessionals corresponding to work load increases from continuing education, new publication commitments, and economic constraints. All tend to interfere with the quality of the reference services.

The second conclusion is that arguments exist favoring the use of nonprofessionals. Examples include their lower cost per hour, some patrons' peer preferences, the high rate and simplicity of most questions, the ease of diverting simple questions to directional assistance desks, and the librarians' conviction that their professional stature would be enhanced by dealing only with true reference and research questions.

The third conclusion is that arguments exist opposing the use of nonprofessionals. One example is the difficulty detecting the need for a thorough reference interview. Nonprofessionals have been shown to be very inconsistent in this detection—even when initially trained to do so. They do not resist the temptation to satisfy the patron themselves and to "muddle through" on their own. Librarians tend to prefer to treat the nonprofessionals as equals when at the desk and no attempt is made to differentiate between the staff. Consequently, the patron can not estimate the qualifications of the desk staff.

The fourth conclusion is that this issue is very complex. The 1981 survey, cited earlier, found that all of the following factors influenced the decision to use nonprofessionals: geographic location, student body size, degree levels offered, library holdings, state of the economy, librarians' faculty status, rate of change in student body size, query rates at the desk, and even the percentage of directional questions. The choice is not easy and must ultimately depend on the particular circumstances at each library.

Current economic pressures, the rate of technological change, and the growing acceptance of reference librarianship as a profession worthy of faculty status have all joined to make it imperative for many libraries to consider the use of nonprofessionals on the desk. But it necessarily follows that, in doing so, a clear distinction must be made between professional and nonprofessional duties. Neglecting this distinction will only assure patrons will ultimately be deprived of the benefits of a thorough reference interview and probably will receive incomplete or faulty information about sources.

The distinction between professionals and nonprofessionals must be obvious to the patron. Durrance commented, "Everyone behind a desk, from the lowest paid clerical to the head librarian, is perceived by the library user as 'the librarian'. . . . The practice of fostering anonymity . . . is unheard of in the professions."[24] It is important the patron be aware of the distinction so that he/she can seek the specialist best suited to his/her requirements. Techniques are available to clarify the distinction between professionals and nonprofessionals. Separation of directional assistance desks from the reference desk is one. The use of identification badges is another. Signs above service areas may help. Regardless of the means by which the patron is informed of the difference, the intent is the same: the library is obligated to let the patron know about the differences in skill and training levels that exist at the reference desk. If the professional staff resists a policy of differentiation, they should recognize that they are in effect choosing a policy of misleading the library patron.

It is important that distinctions be relatively permanent because it is not the library's intent to slowly transform nonprofessionals into librarians. The best ways to establish these differences are by developing a training manual for nonprofessionals, much as Mitchell did for Mankato State University,[25] or a workshop, as was developed for the California State University at San Diego by Coleman and Margutti.[27] Formal training should be adopted. Clear descriptions, with examples and responses should be included of the types of queries suitable for the nonprofessional to answer, along with typical queries that indicate a need for a reference interview. As important, possibly, is the need for professionals to recognize any tendency to consider the nonprofessional as "one of us" or to "let George do it" rather than get involved, disregarding the fact that the nonprofessional has a natural desire to answer increasingly more difficult questions. Monitoring is required to offset these human tendencies which break down the differentiation between specialties. When the distinctions are not vigorously maintained, the outcome is the same as having reduced the educational and experience standards for hiring reference librarians.

## REFERENCES

1. Jeffrey W. St. Clair and Rao Aluri, "Staffing the Reference Desk: Professionals or Nonprofessionals," *Journal of Academic Librarianship* 3 (July 1977): 149-152.
2. Maureen Pastine, "A Response," (to St. Clair and Aluri), *Journal of Academic Librarianship* 3 (July 1977): 152-153.
3. Rao Aluri and Jeffrey W. St. Clair, "Academic Reference Librarians: An Endangered Species," *Journal of Academic Librarianship* 4 (May 1978): 82-84.
4. Nancy J. Emmick and Luella Hemingway Davis, "A Survey of Academic Library Reference Service Practices," to be published in *RQ* (Summer 1984).
5. Ibid.
6. Laura M. Boyer and William C. Theimer, Jr., "The Use and Training of Nonprofessional Personnel at Reference Desks in Selected College and University Libraries," *College and Research Libraries* 36 (May 1975): 193-200.
7. St. Clair and Aluri, "Staffing the Reference Desk," p. 152.
8. William F. Heinlen, "Using Student Assistants in Academic Reference," *RQ* 15 (Summer 1976): 323-325.
9. Arthur P. Young, "A Report and a Challenge," *RQ* 9 (Summer 1970): 295-297.
10. Victoria T. Kok and Anton R. Pierce, "The Reference Desk Survey: A Management Tool in an Academic Research Library," *RQ* 22 (Winter 1982): 181-187.
11. Young, "A Report," p. 296.
12. Egill Halldorsson and Marjorie E. Murfin, "Performance of Professionals and Nonprofessionals in the Reference Interview," *College and Research Libraries* 38 (September 1977): 383-395.
13. Pastine, "Response," p. 152.
14. Charles Bunge, "Library Education and Reference Performance," *Library Journal* 92 (April 15, 1967): 1578-1581.
15. Halldorsson and Murfin, "Performance," p. 39.
16. Dennis W. Dickinson and Ruta Pempe, "Information Desk: Testing a Prescribed Model in the Local Environment," ERIC (1978) ED168585.
17. Heinlen, "Using Student Assistants," p. 325.
18. Ibid., p. 324.
19. Halldorsson and Murfin, "Performance," p. 394.
20. Young, "A Report," p. 296.
21. David Peele, "Staffing the Reference Desk," *Library Journal* 105 (September 1, 1980): 1708-1711.
22. Emmick and Davis, "A Survey."
23. Boyer and Theimer, "Use and Training," p. 196.
24. Joan C. Durrance, "The Generic Librarian: Anonymity versus Accountability," *RQ* 22 (Summer 1983): 279-283.
25. Sandra F. Mitchell, "Development of a Handbook for Student Assistants in the Memorial Library Reference Room at Mankato State University," Mankato State University, ERIC (August 1981) ED212256.
26. Kathleen Coleman and E. Margutti, "Training Nonprofessionals for Reference Service," *RQ* 16 (1977): 217-219.

## ADDITIONAL REFERENCES

Eyman, David H., "Student Assistants and Reference Questions," *Michigan Librarian,* Autumn 1970, pp. 14, 19.

Goodrich, Susan, "No, I'm Not a Librarian, But May I Help You?" *Michigan Librarian,* Winter 1972, pp. 24-25.

Kleimer, Jane P., "The Information Desk: The Library's Gateway to Service," *College and Research Libraries,* November 1968, pp. 496-501.

Neill, Samuel D., "Who Needs to Go to a Graduate Library School," *Journal of Education for Librarianship,* Spring 1973, pp. 212-225.

# Self-Conflict in the Academic Reference Librarian: Or Help! We Need a Better Word for What We Do!

Paul B. Weiner

Conflict is a natural part of every organization that employs more than a few people and is productive only insofar as it interacts with people. Conflict is thus part of nearly every organization. It arises when the success of a work effort requires cooperation. Often it is abetted by the separation of co-workers by function, department, social standing, skill level, ability to communicate, self-interest and style. If we substitute line of work for function and department, these same separations also generate conflict between workers and clients.

Almost all conflict within organizations, or between organizations, is perceived as externalized, acted out. That is, two or more people experience and manifest some difficulty working together. Much of this conflict is not only ultimately productive; it is necessary, for it is a byproduct of communication, goal-setting, group formation, creativity. It is one of the chief ways people have of making known their problems, interests and needs, and of seeking help satisfying them. Without this kind of conflict workers in an organization can become smug, self-satisfied, stuck with habits, frustrated, lonely, and may ignore organizational or client interests while favoring their own.

Some conflict is non-productive, even harmful. Often it is the result of poor communication and the lack of an intelligent facilitator. It may be due to inherent weaknesses or imbalances in the organizational structure, to a confused assignment of responsibilities, or to

---

Paul B. Wiener, Special Services Librarian, SUNY at Stony Brook, NY 11794.

© 1985 by The Haworth Press, Inc. All rights reserved.

one group's unreasonable or impossible expectations of another. An intractable individual may present insoluble conflict. When nonproductive conflict persists, organizations and individuals may deal with it by scapegoating, by avoiding it, or by overcompensating for its damage. Tasks may be left undone, or poorly done. Anomie, cynicism, burnout and performance problems may set in. Eventually, a "philosophy" may evolve to explain the inevitability, eternity or even the justice of the situation, and it will become part of the myth of the workplace and the service, one that affects future workers and clients.

There is another kind of conflict that is almost always non-productive, one most inaccessible to traditional resolution. That is conflict within an individual, conflict between what he wishes to think of himself, wishes to feel, and what he actually sees or feels himself doing or becoming. Almost everyone has to deal with adjusting early, private hopes and illusions of their importance in the workplace to the compromising realities of social survival and human nature. This process of adjustment shapes a major part of our identity, and shapes our strategies for continually resolving the conflict, if circumstances renew it. I believe librarians are burdened by this conflict more than most workers, for a variety of well-known reasons, and that reference librarians suffer especially from self-conflict because their public visibility and helping functions rest uneasily on the essentially private dramas of librarianship. It is the purpose of this paper to explore the nature of the reference librarian's conflict with himself by trying to distinguish what reference librarians actually do from what they think they do.

## *BACKGROUND*

Before I continue, though, it might help the reader to know something of my own background, since I believe it has strongly influenced my views. I've been an academic librarian at a large state university for 4½ years; I have about 30 professional colleagues. I'm not a reference librarian, although I work on the reference desk about six hours a week and most of my workplace friends are on the reference staff. My primary duties are selecting, buying and distributing audiovisual materials and managing the audiovisual services of the library. My wife is an occupational therapist, a healthcaring job she and I frequently discuss in terms of the help she provides and the rewards she reaps: she teaches severely handicapped infants and adults to use what they have so that they can achieve some measure of independence.

I've had several careers—as public school English teacher in a poverty pocket, as editor, free-lance writer, cab driver, medical secretary, radio performer, psychiatric hospital worker. Many of my views are drawn from observation, conversation, professional journals, seminars, and from comparing my own work experiences. I'm an extensive reader and went into librarianship partly because I love books, films—and libraries. I felt I would be happy if I could help people by sharing this love as a librarian, by grounding my rarefied interests in the practical management of media. But I never wondered what this "help" would look like, or should.

## WHAT IS HELP?

Among reference librarians it is virtually axiomatic that their work consists of helping people, though many would hesitate to call theirs one of the "helping professions." They provide information, directions, study guides, bibliographies, assistance and instruction in finding information and information sources, building orientation and, less formally, moral and emotional support for the purposes that led the patron to the library. Most of these are person-to-person transactions. The percentage of the workday each reference librarian actually spends with clients or working for them, however, in any but the smallest college libraries, is significantly less than that of other "helping" professions, e.g., nurses, policemen, school teachers, social workers, secretaries, therapists, though it is easy to inflate this percentage retrospectively. This suggests that when reference librarians see themselves as helpers they are expressing a need and a wish at least as much as a description of their work.

That this creates an inner conflict is suggested by the enormous amount of professional literature studying and promoting the *proper* relationship between the reference librarian and the patron. (Indeed, librarians may be the only profession that also worries about its nonclients!) No one is quite certain what this relationship should look or feel like; most are convinced it should not be taken for granted. Most feel it is at the heart of meaningful and fulfilling work, essential to one's positive self-image.

But is what reference librarians do enough to call theirs a helping profession? Almost every exchange between two people confers a benefit on one or both. When money changes hands the exchange as well as the benefit is visibly symbolized. We don't call bank tellers, auto mechanics, sportswear salesmen, bartenders, butchers, train conductors helping professionals, partly because they handle our money, leaving us with no further obligation, but mostly because neither their interpersonal skills nor their education are essential to their successful work performance.

The helping professions, on the other hand, rarely necessitate on-site payment (if any) from clients, and require their practitioners to meet fairly strict educational and characterological guidelines. Helping professionals spend little time alone on the job, their role is perceived as essential to society's well-being, the benefits of their technical expertise are usually enhanced by their personal style, and the actual benefits conferred on clients are almost always visible, verifiable, unambiguous.

Some of these factors characterize reference librarianship. What is missing—and this distresses those anxious to feel helpful, necessary and powerful—is the urgency of client need. It is simply rarely there, and if it isn't, librarians can't negotiate with it for greater rewards. The traditional image of the profession can't really be blamed; other helping professions have overcome stereotypes. Rather, to do their job well reference librarians just don't have to spend most of their time with clients. They can also occupy themselves with preparing study guides and bibliographies, committee work, computer searching (without patrons), desk duty even when no one approaches the desk, collection development, professional reading, and with coordinating the efforts of other library departments with theirs. At times, though, all of these functions are not sufficient to fill the workday, every day, and boredom, self-doubt and inertia may arise.

## *PERSONALITY*

That the personality, or interpersonality, of the reference librarian is rarely a factor in his successful job performance is probably welcomed by librarians as much as it is regretted by those seeking to improve the profession's self-image. Though they can't really be described, there can be little doubt that certain kinds of people become librarians. If these seem reclusive and mental and orderly, reference librarians seem comparatively social and verbal. Yet for many, their actual work draws upon their sociability and benevolence less than they would wish, and less than is good for them. Sometimes you will see a reference librarian acting with great animation and almost absurd familiarity with a patron, though the information sought was basic and could have been supplied in a few short sentences. It is heartening to witness this welcome crossing of barriers and the good feeling that is exchanged. It looks good and promises a repeat customer. But I sometimes wonder if this librarian is not a desperate soul, too eager to show his capabilities, embracing like a choosy psychiatrist a client whose problems are most easily talked away.

## *WHAT IS REFERENCE WORK?*

There has arisen in the last two decades what can almost be called a cult of reference librarianship in academic libraries, and it may come as a shock to remember that only 30 years ago the first reference librarian was appointed to the University of Cincinnati. The rituals of this cult center chiefly around the theory and practise of service—helping patrons, when "service" gets too abstract. Rituals of departmental administration and self-evaluation, statistics-keeping, practising "doctor-patient" relations, and task-sharing are now the concerns of most conscientious reference librarians and compete for time spent in actually providing assistance to flesh-and-blood users.

This situation has several origins: in the fight for faculty status, which often requires a shift in one's self-image (and responsibility) from public servant to teacher, from human databank to scholar; in the emphasis on self-fulfillment that began in the mid-sixties; and in the growth of reference departments and concurrent task specialization that fosters the assertiveness of expertise in reference staffers. The result is that it is frequently easier to define the reference department than to define reference work and the reference worker. Unless he or she works in a small facility, the reference librarian no longer works only for the library, or the college; he also works for the reference room, the department, the department head, the patron, and the philosophy of reference service. Somewhere in there is an individual doing a job and wondering exactly what it is.

Much of the gloss of reference librarianship that temporarily blinds librarians to the reality of what they do is removed when we think of the work in its germinal sense: providing assistance to patrons in their library and informational needs, "the process of establishing contact between a reader and his documents in a personal way," as S.R. Ranganathan said. True, the "library" is now the reference area, the "user" or "reader" is now the researcher or the student in need of research and library skills, and the "documents" may be a phone number, a celluloid strip, a screen display, an address, a time schedule, travel directions, or another person. But "assistance" remains constant. And it feels good to give assistance. It's usually rewarding, and the interaction seems one worth repeating. One can become satisfied with feeling it. But what of the librarian who wishes to give more than assistance, to be more to a client? Is it possible?

It is not providing the information, search strategy, document or book that distinguishes reference work and reference librarians from cataloguers, collection developers, serials, circulation, or acquisition librarians; it is providing direct assistance, interfacing with library users themselves and all the uncertainties they bring. It is this function that is also the source of conflict, between reference and other librarians, between philosophies of service, between professionals and clients, and within reference librarians themselves. For balancing using and dispensing knowledge with anticipating and satisfying human needs, can be a high-wire act that at times will bring down those neither skilled in both areas nor comfortable with the acrobatics of serving a quiet minority. The librarian whose personal, social and intellectual resources are most frequently challenged in reference work finds himself uniquely positioned to assess the traditions, practises and goals that separate academic librarians from themselves. Often seen as the symbol of his profession, the reference librarian may have too many professional selves to choose among.

## *SELF-CONFLICT PECULIAR TO REFERENCE WORK*

It is said that every occupation knows its own particular anguish leading to times when the worker, be he doctor or company president, waiter or shortstop, wonders how he ever got into that position, and why. This anguish is usually generated by situations that make one aware that self-will is not enough to control, or overcome, or sometimes even understand, unpleasant circumstances. Librarians are no different, and reference librarians, being the most public, are most sensitive to this feeling, for they are confronted daily by people and needs far removed from the routines and demands of the workplace.

A number of factors conspire to create self-consciousness in reference librarians: (1) In most academic libraries they are separated by location, function and interests from "technical service" librarians (i.e., those who don't have to work with nonlibrarians). Misunderstanding, competitiveness, resentment and mutual ignorance may characterize the relations between these two groups: who is the "real" librarian? The public has its own answers too, and imposes them on all. (2) Much of reference work is mental, intellectual and interpersonal. There is often little to "document" or verify the success or importance or amount of the work performed. Workflow statistics can be created and research undertaken to codify and quantify everything that happens—the journals are full of such studies. But much of reference librarian effectiveness remains intangible, with output often tied to the demands of ignorant, frantic or erratic users. Though it touts itself as an art, reference work produces few artifacts. Its practitioners sometimes don't know what to show for themselves.

(3) Many reference librarians give their allegiance to their room, their department head and their patrons. Less space is allotted to accomplishing personal projects and goals, perfecting intellectual skills, or intralibrary cooperation. The public servant is at odds with the conscientious individual. (4) The satisfaction to be gained from helping a user—whether providing B.I., information, research guidance, a physical document—though greatly sought and regarded by reference librarians as their *raison d'être,* is simply not to be compared with the satisfaction gained from saving a person from injury, pain, death, guilt, insult, loss, penury or loneliness. Reference librarians often wish their service had monumental significance and impact, and brag about successes like athletes and lawyers. What they offer *is* important and *can* have far-reaching effects; it simply offers limited rewards. Reference librarians are forced to look beyond "service" for complete job fulfillment, and it can be a lonely search.

(5) Like other, but not all, librarian functions, much of reference work is a low-key operation. Demands are rarely put stridently or threateningly, the pace is gradual, concerns are humanistic. Deci-

sions are never motivated by profit-making. Unless one is on the reference desk human dialogue and interaction may be frequent, but often it is not essential to job performance. Such a low-key environment, while consciously sought and sustained by many librarians, does not exercise one's social, conversational, communicative or cooperative capabilities. Without use, these abilities can atrophy or become highly ritualized, while inner, unsatisfied social and emotional needs remain. Workers can become finicky, idiosyncratic, self-important, bored, passive and skeptical of others' efforts. And they resent their superiors' and colleagues' inability to make them feel better or accomplish more.

(6) The reference librarian, working frequently with students, teaching library skills, helping instructors with class assignments, is highly sensitive to the issue of faculty status. It rankles him not merely as a professional/moral issue but as a practical one, for he often sees himself literally performing the same educative function as teaching faculty, albeit usually in a different setting. There is little a librarian can do, however, in his workplace or in the academic community, to bolster his convictions of being "equal" to faculty other than fight for a dubious "status" of equality based on contractual demands, and address peers as if the matter were beyond dispute.

(7) As noted previously, the reference librarian is seen, and usually sees himself, as the person through whom the library is known, the most visible and accessible contact point. This is both a source of pride and of anxiety: pride, for he is granted recognition and power; anxiety, because he feels obligated. He is burdened by expectations, many of them false, from users, and burdened by resentment from non-reference colleagues who may feel their own roles are unknown and unacknowledged publicly. Prioritization by administrators of needs, expansion and budgets among library departments is also an obvious source of conflict when departmental visibility is involved. Reference departments win some and lose some. Many reference librarians, in the course of giving normal service, are made aware of the operations and problems of other library departments. This awareness encourages a utopian vision of integrated library functioning which they may see, or imagine, undermined or neglected in the actual world of specialized, self-interested departments, including their own.

(8) Finally, unlike most librarians, reference people are called upon to perform a wide variety of roles: as teacher, information spe-

cialist, bibliographer, public servant, reference desk sitter, phone and file clerk, computer operator, subject specialist, problem solver. Rare indeed is the person who excels, or is even competent, in all these areas. Weakness in some leads to self-consciousness. It also gives rise to a confused identity: there are many to choose among. When the reference librarian acts or argues from a wrong, or insufficient, identity, conflict may arise—with others who think he's overstepping himself, and with himself, for feeling unsure of where his best interests lie. He may need help and not know where to find it. He may not be alone.

## *LURCHING TOWARD HAPPINESS*

Because it has for so long enjoyed a questionable social/occupational status, and because the nature of its work appeals to both elitist and democratic, ministering and retiring instincts, librarianship has attracted people who are no strangers to ambivalence. They are also people who are determined, intelligent and self-respecting. Most have come to terms with their ambivalence and have learned, as we all must, to accept a certain amount of conflict on the job. But when work generates self-conflict, the amount is rarely certain enough to control. Nevertheless, most reference librarians working in an active environment can keep busy enough to forget the problems and vague dissatisfactions that more quiet periods thrust into consciousness. Is this the answer, then: to learn to accept our fate, to enjoy what we can enjoy of work, and for the rest, keep busy?

There are conceivable a number of "solutions" to the problem of the self-conflicted reference librarian, but only one or two stand the test of practicality: (1) Abandon efforts to gain or retain faculty status. It drains energy and appeals primarily to false pride. Work for either a full faculty appointment, or an enhanced librarian position. (2) Establish a moratorium on reference librarian-patron interaction studies. Most are ludicrous parodies of the obvious. Successful interactions are not rituals. (3) Develop through the library schools a psychology and sociology of librarians and library work that can stand alongside those developed for the other professions. This should include coursework, field trips, a substantial literature, a multidisciplinary approach to library research, and a set of axioms and hypotheses that would enable fledgling as well as burned librarians to center themselves in the profession, its priesthood, and in society.

(4) Identify and employ those with leadership abilities, admittedly a tall order for a bureaucracy. A department or library head who, by the force of intelligence and personality, can rally subordinates, establish goals and see them through, and can himself or herself model the fullness of character and achievement desired by all, can make a tremendous difference, and render the stirrings of self-conflict inconsequential. Unfortunately, we can't create leaders, only administrators. In their absence, though, librarians might at least read what our profession's leaders have had to say—people like Lawrence Clark Powell, Ranganathan, Lester Asheim, Louis Shores.

(5) Require, as has long been recommended, all librarians to work periodically in other library departments—to learn new skills or exercise old ones, to entertain other points of view, to talk to other staffers. The nature of our work is such that most of us can still learn most of its tasks and skills. Since no Japanese paternalism from our employers is likely to guarantee our loyalty, high productivity and personal fulfillment, perhaps an American immersion in holistic job performance will. We are not yet tied to the unions that forbid it, yet few reference librarians are general practitioners.

My most serious "solution," though, is a simple one and has its roots in the origins of culture: foster creativity. There is so much less room for feelings of self-conflict when one is aggressively tapping his own skills, invention, vision, talent and authority. Make something, share something, leave something at work that wasn't there before. It can be a bibliography, an article, or organization, a staff, a procedure, a manual, a course, a new service or technology, a cooperative relationship. It can even be a personal style, a willingness to share one's self, one's humor, philosophy and energy. Such non-documentable creativity acts as an example, a precedent for reference librarians who feel their character is still their most reliable resource, the best medium between the library and the library user. In every line of work creative effort has advanced that profession's ability to help others, to improve its efficiency, economy and productivity, to attract new workers, to keep clients happy. Libraries are no different, and reference librarians, having daily access to much of the world's treasury of intellect and culture, are in an excellent position to invest it in themselves, and thus increase its interest.

# Why Didn't They Teach Us That? The Credibility Gap in Library Education

## Michael McCoy

It seemed so easy at the time. A single sheet of paper filled with questions like, "How much money did IBM make in 1978?" and "How much is a first edition of *A Farewell to Arms* worth?" At the bottom of the sheet were a dozen or more sources to be found in the university library. Twelve weeks of this, and I had completed my coursework in reference services: all at my own pace, all at my own leisure.

Looking back, I had a pretty good ratio of found answers to those not found. I even managed to score a minor coup when one of the questions was "Find a biography of Jack Smith." No one else seemed to remember that Jack Smith was the host of the television show, "You Asked for It." Even though there were at least three other Jack Smiths to be had, I'd found one, and that made my day. Even if I hadn't found it, someone else would have, and I would have made a notation in my notebook to remind me where they'd come across the information. It seemed very methodical at the time, and pretty straightforward. I came out of school a reference librarian.

Eventually, I landed a job as adult services librarian at the Tarrytown (NY) Public Library, a job which includes a great deal of time at the reference desk. Serving a community of 18,642, in 1982 we answered a total of 19,718[1] reference questions, or a little more than one inquiry per person. Questions typically range from ready-reference ("What is the circumference of the Earth?") to school assignments ("What do you have on glaciers, volcanoes, and con-

---

The author, a frequent contributor to this journal, is Reference Librarian at the Warner Library, Tarrytown, NY 10591.

tinental drift?'') to dissertations (''I'm looking for articles and books on the attitudes of students toward mentally and physically handicapped peers.''). Thrown in for good measure are requests for company profiles, census material, information on any particularly hot topic, and trivia. (The last two sometimes merge for an interesting question. Last St. Patrick's Day, for example, a caller wanted to know the name of Parnell's mistress.)

Having worked at several libraries for the past six years, I know that—aside from number—these questions differ little from what any other public library is likely to receive. So why do I feel that so much of what I've needed to know has been learned on the job, and not from my classwork? What did my reference coursework prepare me for? Did it prepare me at all?

A look at some of the literature from the past three years (since my graduation) indicates I'm not alone in these feelings. Under various headings in ''Library Literature Index''—''Library schools— Evaluation'' and ''Education for librarianship—Evaluation,'' for example—I was able to turn up fifteen articles dealing with the same general frustration, that library schools aren't preparing students for what they'll be facing once they graduate. John Calvin Colson, in his article, ''Professional Ideals and Social Realities: Some Questions about the Education of Librarians''[2] asks the question: ''what does a librarian need to know; when does the librarian need to know it?'' He continues:

> Our curricula in librarianship do not appear to have been devised with these questions firmly in mind, except the assumption that the librarian needs to know about books, whatever that may mean. Also, it appears that our curricula are based on an assumption that a librarian is a librarian is a librarian—that is, any librarian's (hence, all librarians') formal education needs may be met by passage through a standardized curriculum for entry into the field . . .

This same attitude is voiced (albeit humorously) in Pauline Anderson's 1982 article ''Creative Coping: Things You Never Taught Me,''[3] in which she relates several problems that may typically confront the young reference librarian. For example, ''Which way is Mecca?'' And though I don't believe for a minute that Ms. Anderson handles all inquiries the way she did this one (she faked it), the day-to-day reference service does confront us with situations that we were never taught in school; that were never mentioned in school.

## *ETHICS*

For example, the problem of ethics. In a medium-sized library, it becomes hard not to develop favorites among the patrons, just as a teacher has a "teacher's pet." And conversely, there are always those patrons who make us want to run for the hills when we see them coming. If this had been brought up in a classroom situation, we could all have written down "Play no favorites" in our notebooks, and gone on to something else. But which of us has not found himself bending over backwards for a trustee or a board member, when we may not have bent quite so far for the assembly-line worker from down the block? Unethical, of course, in the purest sense. But also very human, and sometimes apparently necessary. It's a reality that some patrons do carry more influence than others, and who wants to go through the day feeling that they've let down the person who pays their salary? And as far as the unfavorite patron is concerned? We do our best, and grin and bear it. But it does point out that, to paraphrase Orwell, all patrons are equal, but some are more equal than others.

Another conflict arises when it comes to the reference interview. Anyone who has had to deal with the public realizes that many times what they ask for is not at all what they want. This arises from either reticence, or an unclear picture in their own minds of the type of information available. For example, a request for information about Pan-American Day may eventually become a list of countries in the Pan-American Union. Any confusion about what the patron needs is theoretically cleared up in the reference interview. Charts, films, and articles abounded in library school when the mention of the interview was brought up.

The problem becomes, how to handle an effective interview when there are three people waiting at the desk to be helped, the phone is ringing off the wall, newspapers have to be brought up from downstairs, and someone can't turn on the public computer? Against my better judgement, I've resorted to becoming a pointer: I point to the card catalog, I point to the spot on the shelves where they might browse. It seems more productive than having them wait at the desk while I handle everyone else, or making everyone else wait while I probe them with endless questions. The hope is always that, if they're still looking for material in five or ten minutes, it may have quieted down enough so that I can follow up on their initial request, asking if they're finding what they've been looking for; if they feel they need more help. Not according to library rules, I admit, but the only effective way to get through the day sometimes.

And maybe it's time we gave the patron more credit than we do. I'm beginning to feel that the reference interview isn't always necessary, at least not to the extent that we were led to believe in class. I find the average reference exchange might be:

"I'd like some information on Pan-American Day."
"Are you interested in how the day came about?"
"Well, what I'd like to find are books I can use in a school exhibit."
"Books on the Americas?"
"Books on the countries, yes."

It may seem a bit simplistic (nothing to chart, surely) but very common. And while the reference interview does come in handy for anyone working on a paper, or for any information that might involve inter-library loans, subject requests, and data-base searches, it's likewise idiotic to question someone who comes in asking for last Sunday's edition of "The New York Times." I can't speak for academic or special libraries, but the reference interview can't—and shouldn't—be applied as readily in public libraries as we were taught. Time and common sense won't permit it.

## *CONFLICTS*

Another conflict in reference service is one that I never had to worry about in school: the currency and availability of the information I was using. With a million-volume collection at the State University of New York at Albany, I had generally the most up-to-date material, in more subjects than I could hope to cover. But in the library where I now work, the adult collection numbers around 60,000 and, being a public library, a tight rein is kept on our budget. How to handle, then, the patron who comes in asking for a copy of "New England Journal of Medicine," or annual reports from a small company in Illinois? While Thomas Childers, in a 1980 article,[4] classified steering as a "non answer," I feel that the prime consideration is to get the right information to the patron with the least amount of time and bother, and so better to be steered than turned away. As part of the Westchester Library System, we are one of thirty-eight public libraries, and we do rely on inter-library loan and such steering when necessary. But the consensus in school seemed to be that if the material wasn't on the shelf, it wasn't to be found. Admittedly, this is not as much a fault of the education as it was of our own inexperience, but I don't think it would do any harm to mention the possibility of working as part of a network, as opposed to a self-contained unit. The literature certainly bears out that the inter-library loan has been with us a while, and will probably stay a while longer.

Which brings me to a particular pet peeve, which is that all the information we needed was to be found in books. What about periodicals, pamphlets, and other non-book materials? Would it have counted against us if we had used a data-base search to answer one or more of our reference assignments? To be fair, there is a limit to what one teacher can reasonably be expected to cover, but I find that the most recent, the most accurate, and the easiest information isn't always in a book. A few questions about the most recent developments in teenage drinking and driving will find you at the vertical file or the "Magazine Index," not at the card catalog.

There are, of course, those things that school can't be expected to teach: politicking, soothing ruffled feathers, and making it through those days when you just should have stayed in bed. It's on those days when the reference librarian needs a degree somewhere between psychology and political science. Only experience will help you deal with the woman who is looking for a pain clinic and then explains why she thinks her doctor is giving her the wrong medication after her mastectomy. Or the cartoonist who regales you with the stories of what it was like to draw Felix the Cat back in 1920. Or even the endless patrons who come in to shoot the breeze about the latest mystery books or spy fiction. One thing library school didn't need to teach me was when to listen.

## *TRIVIA QUESTIONS*

One thing they *did* teach us, more as warning than a promise, was to beware of the trivia question, the barroom bet-settler. On a deadly dull Friday, I don't really mind looking through our books to see who played the Shadow on radio, but I was a bit less enthusiastic when, on a busy day, I got a reference call that went: "There are three words in the English language that end in -gry. One is angry and the other is hungry. What is the third?" Visions of "Do you have Prince Albert in a can?" danced through my head. But, I felt compelled to give as much time as I could. Which leads me to sometimes agree with Will Manley who, in his October, 1982 article in "Wilson Library Bulletin," wrote of his distaste for the ALA "Call Your Library" campaign, and the similar emphasis on trivia that he found in segments on "The Tonight Show." Manley went on to say:[5]

> Why should we waste our time counting the dimples on a golf ball when we don't waste either our time or money providing trashy novels or tabloids? Why isn't it valid to apply the same standards of quality that we use in book selection to reference question selection? Perhaps the one constructive thing that the "Call Your Library" campaign will accomplish will be to embarrass librarians into taking as strong a stand toward developing reference question policies . . . as we have in developing materials selection policies.

But even here there are some other considerations to make. I've been able to see how the public does, indeed, respond to some of the publicity gimmicks that ALA and other libraries have attempted from time to time. My own library is about to undertake what others seem to be doing more and more often, a contest to see if any of the patrons can come up with a legitimate question that our reference staff can't answer. And while I admit I was hesitant about this, I have to concede that it really has struck a chord in the community, and I'm looking forward to a fairly large rise in the amount of reference questions this March. And from the few that I've seen already, they do seem to be legitimate, as opposed to the *Guinness Book* variety.

But the question still remains: what could school have done, if anything, to prepare me for some of these problems that I encounter on a day-to-day basis? I think there are three solutions, all effective to varying degrees.

The first is the push toward continuing education. Several times in the Spring and Fall, brochures will cross my desk with courses ranging from computer training to the psychology of the reference interview. And while they may be, as Colson states, "symptomatic rather than systematic, stemming from recognition that the M.L.S.

is inadequate for an entire career,"[6] they also serve to keep the librarian in touch with others in the field, which sometimes can accomplish more than a semester of course-work. And it does provide the librarian with an opportunity to enjoy some hands-on experience with computers, microforms, and other technologies, not to mention some personally rewarding topics (e.g., dealing with stress, how to prevent burn-out, etc.). If the M.L.S. isn't—or can't—provide all that a librarian needs to know, this sort of program seems to be the next best thing.

## *POSSIBILITIES*

But there are some possibilities that could take place in the library school, before the degree is granted and the job is taken. For example, there could be more of an emphasis placed on internships. While more common with the special librarian, there shouldn't be any reason why reference librarians shouldn't have some on-the-job training while they're still in school. There's no better way to prepare oneself for the day-to-day handlings of the reference desk. The lack of a degree shouldn't be an obstacle: there are many libraries with non-degree personnel handling reference questions. As a matter of fact, the coursework already completed could be considered an advantage. And there are plenty of libraries—particularly public libraries—who would probably be glad to have an extra person on staff. From such a program, all could benefit.

The third possibility of bringing library schools more in line with the world of libraries is to use the librarian who is out there everyday as an adjunct professor, either on an occasional basis (perhaps part of a round-table), or on a semester-long temporary assignment. Short of placing the student in an actual library situation, it would serve to bring the library to the school. This was done in a course I took in collection development, and the effect it had on the class was swift and dramatic. It took us away from our desks and into the library. Perhaps librarians taking part in the program could then have tuition waived for any courses they may wish to take as part of their own continuing education. This would make it mutually profitable for both parties.

None of these ideas is meant to suggest that there is anything fundamentally wrong with our library education. Nothing needs to be changed or omitted. What is needed is merely a look at the desired ends, and then perhaps adding a few things. And even if all three suggestions I've made could some how be implemented, I have no illusions that all the conflicts between what is taught and what is, would suddenly disappear. There will always be those situations when the librarian will have nothing to rely on but experience, a good nature, and more than a little luck. But when most situations do occur, the response shouldn't be "Why didn't they teach us that?" but rather, "Now where have I heard this before?" It can work wonders.

## REFERENCES

1. Westchester Library System, *Member Library Statistics: 1982*, p. 8.
2. John Calvin Colson, "Professional Ideals and Social Realities: Some Questions about the Education of Librarians," in *Library Lit. 12—The Best of 1981*, edited by Bill Katz and Kathleen Weibel, Metuchen, NJ, Scarecrow Press, 1982, p. 57.
3. Pauline Anderson, "Creatived Coping: Things You Never Taught Me," *VOYA*, 5: 14-15, August, 1982.
4. Thomas Childers, "The Test of Reference," in *Library Lit. 11—The Best of 1980* edited by Bill Katz, Metuchen, N.J., Scarecrow Press, 1981, p. 18.
5. Will Manley, "Facing the Public," *Wilson Library Bulletin,* October 1982, p. 147.
6. Colson, *loc. cit.*

# Role Conflict and Ambiguity in Reference Librarianship

Henry N. Mendelsohn

When asked to write about an aspect of conflicts in reference service it seemed like a good opportunity to clarify some thoughts that have been bothering me since graduate school days. The problems which I wish to address are based on my perception that reference librarians frequently find themselves in situations where there are no rules to follow or if there are rules they may conflict with what the reference librarian is being asked to do. It is the reference librarian who usually bears the brunt of the public's demands on the library. The public being served may not understand the nature of a complex organization such as a library nor may persons working in other units of a library understand the demands of public service.

It seemed a good idea to list both potential conflicts and actual situations I have been involved in. However, the list began to sound like a description of Civil War battles. Could these horror stories be a result of a lack of interpersonal skills on my part, some deficiency in my professional training or perhaps some lurking unsuspected conspiracy on the part of some radical anti-intellectual group out to get reference librarians?

Although communication breakdowns can and do occur and my professional training was not all it could have been I am sure such problems cannot account for all of the conflicts I have encountered or heard about. And while Americans love conspiracy theories not all of our problems can be solved by looking under rocks for agitators.

A more productive approach would be to use a little "sociological imagination" and look for institutional variables that may affect how reference librarians do their job. The concept of "sociological

---

The author is Bibliographer and Reference Librarian, Graduate Library for Public Affairs and Policy, State University of New York at Albany, Albany, NY 12222.

imagination" refers to the distinction between personal troubles or private problems and public issues (Mills, 1959). Mills used "public issues" to refer to the problems of the macrostructure of society. For the purpose of this essay I am narrowing this perspective to refer to organizational issues that may affect an individual's behavior. The way in which libraries organize themselves and the behavioral prescriptions administrators place on their employees, including reference librarians, affect the delivery of services.

Reference librarians are often caught in the middle of conflicting institutional and patron pressures. Most reference librarians work in complex organizations and must meet the expectations of their supervisors, cooperate with other units of a library and at the same time please the customers or patrons. In order to describe this "between a rock and a hard place" phenomenon I am employing two sociological concepts: role conflict and role ambiguity.

Role conflict results when incompatible goals and expectations are imposed on a role, or occur between the roles that a particular individual occupies. The information supplied to the employee is clear but it conflicts with the role the employee must play.

Role ambiguity refers to the situation a person finds himself/herself in when unclear about whose expectations he/she is required to meet. That is, must he/she meet the demands of the employing institution or the demands of the public that may conflict with the required institutional role. The needed information is not forthcoming from the employing organizations and the person is left wondering what to do. It follows that there may also be uncertainty about how the role incumbant will be evaluated. If the expectations for behavior are not clear the evaluative process may also be unclear.

## *LITERATURE REVIEW*

Role conflict and role ambiguity are concepts developed by sociologists. Only one major study has surfaced in the library literature. White (1970) addressed himself to the problem of ideological role conflict as well as sex role conflict within librarianship. He points out that librarians experience differing role expectations within their role sets but have competing role models and loyalties which make it difficult to select appropriate role behaviors.

White thought that many librarians ultimately aspire towards the higher levels of library work, that is, management and administration. Career-oriented library students and working librarians view senior library administrators as role models. However, since most library administrators are male and the bulk of librarians female, White believes sex role conflict can ensue.

Another situation exists in university and college librarianship that is ripe for the development of role conflict. College and university librarians work in institutions whose norms favor research, writing and teaching rather than administration. As more emphasis is placed on research, writing and subject area specialization the situation will be compounded when librarians seek or attempt to live up to faculty status or seek to enter the highest ranks of their profession.

Furthermore, as DeWeese (1972) pointed out, librarians are still all too often regarded as second class citizens by fellow faculty members even when faculty status has been achieved.

## *EXAMPLES*

It has been my experience from having worked in three different academic libraries that reference librarians are frequently faced with ambiguous or conflicting role situations. Employing institutions do not always make clear to their reference librarians exactly what is expected of them. The reference librarian may have one idea of what their job is about, their supervisor may have a slightly different idea while the library director may have yet another idea about appropriate role behavior.

My approach to reference service at the college and university level is to explain to patrons where to start to look for information by showing them sources, explaining their use and then letting the patron do their own research. However, my arrival in my first professional position coincided with the arrival of the new assistant director for public services who announced that he was a "closet public librarian" who believed that reference librarians should do the research and hand everything to the patron on a silver platter.

This issue continued to plague the overworked reference librarians throughout this particular administrator's tenure. The assistant director continued to hint that we should follow his philosophy but never actually made it a clear-cut policy. The Head of Reference thought it to be a ludicrous position and told his staff to ignore the assistant director. Thus, the reference librarians worked in an organization that failed to clearly delineate the role expectations of its employees. It was clearly a case of role ambiguity.

An example of role conflict is illustrated by a situation in which a highly trained reference specialist has to spend a great deal of time with patrons working on complex reference problems while simultaneously performing clerical duties such as changing copy machine paper and making change. Two clearly opposed role behaviors are expected to be performed at the same time, one by patrons and the other by the employing institution. Role conflict results and the reference librarian may be unable to adequately perform either role. Reference questions are not sufficiently answered and change is incorrectly counted. The role conflict has resulted because institutional support (such as the provision of a change machine or sufficient support staff) has not been provided.

Furthermore, patrons may be confused as to exactly what a librarian does when they see a librarian performing essentially unprofessional, subservient role behavior. It is little wonder that many teaching faculty have trouble viewing librarians as colleagues when they see librarians making change or continually pointing patrons to the bathroom.

Another problematic aspect of reference that is potentially fraught with conflict occurs when the assistance of other units within the library is needed in order to provide services or materials for patrons. If a library does not own a book or article or it is lost or missing or whatever, a reference librarian is usually the first one to hear about it. He or she must then marshall the resources of the library to meet the needs of the patron. This may not be an easy thing to do.

In many large (and not so large) libraries there are schisms between reference services and technical services departments which inhibit cooperation and even understanding of other units' goals and problems. A reference librarian is usually powerless to force a reluctant acquisitions librarian to rush order a book or an interlibrary loan librarian to fill a particularly troublesome order. Yet, the reference librarian is the one who must apologize to the patron if another unit in the backroom is uncooperative.

Such problems will be compounded if the reference librarian finds himself/herself without clear guidelines to follow. If the library administration cannot resolve internal bickering, a lowly reference librarian certainly cannot. He/she may have to rely on affective bonds with members of other units but if those bonds are not or cannot be established the reference librarians will be caught in the ensuing conflict. The required role behavior is either ambiguous or clearly in conflict with others' roles in the institution.

## ORGANIZATIONAL PROCESS IN ROLE STRAIN

It can be seen from such anecdotes that the employing organization affects for better or worse how employees perform their roles. Repeated local instances of role conflict and ambiguity frequently reflect the failure to solve or even recognize problems inherent in the functioning of any complex organization.

As illustrated above, persons who may be particularly caught up in structurally induced conflict and ambiguity are those who occupy statuses that must deal with people in other units of an organization or outside of the organization entirely. This is particularly true in service occupations where patrons are in need of a certain role behavior from the organization's focal person.

When the role incumbant lacks the ability to control the behavior of others outside the immediate work unit the person cannot guarantee that the role performance of those outsiders will be as he/she needs and wishes.

In the above example the patron views the reference librarian as the focal point for the library. The success or failure of the library to obtain the needed information or service will reflect on the reference librarian whether or not he/she was actually instrumental in performing the service.

## BOUNDARY ROLES

When a person occupies a status whose successful role performance depends on others outside the immediate work unit such a status may be thought of as a boundary status and role. It is on the periphery or boundary of a work unit or units.

When a reference librarian occupies such a role he/she must, all too often, walk a thin line between the needs of the organization and the demands of the patrons. And most reference librarians are powerless to influence the roles of others they depend on.

In order to reduce the potential conflict and to compensate for a lack of power or formal authority the person occupying a boundary status should rely to a great extent on the affective bonds of trust, respect, and liking which can be developed among outsiders, both the public and within other work units. The reference librarian may court the acquisitions clerk who can be relied on to place an order for a needed item and to follow through to see that the reference librarian and ultimately the patron is satisfied. However, such bonds are difficult to create and maintain. To the public the failings of a person's unit or that of another unit within the library are all too easily identified as failures of the role incumbent. Any affective bonds that may have been developed will weaken to some extent.

An additional result of such problems is the failure of those in other units whom the role incumbent is dependent upon to appreciate the urgency or necessity of a boundary person's requests to them.

The incumbent of a boundary role is faced with a number of people demanding certain role behaviors. The public wants one thing while people in other work units want another. The demands are hard to predict and hard to control. These demands are usually generated by the dynamics of other departments or organizations and will shift with the vicissitudes of those groups. Compounding the situation is the likelihood that such demands are not going to be tempered by an adequate understanding of what such shifts mean for the boundary person. Thus, the boundary person is faced with conflicting demands but has limited resources to reduce the conflict.

## *INNOVATIVE ROLES*

Another set of institutionally created conflicts may be experienced by persons occupying roles that demand innovative and creative behavior in reaction to routine problems. This may particularly occur in a bureaucracy. Persons who hold innovative positions in basically conservative, rule-oriented organizations may find themselves in open conflict with those who have a vested interest in the status quo. The innovators are usually placed on the defensive and must continually provide justification for their existence.

An illustration of this problem might be found when a library director decides to initiate and implement a database search service within a traditional reference department. The head of reference may not be receptive to the idea for various reasons. However, the director forces the issue and may hire a new person to come in and set up the service and report to the reluctant reference head. The harried reference head and director may send conflicting signals to the innovator who finds that neither superior can be pleased no matter what behavior the innovator adopts.

Such a role conflict may have a slightly different twist. A person on the staff may be asked to set up a new service that he/she is essentially unfamiliar with. A director or unit head may tell the person to do it, but not how to do it and may not provide any personal or institutional support. Thus, the role incumbant is faced with an ambiguous situation. It is not clear what is expected for adequate performance. This is role ambiguity.

## CONSEQUENCES

What are the consequences of structurally induced role conflict and role ambiguity to the organization and to the individual? No doubt the presence of conflicting role expectations in one's occupational environment tends to produce internal motivational conflicts. Roles which are unclear or ambiguous may also have emotional and motivational consequences. Role ambiguities and conflicts tend to reduce one's general satisfaction with the job and conditions surrounding it and to undermine confidence in superiors and in the organization as a whole. There may be a weakening of interpersonal bonds, a curtailment of interaction and a denial of power. Rather than seeking solutions to conflict and ambiguity people may tend to withdraw and avoid contact.

Of course, emotional reactions will vary. One person may become apathetic while another becomes hostile. A great effort on the part of an individual may be exerted in order to change a bad organizational situation. While this may be productive in the long run if the conflicts are successfully resolved it will also distract the person from routine work and may take a heavy emotional toll on those involved.

In order to cope with such stress a person must deal with the situation so as to reduce or eliminate its stressful aspects. They must master the tension and negative emotions which may develop. And such persons may have to confront problems which may derive from the original coping efforts, e.g. an angry boss who may or may not want to resolve the situation.

## CONCLUSIONS

Finding resolutions to role conflict and ambiguity in complex organizations such as libraries will not be an easy task. It is doubtful whether any work situation can be or should be entirely free of conflict. It would help if library administrators would be aware that the way in which a library is structured affects employees' behavior. Libraries are not merely hierarchical lines on an organization chart but also a complex set of human relationships. Administrators should also pay particular attention to the schisms that can occur between reference services and technical services. Technical service librarians should show a greater awareness of how their actions affect reference services. In addition, evaluations of reference librarians need to be based on clearly defined role expectations and not criteria pulled out of a hat after the fact.

It is doubtful that the current generation of unenlightened library leadership, preoccupied with declining budgets, can begin to address sociological and psychological problems faced by employees working in complex organizations. Structurally induced stress will continue to plague reference librarians until some attention is paid to the sociological factors inherent in complex library organizations.

There is a definite need for social psychological research in libraries. The paucity of such research is surprising since university researchers often exploit convenient populations, such as students, for data gathering. Libraries provide a conveniently close complex organization in which to conduct social and psychological research. Library directors should seek out interested researchers and allow research with the aim of improving the quality of working life to be conducted within their libraries.

As the nature of librarianship changes and the role of the librarian evolves, working conditions will have to be structured in a fashion to contain and minimize structurally induced role stress.

## REFERENCES

DeWeese, L.C., "Status Concerns and Library Professionalism," *College and Research Libraries*, 33: 31-8, January, 1972.

Kahn, Robert L., et al., *Organizational Stress: Studies in Role Conflict and Ambiguity*. New York: John Wiley and Sons, 1964.

Mills, C. Wright, *The Sociological Imagination*. Oxford University Press, 1959.

White, Rodney, F., and David B. Macklin, *Education, Careers and Professionalization in Librarianship and Information Science*. Bethesda, MD: National Library of Medicine, 1970.

# ABOUT THE RESOURCES

## In This Conflict of Opinions and Sentiments I Find Delight

Donald Davinson

According to the many academic references and testimonials reaching at least one school of librarianship in support of aspirants to librarianship, conflict is not something ever experienced in such havens of tranquility as libraries. Gentle, rather low powered, little flowers who are 'avid readers' and 'like English' but 'are not strong enough for far more demanding work' are enthusiastically recommended by School and University tutors for our oases of cloistered calm. It is all rather a compliment to us in a way that people who, by definition, must be or have been, considerable users of libraries, to think like that. It implies we have so arranged our housekeeping that the truculent drunk wanting information to settle a bet, the furtive flasher lurking behind the map case, the zealous vandal carving up the fine art collection and the hysterical assistant recently flashed at are dealt with so firmly and quietly that this aspect of our constant conflict with what P.G. Wodehouse called 'the great unwashed' is hidden from open view.

The dirty in-fighting indivisible from the Budget Committee tussling for resources in an academic library and the sheer unpleasant-

---

The author is Head, School of Librarianship, Leeds Polytechnic, England. The title, as most readers recognize, is a quote from Dr. Johnson.

ness often associated with Trustee or Committee person claims for special service from a Public Library are likewise hidden from public view. The public image of semi-soporific silence and absence of stress is perhaps our greatest area of personal conflict in librarianship. We need to maintain such an appearance of ordered calm in our environment without being regarded, ourselves, as so many automaton-like dwellers in safe, gilded cages over whom a green baize cloth is thrown every evening like so many parlour parrots until the human race needs them again in the morning. We need people to know that we too are creatures of the switched-on electronic age. Purely to protect our status in society, we need to dispel the image of the dumpy, myopic, pedantic frump to attract the quality of personnel we need and yet this is all a matter of total irrelevance to our users. If they are obtaining what they see as a satisfactory service, fitted to their needs from the dim, the dumb and the daft they appear to perceive our ranks to be populated with, perhaps all is at its best in the best of possible worlds? But it isn't is it? The apparently satisfied are only so because they have no idea what a first class library service could do for them—and we have not been able to show them. Those we have shown, or who knew already what they ought to expect, we are really not very good at giving service to because their demands often exceed our capacity to supply.

The biggest conflict of all in our work is that were we to have a user population all of whom demanded of us the sort of service we tell each other we can supply, then we should not be able to do so. Our resources and, more importantly, the abilities of our staffs would not cope with the demands made. We tell the world we can do things which we know, deep down, we can only do for some of the time for some of the users. We *need* the non-users we agonize over not having in order to provide adequate service to the more vociferous users we have. This is the ultimate conflict in the Reference Librarian's working life.

## CONFLICT IN REFERENCE SERVICE

Conflict in Reference Service is a thing of many dimensions. Public punch-ups with clients at the service desk are the most manifest of conflicts. Every Library seems to have at least one staff member who, though pleasantness itself in the staff room, only has to appear at the public counter for a row to commence. Disputes with colleagues, superiors and resource providers are ever present and on the increase in these days of declining resource bases. Equally potent, however, as a source of conflict and certainly little aired are inconsistencies in our service policies in which our objectives and actions take two different courses depending upon whether we look, in the abstract, at overall policies of a national/international information system or whether we think of our own Library. It is two such apparent conflicts which are outlined here. One concerns the Public Library reference department and its aspirations and the other the magpie-like instinct inherent in many librarians to knock down and drag back to their bibliothecal caves, goodies that they really should not covet in the first place. The British context of these remarks might not perhaps be fully understood elsewhere but the problems are universal even if the fine detail is not fully comprehensible in a non-British context.

The British Public Library movement began its life with the tag 'The Poor Man's University' attached to it. There is no doubt, from the testimony of many major public figures of the past 100-150 years, that such it was to many people. The tag has, though, tended to stay attached long after it has ceased to be necessary—in the minds of Public Library Reference Librarians even if not in the minds of their users.

Unlike the situation in the United States, where by 1900 there were nearly a quarter of a million people enjoying a University education—1 in every 300 of the total population—the situation in the U.K. was that only 1 person in 5000 was enjoying the privileges of University life. The role of the Public Reference Library as a surrogate academic library was, therefore, a significant one in Britain. Some of the major Public Reference Libraries such as Manchester, the Picton Library at Liverpool and the Mitchell Library at Glasgow were, after the National Libraries, the best in the country. The fact was that they had very little competition from the University Libraries of the time other than Oxford and Cambridge. In terms of user service they were superior to any Libraries. It is an heritage which has left the acquisition policies of the Public Library Reference Departments in a strangely mixed up state. No longer needed as 'academic' libraries because of the rapid spread of tertiary education in the past 30 years, they still behave in such a way as to try to retain the old 'Poor Man's University' tag. The conflict, in these circumstances, is between the aspirations of the Library staff and their user's real needs.

## PERIODICAL RESEARCH

A few years ago a piece of research into the nature of periodical literature collections and their usage in Public Libraries in England revealed a very interesting—even startling—situation.[1] The bulk of the use of the periodical material supplied was confined to the relatively small proportion of the collection which dealt with hobby, current affairs, recreation and leisure interests. The bulk of the provision, however, was much more heavy weight and academic in tone and seriously underused if compared with the use made of the rest of the supplied material. Showing the librarians concerned the evidence (and none of those librarians had ever attempted to survey usage) made no difference to their attitudes. They had the feeling that it was fitting and proper to supply academic material even if it was underused or not used at all and then to bind it and store it for posterity. The attitude of the Librarians to the research evidence was, in effect, 'Please do not confuse us with facts. We have made our minds up.' The conflict of objectives is a serious one. On the one hand the Librarian must supply the service the Library user wants but, on the other hand, needs also to support an ideal, long outmoded, that the Public Library Reference Department be the major research collection in the area. In other words, the acquisition policy serves the need the Librarian feels the users *ought* to have if the self-image formed is to be seen to be an important one. After all it is so much more prestigious to display *The Structural Engineer* on the shelves than *Do-it-Yourself Magazine*.

## IMAGE BOLSTER

This desire on the part of the Public Reference Librarian to bolster up the image creates a curious little piece of further dissonance in the creation of sensible and sensitive provision policies in a particular City or Region where the last 20-30 years has seen the establishment of major academic libraries in many parts of the country previously without Higher Education Institutions. Most towns or cities of 150,000 population and upwards have a University, a Polytechnic or a College or Higher Education if not one of each. One way or another all of the funding for all of the various academic libraries generated recently, as well as the Public Library, comes from the same place—the taxpayer via the National

Treasury. Despite a substantial amount of discussion and research about the need to ensure that, where a number of libraries drawing public funds and within easy geographical reach of each other, cooperate together and attempt to provide a service based upon joint policies little has actually happened.[2,3,4] Indeed, recently SCONUL (the Standing Conference of National and University Librarians) announced that, in response to Government cuts in their levels of financial support, they had decided to make substantial reduction in their provision of services to other libraries and to non-university member use of their libraries. This decision was less than totally devastating to the morale of Public Libraries and others who might have designs upon the use of University Library stocks. British University Librarians have not, speaking generally, exactly put themselves at risk of bursting the smallest blood vessels in the support of any but their own internal community (and it is only within the last generation that they have been happy to serve *them* with any great enthusiasm!).

Each Library, then, in a particular City/Region will draw funding from essentially the same source and then pursue separate acquisition policies in three or four different libraries only a few blocks apart. More importantly still perhaps, each will take the decision that, in order to afford to purchase a particular item they must reject another, and so it could happen that four libraries virtually replicate each other's stocks when creative cooperation could have greatly extended the range of material available in the region. The conflict between the Librarian's stated desires to provide free access to information and an urge to be independent and self-sufficient is a profound one. It is this same kind of conflict which manifests itself in the second of the two areas noted earlier.

Free access to information as a desired goal of Library provision can, in certain circumstances, be deeply at variance with the desire to acquire and preserve so-called 'special collections'. The following example illustrates the potential for conflict of aims. Many British Public Libraries were established in the last two decades of the Victorian era—1880-1900. It was a time of great affluence (or rather a time when a minority acquired great affluence and the National Exchequer had not yet worked out how to extinguish it with punitive taxation). Many newly established Public Libraries received as donations valuable collections of local or even national significance. Public benefaction was, in those days, a sure road to honour and preferment. Aspirants to Knighthood or a Baronetcy fell over themselves to present, with great ceremony, collections of books, curios or museum pieces to their local Public Library on the occasion of the official opening performed (as they almost always were) by one of the superfluity of Princes or Princesses produced by Victoria in her prime.

## *PROUD POSSESSOR*

At that time one British Public Library in a very grimy and rather godless town found itself the proud possessor of one of the finest collections of early printed Bibles in the country. They are still there. Every beautifully printed vellum page proclaims pride of ownership with an indelible ink rubber stamp 'The property of . . . . . . . Public Library. Not to be taken away'! And they never have been. They were found floating in six feet of water once when a water pipe burst in the cellar in which they were stored during the Second World War and it did not do a lot for them but they are still there. Another Public Library of the same vintage has what is probably a unique collection of manuscripts providing the keys to a large number of early shorthand systems. Yet another has a series of manuscript notebooks belonging to an early Christian missionary amongst the North American Indians in which he set down the grammar of the various languages he encountered. Throughout the North and Midlands of England several libraries have 'Priestley Collections'. The somewhat footloose Joseph Priestly, like others of the 18th century learned dissenters, left substantial collections of papers in various places which, having found their ways into different libraries, represent a real chore to the scholar attempting to use them. Many of the towns where they have found a home are hardly meccas for the itinerant scholar. The local pride of ownership of such collections is often profound. The conflict, however, lies in the fact that the desire to keep such treasures locally usually militates against an adequate knowledge of their availability. They are often poorly housed and looked after and their accessibility is, for all of these reasons, questionable. An enlightened library autocrat determined to improve facilities for scholars and render their tools optimally accessible would never contemplate allowing the present scatter and chaos of primary materials to continue. No amount of carefully produced 'guides to resources' can adequately replace convenient accessibility of the original sources and anyway it does not solve the basic problem of scatter, travel difficulties and inexpert husbandry inevitable when the library staff concerned are not constantly in the business of serving the scholar. What can be done, in practice, to solve this conflict? Probably nothing unless it could be made an item of resource providing policy by Government that additional resources are available to libraries who give up odds and ends of special collections to the National Libraries. That might do it?

## REFERENCES

1. Oldman, C. *and* Davinson, D.E. *The usage of periodicals in Public Libraries,* Leeds, Leeds Polytechnic 1975.
2. Masterson, W.A.J. *and* Wilson, T.D. *Local Library Cooperation Project: Final Report,* Sheffield, The University of Sheffield 1974.
3. Garthwaite, G.D.V. *and* James, A.M. *Regional access to libraries and information studies,* Leeds, Leeds Polytechnic 1976. (BLR & D Report 5339)
4. Urquhart D. *and* Irving, A. *Access to Libraries: a study of methodology,* Loughborough, The University of Loughborough 1978.

# Access to Consumer Health Information

Robert Berk

A number of articles, reports, and books have been written on the subject of providing health related information to consumers.[1-5] Consumers who are members of the general public and who, until recently, have had little means of access to such information in a timely and authoritative fashion.

More attention in recent years has focused on the provision of health related information to patients. This has been mandated by a number of conditions including the need for informed consent, the patient's rights as indicated in documents such as the "Bill of Patients' Rights" of the American Hospital Association, and by interest from health insurers in the potential for reduced health care costs through improved patient compliance brought about by a better informed patient population.

The same general arguments could be brought to bear upon the right of the general public to have access to similar types of information prior to the time that they become ill and fall under the care of organized medicine. What is needed is an information system that will respond to information needs associated with "wellness," which are recognized as distinct and separate from the patient education systems provided as part of the medical system's response to those who are sick.

This paper will briefly trace some of the trends that have developed regarding the role of different types of libraries in the provision of consumer related health information. In addition, it will discuss what may or may not be a valid cause for potential concern by librarians—malpractice and the possibility of legal action. Finally, it will discuss appropriate ways for dealing with the provision of consumer related information and the part that all reference librarians can play in this important area.

---

The author is a Professor at the School of Library & Information Science, University of Missouri, Columbia, 65211.

© 1985 by The Haworth Press, Inc. All rights reserved.

## PUBLIC LIBRARIES AND CONSUMER HEALTH INFORMATION

Public libraries have long addressed themselves to inquiries relating to the health of their local users. Unfortunately, until recently, the problem has been the inadequacy of public library collections in health subjects and the lack of specialized knowledge on the part of public library staffs needed to cope with the myriad requests for health related information. An interesting study by Eaton and others[6] showed that during a four week period, the Houston Public Library Science and Technology Division responded to 361 health related reference questions. This would appear to be a sizeable number except that when compared to the total number of information requests during the same period, health related inquiries amounted to only 5 percent of the total. Even so, the fact that 361 were related to health information indicates that there is a role for public librarians to play in the provision of health related information. In response to such a need in other parts of the country, a number of cooperative ventures have been formed linking public libraries with other types of health sciences libraries.[7-9] Some of the thrust of such cooperative ventures has been to aid public librarians in acquiring quality materials in the health field while at the same time making the public librarians more aware of sources for meeting consumer health information needs. When necessary this includes the referral of users to other more appropriate libraries. Some of these cooperative ventures have received federal funding indicating the government's continuing concern for an informed public with access to appropriate information sources.

## HOSPITAL LIBRARIES AND CONSUMER HEALTH INFORMATION

Hospitals have been very much involved with consumer health information issues over the past few years. This has largely been confined to areas pertaining to patient education necessitated by the requirements of informed consent and to insure patient compliance with physician instructions. The threat of medical malpractice has, of course, been instrumental in identifying the relationship between required information and the ability of individuals to assume responsibility for their health related actions. In some instances, hospital libraries have taken an active leadership role in providing patient education. Now consumer health information activities are beginning to immerge more and more in the hospital library setting. As an example, the Overlook Hospital in Summit, New Jersey recently designed and constructed a new hospital library that had a consumer health information center as part of its design and the provision of consumer health information as a major goal for library operations.[10] Similar services have been part of the library operations at Central DuPage Hospital in Winfield, Illinois since 1976.[11] In lieu of providing direct and free access to health related materials, other hospitals have placed the library on an "access by permission" basis so that information becomes available to consumers if they are referred by a health professional—usually a physician. Other hospital libraries have cooperated with public libraries to provide expertise regarding health problems and health related information sources. Still other hospital libraries have joined in cooperative ventures to provide backup resources for inquiries that cannot be handled successfully at local public libraries. Unfortunately the number of hospital libraries concerned with consumer health information needs is probably quite small. As noted in an editorial in *Library Journal*,[12] the picture with regard to public access to adequate and comprehensive health information resources in health sciences libraries is a dismal one. The majority of hospital health sciences libraries do not want the public accessing the materials in their collections. It is bad enough that they are being forced to make information available for patient education purposes. They have no intention of opening their doors to the public. Such an attitude can be condoned for at least a couple of reasons. First, most hospital libraries are quite small and cramped for space. They hardly have enough room for use by professional staffs and consequently, the idea of opening the library to outsiders is not practical. The second reason for their reluctance to participate in educating the consumer has to do with the lack of staff time to insure that appropriate materials are in the hands of these users and that their inquiries are dealt with in a competent and professional manner. Hospital libraries are simply understaffed for the many functions they are required to perform for their primary user groups.

How legitimate the above caveats may be will depend largely upon the individual hospital library. For example, at the Central

DuPage Hospital in Illinois, it was found that consumers from outside the hospital made very little difference in the ability of the library to perform its other functions.[13] Still, if a library is full to overflowing, and understaffed to the point of exhaustion, it makes little sense to add in another user group and then be forced to respond to their health related information needs in less than a thorough and effective manner. In spite of these reservations, one must ask how many hospital libraries do not participate in consumer health information activities for other reasons more closely related to a philosophical difference in who has the right to access health related information? Anyone who is convinced that such information is the sole province of the health professionals is out of touch with the concept of freedom of information and the entire consumerism movement.

## ACADEMIC HEALTH SCIENCES LIBRARIES AND CONSUMER HEALTH INFORMATION

Despite what consumers might have perceived as an attitude of indifference or one of elitism, academic health sciences libraries have been widely concerned with meeting the health related information needs of the general public. This is clearly evident in the results of two surveys conducted by Jeuell and others, of public information services offered in such settings.[14,15] Findings show that 94 percent of the privately supported medical schools were open to " . . . some or all of the general public . . . ," while 91 percent of the publicly supported medical schools have library facilities that are open to the general public. However, there are restrictions as to which public user groups may access the library and these are more stringent in private than public medical schools. For purposes of this paper, a more important figure is the degree to which library services are available to all members of the general public. For public medical school libraries such access was provided by 32 percent who made extensive reference service available to the general public. For privately operated medical schools the figure was only 23 percent. Unfortunately, the survey did not examine the lending policies of these academic health sciences libraries. The conclusions from this survey indicate that many academic health sciences libraries do feel a responsibility for providing consumer health related information. However, it appears that many of these libraries would rather "... deal with public or university libraries as intermediaries, rather than directly with individuals, as far as reference services are concerned."[16] As positive as these figures might be linking the medical school libraries or academic health sciences center libraries to the consumer information network, one of the final comments from the survey report must be emphasized: "Many libraries in both public and private medical schools do not give out information to patients about their illnesses without a physician's note.[17]

This comment is of direct concern to those interested in patient education, but it is also applicable to consumer health information. How does the librarian know which user is a patient and which user represents a member of the public with a health related information need? In the hospital setting it may virtually be impossible to distinguish between the two. For any library with a walk-in user group, there should be no reason to distinguish between patients and consumers unless the library user volunteers such information.

As with hospital libraries, academic health sciences libraries are also faced with staff shortages. The same argument may be applied for not providing more in the way of consumer health information; without adequate staff support such a service would actually be a disservice. A library must be adequately staffed if the general public is to receive thorough and effective information services. However, as with hospital librarians, a philosophical prohibition on access to health related information by the general public cannot be condoned.

## UNIVERSITY LIBRARIES AND CONSUMER HEALTH INFORMATION

Of all the library groups discussed in this paper, the general reference departments of university libraries are now and have been the least interested in providing consumer health related information. This may be largely due to the lack of access by the general public and the fact that the student population is assumed to be a generally "healthy" group. However, there are faculty and staff groups on campus as well, and the university populace in its entirety closely represents the general public with the exception of the very young and the very old. From personal observation it would appear that most academic general reference services get by with a very minimum of health related information sources. The argument may be that, after all, the university has already purchased these sources for the health sciences library. Even so, if the health sciences library is not easily accessible then such information is beyond the reach of the vast majority on campus. It seems that if academic health sciences libraries have, to a limited extent, recognized the need to assist public libraries in providing adequate services and collections related to consumer health information, then they might also recognize a similar need in the general reference departments of their own institutions. How can an undergraduate who is interested in the nutritional aspects of a particular diet easily pursue this topic? How can a staff member evaluate various exercise plans prior to adopting one? How can a faculty member determine the possible adverse effects of combining certain foods with prescribed medications? All of these are consumer related health information needs that should be readily answered within the resources of the general reference library. The same type of information may be available in public, hospital, and academic health sciences libraries, but the difficulty entailed in accessing such collections may preclude the academic consumer from ever acquiring the needed information.

For the academic library the question becomes one of identifying the needs of library users. Secondly it means a decision must be made as to whether or not health related information requests are a legitimate concern of the academic library. With regard to this second question, many of the other areas in which libraries provide information might also appear to be peripheral to their educational mission. One might make the case that academic general reference libraries have no more reason to provide employment information than health related information. The case should be made that both employment and health are areas of concern to library users and both effect the educational process.

## HEALTH INFORMATION CENTERS AND CONSUMER HEALTH INFORMATION

A different type of facility providing consumer health related information is one that is not library affiliated, although it may have a library of its own. This is the free standing health information center designed solely for the purpose of providing the consumer with health related information. It appears that this type of service has arisen largely because of the gap in the provision of health information caused by the failure of libraries to accept their responsibility in this area. Although there are many centers of this type, the only one to be mentioned in this paper is the Consumer Health Information Center (CHIC) in Salt Lake City. This center is a fair representation of the growth that has taken place in this type of activity. CHIC provides a free resource library of both books and pamphlets relating to health. They also serve as a clearinghouse for community health agencies and organizations and related services. CHIC provides a calendar of community health-related events, free periodic health screenings, and an educational lecture series. The center is staffed by a health educator and a coordinator, but most of the public contact work is done with trained volunteers. As effective as these volunteers may be, they are still without the training in reference work and materials evaluation that is the stock in trade of every librarian. Also, such a collection as that of CHIC must necessarily be limited and there must be recourse to the variety of information resources one would find in an academic health sciences library. Although it is clear that information agencies such as CHIC can provide a valuable service to the public, it is also clear that existing libraries could well be utilized to provide comparable services. Public libraries are already used for a variety of information needs, why should the consumer have to go elsewhere for needs related to health? Some of the reluctance of librarians to undertake library functions with regard to health information may be related to a fear of being forced to deal with an unfamiliar subject area and the possibility of being charged with some illegal practice.

## LEGAL IMPLICATIONS OF PROVIDING CONSUMER HEALTH INFORMATION

A number of articles have addressed the topic of malpractice by librarians who provide medical information to the public.[18-21] Although there are apparently no known cases where a librarian has been the target of legal action, nevertheless, many librarians have expressed a fear that by providing health related information they might be subject to legal action, or at least charged with practicing medicine without a license. The basic distinction which will govern acceptable practice by librarians and deter any legal recourse has to do with the difference between providing health related information and providing health related advice. If a librarian is asked to define a medical term and responds by reading the user a definition from an authoritative medical dictionary, then the librarian has provided only information. If the user is not satisfied and wants to have the definition interpreted, then the librarian could be providing advice. The picture is clearer when the librarian is faced with the question, "What do you think I ought to do?" Obviously the librarian answering this question could be providing medical advice—the responsibility of a physician.

Librarianship is a helping profession and librarians want to go out of their way to aid a user in search of information. Consequently, it is extremely difficult for a librarian to draw a line between providing medical advice and seeking to amplify and clarify information so that it is of more direct use to the library user. One must learn to gauge one's response in this particular type of information work just as one is required to do in other areas relating to reference work. For example, legal advice is not the domain of the librarian, legal librarian or not. The ability to gauge the needs of users and the desire to provide additional amplifying information from authoritative sources should guide the librarian in the provision of health related information without cause for fear of legal action. The problem and the solution is summed up nicely in the "Factsheet" produced by the Community Health Information Network (CHIN): "Our own working policy is that librarians must communicate that they are librarians and not health care providers and that they are giving (1) information from published materials and/or (2) referral to recognized service agencies and organizations."[22] A librarian need not fear any legal repercussions if he or she draws an imaginary line between providing information and providing advice and then stays on the information side of that line.

## A MODEL FOR LIBRARY PROVISION OF CONSUMER HEALTH INFORMATION

As a prelude to providing health related information, librarians must have the correct mind set. The general public has a right to health related information on any level of difficulty. Whether or not an individual can "understand" the information he or she receives is ultimately their own concern. If they seek clarification or additional information, then the librarian can be of further assistance, but the type of information sought and its uses are clearly the responsibility of the consumer. Once the library has accepted this "right to information" philosophy, then each library can respond to meet this information need according to its mission statement and its resources.

Public libraries must take the lead role in providing the initial contact point for most consumer health information requests. In many communities, the public library serves as the sole information resource while in virtually all communities, its information role is well recognized and need only be extended to the provision of accurate, timely, and appropriate health related information.

This is not to say that other types of libraries can or should abdicate this responsibility. Public libraries need help in training their staffs to handle requests in this area and help in evaluating materials for their authority and appropriateness. Hospital and academic health sciences libraries can provide their collections and staff resources as a backup for requests that cannot be dealt with adequately at the public library level. This means that some method of referral must be worked out. Even without a public library referral, hospital and academic health sciences libraries should willingly provide for consumer related health information as their resources allow. Their primary obligation will be to provide for patient information services. But as more staff become available, the general public should also receive information services. At the very least, these services should provide access to library materials with a willing and cooperative spirit on the part of the librarian. Librarians need to get as far away as possible from the idea that the public is " . . . insufficiently educated or knowledgeable to properly handle full disclosure of information about their illnesses, or the potential emotional strain caused by it."[23] They also need to get away from the idea that the consequence of access of health information would lead the public to " . . . self-diagnose itself into a frenzy of disease states."[24]

With a well established cooperative agreement regarding the provision of health related information, all types of libraries should feel free to refer users between different types of libraries according to specific information needs.

Somewhere in this model there is a need for expert advice from the health community. Materials need content evaluation and policy matters will need review. There must also be some means of medical and health related advice for those users with needs that do not meet the ability or resources of the library to provide. It has always been easy for librarians to refer users back to their physicians, but many individuals do not have physicians and a good many others do not want to discuss the matter any further with their own physicians. There must be some way within this information network model for a library user to discuss his or her information need with a health professional or an appropriate agency. This referral function need not be used frequently nor is it a replacement for seeking the services of a physician when required. It does, however, keep librarians from resorting solely to their own subject expertise in building collections and from limiting the library user to only those resources available in libraries.

As a specific measure, academic general reference libraries need to become part of the health information network by building adequate collections of consumer health materials and by making these materials available to students, faculty, staff, and in some cases, the local community. These libraries also need to be able to plug into the broader network of sources in public and health sciences libraries. There is no reason why individuals on campus should not be able to satisfy many of their health information needs in the university library.

## *CONCLUSION*

With public libraries providing for most of the initial contact for seekers of health related information and with their ability to respond to a majority of these needs effectively, there will be limited need to refer users to academic or hospital based health sciences libraries. But when referral is needed, users can be assured that they will be welcome and that their needs will be addressed. If a consumer health information center such as CHIC is available in the community, this resource can also be part of the referral process beginning with the public library. If and when more staff become available in health sciences libraries, the provision of health related information for the general public should be considered as an area in which to establish more comprehensive service. By connecting the entire library network to a health professional or health agency for content evaluation and individual referral, users should never fail to find someone to aid them in their quest for health information. Even academic libraries through their general reference departments have a more aggressive role to play in providing for the health related needs of the academic community.

The model presented does represent what has already taken place in some locations and between selection institutions. Once librarians of all types have recognized the legitimacy of providing health related information, and have accepted this as part of their reference philosophy, a variety of network configurations and cooperative ventures may develop. The long range goal is a better informed and consequently a healthier public.

## REFERENCES

1. Gardner, T.A. and Siebert, J.A. "Consumer health information needs and access through existing indexes." *RQ* 1981, 20 (Summer): 366-72.
2. Knowles, J.H. "Responsibility for health." *Science* 1977, 198 (Dec. 16): 1103.
3. Heifetz, R.M. "Information and the public's health: are they related?" *California Librarian* 1978, 39 (Jan.): 8-18.
4. Rees, A.M. (ed.) *Developing Consumer Health Information Services.* New York: R.R. Bowker, 1982.
5. Larson, M.T. (ed.) "Patient/health education-the librarian's role." *Proceedings of an Invitational Institute,* Feb. 5-9, 1979. Detroit: Wayne State Univ., 1979.
6. Eaton, Dottie and others. "Consumer health information: libraries as partners." *Bulletin of the Medical Library Association* 1980, 68 (April): 220-29.
7. Goodchild, Eleanor. CHIPS—consumer health information program and services." *California Librarian* 1978, 39 (Jan.): 19-24.
8. Goodchild, E.Y. and others. "The CHIPS project: a health information network to serve the consumer." *Bulletin of the Medical Library Association* 1978, 66 (Oct.): 432-6.
9. Gartenfeld, Ellen and Witte, L.M. "Hospital, public libraries join forces to make reliable health information more accessible to public." *Promoting Health* 1982, 3 (July-Aug.): 8-10.
10. Moeller, K.A. and Deeney, K.E. "Documenting the need for consumer health information: results of a community survey." *Bulletin of the Medical Library Association* 1982, 70 (April): 236-39.
11. Rowe, D.B. "Open medical library provides valuable community service." *Hospitals* 1980, 54 (Dec.16): 115-17.
12. Berry, John. "Medical information taboos." *Library Journal* 1978, 103 (Jan. 1): 7.
13. Rowe. "Open medical library." pp. 115-17.
14. Jeuell, C.A. and others. "Public information services at state-supported medical school libraries: a brief survey." *Bulletin of the Medical Library Association* 1967, 64 (Oct.): 415-17.
15. Jeuell, C.A. and others. "Brief survey of public information services at privately-supported medical school libraries: comparison with publicly-supported medical school libraries." *Bulletin of the Medical Library Association* 1977, 65 (April): 292-95.
16. Ibid., p. 293.
17. Ibid., p. 294.
18. Wood, M.S. and Renford, B.L. "Ethical aspects of medical reference." *The Reference Librarian* 1982 (Summer): 75-87.
19. Charney, Norman. "Ethical and legal questions in providing health information." *California Librarian* 1978, 39 (Jan.): 25-33.

20. Foster, Lynn and Self, P.C. "Legal and medical reference: a dilemma for public libraries." *Illinois Libraries* 1978, 60 (March): 243-48.

21. Slovenko, Ralph. "Legal dimensions of library service." In "Patient/health education—the librarian's role." *Proceedings of an Invitational Institute,* Feb. 5-9, 1979. Detroit: Wayne State Univ., 1979. pp. 117-26.

22. Community Health Information Network (CHIN). *Factsheet.* Mount Auburn Hospital: Cambridge, Mass. /no date/.

23. Berry. "Medical Information.", p. 7.

24. Vent, M.S. and Weaver-Meyers, P.L. "Health information sources and services for the small public library." *Oklahoma Librarian* 1978, 28 (Jan.): 17-21.

# Academic Library Service to Physically Disabled Students and Faculty

Gerald Jahoda
Paula Faustini

Questionnaires were sent to heads of public services of 167 academic libraries in the Southeast. Usable returns were obtained from 109 respondents. The questionnaire included ten tasks that might be appropriate for a part-time coordinator of library service to disabled students and faculty. Respondents were asked to indicate whether or not these tasks should be done and are done by either the library or another unit within the institution. The librarians' attitude toward disabled persons appears to be the critical factor in providing service to this group.

Institutions of higher learning in the United States now enroll many physically disabled students. At The Florida State University, for example, there were over 900 physically disabled students enrolled in various programs during the 1981/82 academic year. Once an academic institution admits a student, able-bodied or physically disabled, to one of its academic programs, it is under some obligation to provide the necessary resources and services for completion of the program. One such service is library service.

Library service to disabled persons (students, faculty, and others who use the academic library) calls for modification of existing services, knowledge of special resources, and the ability to work with those who have physical disabilities. Material has to be delivered from the stacks for some who are mobility impaired. Material may have to be provided in special format for the visually disabled. Disabled persons need to feel free to use the library and to ask the li-

---

Both authors are on the faculty of the School of Library and Information Studies, Florida State University, Tallahassee, Florida 32306.

brary staff for help. This in turn requires a library staff that can work comfortably with those who are disabled. Some member of the professional staff, perhaps a public services librarian, needs to be assigned the responsibility for seeing that library service is provided to this part of the library's constituency. Tasks that might be assigned to such a librarian are listed in Table 1. In most academic libraries these tasks can be performed on a part-time basis.

To determine whether academic librarians agree with the need for performing the listed tasks and whether they or some other unit in their institution perform these tasks, a short questionnaire was sent in May 1982 to 167 academic libraries in the Southeast. Academic institutions with an enrollment of at least 2,000 students or a professional staff of at least five librarians were selected from the 1981 *American Libraries Directory*. The questionnaires which include the ten listed tasks of coordinators of library service to disabled students

Table 1 LIST OF TASKS FOR COORDINATOR
OF ACADEMIC LIBRARY SERVICE TO PHYSICALLY DISABLED STUDENTS AND FACULTY

| | SHOULD BE DONE IN AN ACADEMIC LIBRARY | IS BEING DONE BY MY LIBRARY | IS BEING DONE BY MY INSTITUTION |
|---|---|---|---|
| 1. Determine information needs of physically disabled students and faculty | 68% | 35% | 33% |
| 2. Instruct physically disabled students in the use of the library | 75% | 61% | 10% |
| 3. Orient public service library staff on special needs of and resources for physically disabled students and faculty | 79% | 38% | 5% |
| 4. Coordinate work of library staff as it relates to physically disabled students and faculty | 67% | 35% | 2% |
| 5. Coordinate work of volunteers as it relates to library service to disabled students and faculty | 50% | 2% | 9% |
| 6. Provide liaison with organizations serving physically disabled persons | 48% | 16% | 33% |
| 7. Assist in obtaining outside funding for library service to physically disabled persons | 51% | 6% | 20% |
| 8. Keep up with developments in information resources and services to physically disabled persons | 72% | 28% | 24% |
| 9. Conduct a facilities evaluation to identify architectural barriers | 57% | 40% | 62% |
| 10. Assist in the evaluation of library service to physically disabled students and faculty | 76% | 24% | 7% |

and faculty and an open ended question were sent to heads of the library's public services. One hundred nine usable questionnaires, a 65% return rate, were obtained. The results of the survey are summarized in Tables 1 and 2.

TABLE 2  EXAMPLES OF OPEN ENDED COMMENTS

One respondent had previously interviewed some of the physically disabled patrons who " . . . felt they were shunned or avoided by particular librarians and were actually hindered in their use of the library by these people. For example, the public service librarian on duty would not pull books from shelves which were too high or low for the disabled to reach. These librarians seemed to resent having to do anything out of the ordinary to help these people . . . "

" . . . All of the services you list should be done in an academic library—we will welcome results of your study and would hope to be able to implement some of the listed services. More awareness of these users' needs is vital in providing service to them . . . "

" . . . the handicapped are less than 2% of our student body! With the economic situation the way it is, we need funds and positions to serve the other 98%! . . . I feel the emphasis on 'handicapped' will be short lived as we just can't afford it."

" . . . we would appreciate any tips you might be able to offer on how to improve our service to the disabled. We do not have very many disabled, but they need and deserve the best service we can give."

"How are the information needs of the physically disabled different from those of the physically able? Physical disability limits the person's access to the material, perhaps, but does it affect the kind of information he needs?"

" . . . In the past few years we have had several blind students attend our college, as well as several students with varying degrees of other physical handicaps. Though the college as a whole is not, at this time, really equipped for the handicapped, a ramp was built for entrance to the library. We have no elevator, but all the staff members make every effort possible to assist students in getting books from upper and lower floors. The Student Assistance office has

TABLE 2 (continued)

helped students obtain aid from vocational rehabilitation, Lions Club, etc., for special equipment, e.g., record and tape players. As reference librarian, I usually deal with the informational needs of the handicapped. For particular students I have frequently corresponded with Recording for the Blind. I have gathered resources and personally delivered, or allowed someone other than the handicapped student himself, to pick up the compiled sources—after we have done the checkout procedure—without the student ever coming to the library, when that seemed necessary. . . . ''

## DISCUSSION OF RESULTS

Two thirds or more of the respondents indicated that six of the tasks should be done and almost half of the respondents indicated that all ten of the tasks should be done. On the four tasks with less than two thirds agreement, facilities evaluation had a higher percentage of performance of task than agreement that it should be done. This may be because it is a task imposed by law. The relatively low level of agreement that volunteers should be used along with the low use of volunteers can probably be explained by institutional constraints such as inability to insure such workers.

The relatively low agreement that outside funds should be sought for service to this group and that liaison should be maintained with organizations serving disabled students is more difficult to explain. Service to this group does entail additional expenditures and seeking support from outside sources appears to be a way of obtaining such needed funds. Liaison with organizations serving disabled students is necessary for learning about needed resources and also for learning about the special needs of disabled students.

For two of the six tasks on which two thirds or more of the respondents agree should be done, determining information needs and instructing students in library use, there appears to be good agreement between what should be done and what is being done. On the other four tasks—orienting students to the library, coordinating library staff, keeping up with developments in the field, and evaluation of library service—there is a considerable difference between what should be and what is being done.

Whether a given task is performed and what priority is given to service to this part of the library's constituency depend to some, we are tempted to say to a large, degree on the attitude of the library administration and staff. A sampling of attitudes expressed by the respondents are given in Table 2.

How well are academic libraries doing in terms of library service to disabled persons? This is not a definitive study on the subject; the size of the sample and the subjective nature of the questions prevent us from making such a claim. Nevertheless, there are some indicators that suggest tentative conclusions. The fact that almost half of the respondents agreed that all ten listed tasks should be performed is an indication of concern about academic library service to this group. However, there seems to be a discrepency between what should be done and what is being done, particularly in the evaluation of services, the coordination of the work of the staff, and the orientation of students to the library.

The study suggests that there are tasks usually associated with the library that are performed by other units of the institution, either instead of or in addition to the library. Many academic institutions now have offices of disabled student services that can help in identifying disabled students, review physical facilities for barrier free architecture and serve as sources of information.

One additional consideration, perhaps the most influential, is expressed in several of the open ended comments. Lack of funds, understaffing and even architectural barriers are potential hinderances to the provision of good library service to disabled students but they do not necessarily preclude good service. A willingness to help coupled with flexibility and some creative problem solving can go a long way in overcoming perceived obstacles. A part-time coordinator of library service to disabled students and faculty could be instrumental in heightening staff awareness of attitudinal, architectural, and format barriers that prevent or limit library use by this growing constituency.

# Abstract Thinking: Considerations for the Provision of Statistical Data in Evaluation

Juri Stratford
Jean S. Stratford

Our system of government requires the production and dissemination of a wide variety of statistical data at all levels. For example, the *U.S. Constitution* requires a census of population to determine the apportionment of representation in the House.[1] The distribution of this information provides citizens with the means to judge whether this apportionment is fair. Once published, the data from the census have a broad range of additional applications in the public and private sector. The *Constitution* also requires that the President deliver a State of the Union message before Congress to insure the sharing of information between the executive and legislative branches of government.[2] As this country and its economy have grown in size and complexity, the State of the Union address has been grounded more and more in statistical data. The address itself is complemented by statistical reports required by law including the *Budget of the U.S. Government* and the *Economic Report of the President*.[3]

The resultant body of literature provides a primary information source for librarians that must be properly treated and understood. The present paper provides a foundation for such an understanding by examining the problems of interpretation that must be considered in reference work with statistical data. First, basic statistical concepts will be defined. Second, examples will be drawn to illustrate the limitations of statistical data. These examples include the prob-

---

Ms. Stratford is a graduate of the School of Library and Information Science at SUNY, Albany. Juri is with the Documents Division, Marriott Library, University of Utah, Salt Lake City, 84112.

lems of comparability and bias in compilation. Finally, these principles will be applied to the reference interview.

## *DEFINITIONS*

A statistic can be defined as the numerical representation of a characteristic (or variable) of a sample or population. For example, the National Center for Health Statistics compiles health statistics. These statistics are numerical representations of variables, in this case, the instances of disease in the United States. Some statistics are based on samples that are used to draw inferences for some larger population which the sample was chosen to represent. A population is defined as "any class of phenomena arbitrarily defined on the basis of it unique and observable characteristics."[4] For example, in order to obtain health statistics for New York State, a representative sample of New York hospitals might be chosen and queried with regard to incidence of various diseases. In order for the sample data gathered to accurately represent the population as a whole, the sample must be "a collection of phenomena so selected as to represent some well defined population."[5] It should be composed of a similar distribution of factors, such as distribution by sex, age, income, in order to accurately reflect the larger population. The sample should also be random, chosen in such a way "that each phenomenon in the population [in this instance NYS residents] had an equal chance of being selected."[6]

While the preceding description touches only upon major concepts, it can suffice as an introduction to descriptive statistics. However, there are numerous sources for the librarian, or patron, in need of further explanation, whether to provide an overall understanding of the subject or to illuminate the meaning of specific statistics. Frederick Williams' *Reasoning with Statistics* is a good starting point.[7] This book is intended to provide an understanding of statistical methods rather than to prepare readers to use such methods. Should further or more specialized information be required, several sources may be appropriate. *Library Literature* has several headings for the location of periodical articles on both sources and interpretation of statistics. Unfortunately, these headings are also used for articles on the collection of library statistics. Despite this confusion, the following headings should not be overlooked as a source for further information:

Indexes and abstracts—Statistics
Information services—Special subjects—Census data
Information services—Special subjects—Statistics
Research materials—Special subjects—Census data
Research materials—Special subjects—Statistics
Statistics
Statistics—Bibliography
Statistics—Indexes and abstracts

The *Public Affairs Information Service Bulletin* is another useful indexing source for material on social and economic statistics and their interpretation. Appropriate headings include

Census
Census—Bibliography
Census—Errors
Social statistics
Social statistics—Information processing systems
Statistics—Information sources
Statistics—Research—Bibliography
Statistics—Yearbook

In addition, "Statistics" is also used as a sub-heading under appropriate headings, e.g. "Libraries, depository—Statistics". There are also access points for specific types of statistics such as Gross National Product or market statistics. Indexes like *Social Sciences Index* and *Applied Science and Technology Index* should be consulted for articles on specific statistical methods such as ranking or multivariate analysis.

Statistics provide a basis for comparison. Being the numerical representation of the measurement of a variable, they provide a mathematical means for comparing more than one measurement of the same variable. Using the example of population statistics, individual cities may be compared to one another in terms of population. A hypothetical example will serve to illustrate this point. City X has a population of 500,000 while City Y has a population of 1,000,000. The statistics can be compared to one another and manipulated by means of the mathematical operation of division. From this, the conclusion can be drawn that City Y has twice the population of City X. This type of comparison gives statistics meaning by placing them in context. However, not all comparisons are valid.

Comparisons should be made only when the variable measured in each instance and the context of the statistics are comparable. To judge the comparability of statistics, both the context and the variable measured must be taken into account.

## COMPARABILITY AND BIAS

One important consideration in using statistical data is comparability. Two examples illustrate this point. First, various techniques for determining population figures demonstrate fundamental problems in the comparison of various types of figures. Second, the example of the Consumer Price Index illuminates the limitations of a statistical measurement. In addition, problems of political and social bias in government-produced demographic statistics are considered.

The decennial census of population of the U.S. is an actual enumeration. It has been argued that this is not the most accurate means for determining population figures. Based upon legal precedent, the Census Bureau argues that "the underlying constitutional purpose for the census was to determine as accurately as possible the number of inhabitants of each State." They believe that "it is the *accuracy* of this determination and not the *method* which is of primary constitutional significance."[8] However, if adjustments are made to insure the accuracy of population figures, how are these adjustments to be made? In a prepared statement submitted before the Senate Subcommittee on Energy, Nuclear Proliferation and Federal Services, Vincent P. Barabba, Director of the Census Bureau, indicated that "none of the currently known procedures [for adjustment] have been tested for their capability to measure undercount for all units of government," and therefore were not being used in the decennial census.[9]

In addition to actual enumeration, population figures are determined through estimates and projections. A population estimate is a calculation based upon a combination of existing data. For example, a population estimate might be the result of comparing vital statistics with earlier census figures. Other calculations might consider employment statistics as an indicator of population migration. A third means for calculating population is through population projections. A population projection is similar to a population estimate as it uses current or earlier figures as a base, but a population projection is made when no additional data exist to determine an estimate of population. Population projections most often 'project' into the future based upon current trends, but a population can be made into the past when insufficient data exist for population estimates.[10]

When helping a patron use population statistics, the reference librarian needs to be aware of the comparability of the various types of population figures. If the patron is using figures from a census or similar actual enumeration, comparison is not a problem. However, if the patron wishes to compare these actual figures with population estimates or projections, certain criteria must be considered to insure the comparability of the figures. The source data should be considered when using population estimates or projections. The figures are always comparable to their source data. For example, estimates of population made in cooperation with the Census Bureau and based upon the 1970 Census of Population are comparable with the 1970 Census of Population. However, the estimates based upon the 1970 census are not necessarily comparable to 1980 census figures. In the table below, population figures from the 1970 and 1980 census counts are compared with the population estimates based upon the 1970 census figures in 1979 for the five states having a greater than 30% gain in population between the censuses.

|       | Florida | Wyoming | Arizona | Nevada | Alaska |
|-------|---------|---------|---------|--------|--------|
| 1970* | 6791    | 322     | 1775    | 489    | 303    |
| 1970  | 6851    | 334     | 1795    | 494    | 305    |
| 1971  | 7101    | 339     | 1878    | 514    | 316    |
| 1972  | 7407    | 345     | 1975    | 535    | 326    |
| 1973  | 7757    | 351     | 2075    | 551    | 332    |
| 1974  | 8087    | 362     | 2156    | 573    | 343    |
| 1975  | 8253    | 377     | 2200    | 590    | 379    |
| 1976  | 8348    | 392     | 2244    | 610    | 405    |
| 1977  | 8481    | 407     | 2309    | 634    | 408    |
| 1978  | 8861    | 425     | 2373    | 666    | 411    |
| 1979  | 8860    | 450     | 2450    | 702    | 406    |
| 1980* | 9746    | 470     | 2718    | 800    | 402    |

The population figures are X 1000. Figures for 1970* and 1980* are from the April 1 census. Figures for 1970-1979 are July 1 estimates of population. U.S. Department of Commerce. Bureau of the Census. *Population Estimates and Projections: Annual Estimates of the Population of States: July 1, 1970 to 1979* (February 1980, Series P-25, no.876) and *Characteristics of the Population: 1980 Census of Population* (PC 80-1).

The figures from the 1980 census appear to follow a pattern established in the estimates based upon the 1970 census for Wyoming, Arizona and Alaska. In the case of Florida and Nevada, however, there are significant differences between the population estimates for July 1, 1979 and the census figures for April 1, 1980. While the population estimates were the only figures available prior to the 1980 census, in retrospect they are clearly in error, and the 1979 estimates should not be compared with the 1980 census figures.

A population projection is potentially less accurate than a population estimate because there is less available data for the compilation of a projection. Certain unforeseen factors, such as war, natural disaster or even a change in the economy, can have a tremendous effect on the population. When using population projections, one has to be aware of the data upon which the projection was based. Because a projection draws upon less data than an estimate, the currency of that data becomes more critical. Shyrock and Siegel in *The Methods and Materials of Demography* compare world population projections published by the United Nations in 1966 with an earlier compilation of projections published by the UN in 1957. For the year 1990, there was a 27.5% increase in the population projected for East Asia comparing the 1966 figures with the 1957 figures and a 30.2% decrease in the projection for the Soviet Union. For the year 2000, the differences were a 44% increase in the population projection for East Asia and 32% decrease in the projection for the Soviet Union.[11] It is safe to assume that the further into the future one might wish to draw conclusions from the trends developed in the population projections, the greater the discrepency would be. When using population estimates or projections, one should always seek the most current data available.

## *BASIC LEVEL*

On a more basic level, one also has to be aware of what the statistic itself represents. For example, the Consumer Price Index (CPI) is not a measure of the cost of living, but rather a measure of the *change* in the cost of living.[12] This places limitations upon its use. Approximately every ten years, the Bureau of Labor Statistics (BLS) returns the CPI to a base 100 figure. While historic figures for the CPI are available, like population estimates and projections, these figures are only comparable if they are derived from the same base figure. For example, the CPI for all items for New York in 1960 using 1957-59 = 100 is 103.9 or 3.9% higher than in the base year. Taking 1967 = 100 as the base figure, the CPI for all items for New York for the same year is 87.3 or 12.7% below the 1967 base figure. Both of these calculations took the same set of circumstances into consideration to derive the figure but used different base figures to express them. The same base figure must be used to draw comparisons between CPI measurements.

As the CPI does not measure the cost of living itself but only its rate of change, comparisons of the cost of living between geographic locations cannot be made using the CPI. When comparing CPI figures for St. Louis and Seattle, the CPI figure is higher for St. Louis in 1975 using 1967 = 100 than for Seattle. The figure for 1965 is higher for Seattle than for St. Louis. Is the cost of living higher in St. Louis or Seattle? The Bureau of Labor Statistics explains that "Area indexes do not measure differences in the level of prices among cities: they only measure the average change in prices for each area since the base period."[13] So this question cannot be answered based upon the data given. But because the rate of increase in the cost of living was over a greater number of percentage points for this period in the case of St. Louis, the rate of inflation was higher for St. Louis than for Seattle.

CPI for All Items, 1967 = 100

|  | 1965 | 1975 |
|---|---|---|
| St. Louis | 94.1 | 156.1 |
| Seattle | 94.5 | 155.8 |

Source: Bureau of Labor Statistics. Reprinted in the Bureau of the Census, *Statistical Abstract of the U.S.*, 1982, p.470.

The examples from the census and CPI cited above reinforce the need to understand the context of the published statistical data on a practical level. They establish the need to understand what is measured and what the limits of that measurement are in order to use the data wisely. When dealing with government produced statistical data, there is a further need to take into account the possibility of bias in compilation of the data. In two recent articles, Ramon H.

Meyers and John W. Ratcliffe provide a skeptical vision of government produced statistical data. Their studies focus on statistics of foreign governments and international/intergovernmental organizations.

Dr. Meyers, an East Asian scholar, notes that despite the need for accurate statistical data on China, little exist. This information is needed by the Chinese themselves. Yet, due to political forces historically at work in China, Chinese statistics are generally inaccurate and therefore of little value for the purpose of government or scholarly research. Presently, Dr. Meyers estimates that "published figures might vary as much as plus or minus fifty percent."[14]

## EXPERIENCES

Dr. Ratcliffe's experiences are equally disheartening. He has been a research scientist in East Pakistan and a consultant to international agencies. He notes that the inaccuracy of Near Eastern census figures is due to the fact that "neither Bangladesh [formerly East Pakistan], India, nor Pakistan corrects census data for underenumeration."[15] This underenumeration is due, in part, to the fact that it is the custom among the poor of some Near Eastern areas not to consider children under the age of five to be full-fledged family members and therefore not to report them to census takers. The government does not make any attempt to correct its figures to account for this practice. Not only is this problem in the statistics uncorrected, but it is unmentioned in such widely held and respected reference sources as the UN *Demographic Yearbook* and the UN *Statistical Yearbook*. Even more important for librarians and patrons who make use of statistics published by any of the UN agencies, he notes that these agencies are "allowed to print *only* those statistics approved by the national governments to which they pertain; and statistics likely to reflect negatively on national governments are generally changed to reflect political desires and aspirations instead of reality."[16] Ratcliffe also cites evidence of political manipulation of statistical data in the United States. He asserts that both national and international statistics are of poor quality and subject to manipulation by the political forces which control their compilation and publication. He concludes that "to treat national and international statistics as any more than the most gross and unreliable indices of reality must . . . reflect either naivete due to lack of familiarity with the process of their generation or an absence of good conscience."[17]

## REFERENCE CONSIDERATIONS

Despite the natural impulse, given these accounts, to give up the provision of statistical data altogether, statistics are an important and widely used source of information. Government and business require statistical data to justify operating expenditures and to define populations served. There are certainly techniques for the responsible treatment of reference questions involving statistics, just as there are for reference questions involving legal and medical information.

In his article, "The Uses and Misuses of Information Found in Government Publications," Joe Morehead discusses the librarian's obligation to make the statistics user aware of how statistical data can and cannot be used. Beyond the problems of the acquisition and bibliographic control of government documents for use in libraries, he asks, "Is there a greater professional role in identifying problems of interpretation, of pointing out pitfalls, of warning about the unreliability of statistical data?" While he only raises the question, making no claim to its final solution, he argues that the problem of "*information* retrieval and its uses" has largely been ignored in the library literature; information retrieval being the problem of physical document retrieval. And while much has been written on "the problem of interpretation and reference assistance in legal and medical information," little has been written on the problem of reference questions involving the use of statistics.[18] Morehead indicates that statistical information is often misused because of the user's ignorance of how the information is compiled. In developing this point he recalls that many politicians in this country have commented on the high rate of unemployment in the United States as compared with a much lower figure for Great Britain, while in fact the actual unemployment rate has been consistently lower in the U.S. But he explains that there are many ways to measure unemployment, our own Bureau of Labor Statistics having no less than seven. The result was that "these 'experts' were comparing apples and oranges, and by doing so were misusing government information."[19]

An adequate reference interview is essential to the provision of responsible reference service. The purpose of any reference interview is to clarify the patron's information need. This clarification process is particularly crucial when statistical data are involved. Given the broad range of statistical data available, a variety of possible answers may exist for a given question. Some figures represented in the literature may even be in conflict with one another. So, though a variety of answers may exist in the published sources, not all are appropriate to the patron's information need as will become apparent in the reference interview.

## *REFERENCE INTERVIEW*

First, the reference interview should clarify the patron's objective: *i.e.,* are the data required for knowledge or for confirmation? Does the patron require statistics to reinforce a particular viewpoint or in order to understand an issue? Different objectives require different search strategies. In the search for statistical data to reinforce a particular viewpoint, a variety of statistics may be retrieved from the literature, but only those figures which reinforce the patron's thesis are required. However, in a search for statistical data to illuminate an issue, the "answer" might require an extensive search to insure an accurate perception. Provision of a minimal amount of information, say a figure from the *Statistical Abstract,* may be inaccurate in that it represents an incomplete summation; whereas searching out other measurements of the same variable provide a range within which an accurate answer can be determined.

A second point to clarify by the reference interview is the extensiveness of the patron's need. Information sought to satisfy curiosity, document points made in a doctoral dissertation, a grant application or budget proposal all require different search strategies. In many cases, a figure from an almanac or other compilation may be all that the patron requires. But, as Sheehy notes, such sources "are neither detailed nor authoritative enough for important questions."[20] A clarification of the patron's need will determine the nature of the sources to be consulted and the degree of currency required.

A final point to be clarified in the reference interview is whether or not the statistics are for comparison with other figures. As previously outlined, statistics to be compared must be compatible in terms of the variable that they measure and their context. Often consultation of the sources involved, particularly the prefatory material or user guides, will provide an indication of the comparability of the figures. In questionable or complex cases, the reference librarian should stress that he/she is not a statistician any more than he/she is a doctor or lawyer. Referral to a trained statistician, perhaps a faculty member in the case of a university library or to the government agency responsible for the compilation of the data in question, may be an appropriate course of action.

Certainly one of the more problematic aspects of the reference interview is patron behavior. The phenomenon of the patron who is unwilling or unable to supply the reference librarian with sufficient information to properly answer the question, yet still requires an answer, is sure to arise in reference work involving statistical data. Based upon professional training and experience, the librarian must weigh the patron's need for information against the demands placed upon the patron by an extensive interview. Pressing the patron for details is an inappropriate method for handling the situation when it arises. A few words of explanation as to the problematic nature of reference work with statistics and a manner which indicates that the sole reason for any inquiry is a sincere interest in properly handling the patron's query may be all that is necessary to put the patron at ease. Of course, once the need for clarification has been tactfully outlined and the patron cannot or will not supply further detail, the reference librarian's only course of action is to provide the best possible service given the amount of information supplied.

## *SOURCES*

Reference librarians can adopt an organized search strategy in order to arrive at the degree of accuracy, currency and comparability of statistical data sought. Having clarified the patron's information need in the reference interview, the librarian can work through printed, personal and online sources as need dictates.

Printed sources break down into several categories of materials: compilations, works within specific subject fields, bibliographies and indexes. Compilations of statistics include such commonly held publications as the *Statistical Abstract of the U.S.* and the United Nations *Statistical Yearbook*.[21] Other compilations of statistics might also be appropriate based upon the specific library clientele. For example, a library answering primarily questions within a given subject field might wish to acquire whatever compilations are appropriate to that field. Librarians should also be aware of appropriate monographs or periodicals within that subject field which contain statistics. Appropriate titles may be determined by consulting such works as Paul Wasserman's *Statistics Sources* and the statistical indexes produced by Congressional Information Service,

Inc., including *American Statistics Index, Statistical Reference Index* and *Index to International Statistics*.[22] Librarians working with larger collections should also be aware of these indexes when reference questions require information beyond what can be found in compilations. The *Statistical Abstract* may also be used to locate current sources of statistical data despite the fact that the figures it reports are dated. If the type of statistic desired is provided in one of the *Statistical Abstract*'s tables, the source note for that table can be consulted to determine the source of those figures, and in turn the primary source may be consulted to obtain more current or detailed figures. The same procedure may be used to identify periodical titles in fields of interest for acquisition. Libraries may wish to have statistical abstracts for their own and adjoining states. A list of state statistical abstracts is given in Appendix IV of the *Statistical Abstract*. The list is arranged alphabetically by state and gives the name of the issuing source of the abstract, its title and the latest edition available as of the publication of the *Statistical Abstract*.

## *PERSONAL CONTACTS*

Personal contacts or referrals should not be overlooked when answering statistical reference questions. It should be noted that the above mentioned sources can be useful in determining the provenance of statistical gathering activities. This information can be helpful when the exact figures needed cannot be located in published sources or when complex problems of interpretation arise. In such cases, referral to the agency responsible for the data may be the best course of action. Responsibilities of agencies and individuals can be determined by examining source notes or consulting such works as the *U.S. Government Manual* and the *Federal Regulatory Directory*.[23] Responsible individuals at the state and local level may best be determined through the use of state government telephone directories or governmental listings in the telephone directory for the appropriate locale.

If the appropriate statistical data cannot be found through the methods outlined above, the librarian and patron may decide to continue the search through one or more of the many online bibliographic databases available through commercial search services. Many publishers, such as CIS make their print product available online through DIALOG, Orbit or BRS. In addition, federally produced statistical and bibliographic databases such as ERIC and BLS Consumer Price Index are also available through commercial services. The third edition of Joe Morehead's *Introduction to United States Public Documents* contains an appended table of "Selected Online Databases for Federal Government Information."[24] This table gives the name of the databases, the format of information, the producer and the online services offering access in each instance. It also provides information on commercially produced databases covering government-produced information, such as *American Statistics Index*.

Another factor to consider is the growing amount of government produced statistical data available in machine-readable form only. One important example of this trend is a large amount of information from the 1980 Census of Population. Despite its non-print format, this data should not be overlooked as an information resource. Librarians should contact their state library or the Census Bureau for information on their State Data Center. State Data Centers have been established in many locations to manage machine-readable data from the census. Several sources may be of help in identifying other types of data in machine-readable form. The prefatory material in *Statistics Sources* includes a listing of guides to machine-readable sources.

In conclusion, the library patron requiring statistical data should come away from the reference interview with an understanding of the figures provided. This understanding should include awareness of the currency of data available, the limitations of the statistical measurement and methodology, and the comparability of the data to the extent appropriate. In order for this ideal to be achieved, librarians must adopt an informed and conscientious approach to statistical reference work.

## REFERENCES

1. *U.S. Const.*, art. I, §2.
2. *U.S. Const.*, art. II, §3.
3. Betram M. Gross, "Preface: A Historical Note on Social Indicators," *Social Indicators* (Cambridge: MIT Press, 1966), pp. xi-xii.
4. Frederick Williams, *Reasoning With Statistics*, 2nd edition, (New York: Holt, Rinehart and Winston, 1979), p. 5.
5. *Ibid.*
6. *Ibid.*, p. 39.
7. Williams, *op. cit.*

8. U.S. Senate. Committee on Governmental Affairs. *The Decennial Census: An Analysis and Review,* 96th Congress, 2nd Congress, Committee Print, 1980, p. 73.

9. U.S. Senate. Committee on Governmental Affairs. *Undercount and the 1980 Census: Hearing Before the Subcommittee on Energy, Nuclear Proliferation and Federal Services,* 96th Congress, 2nd Session, 1980, p. 45.

10. Henry S. Shyrock, Jacob S. Siegel and Associates, *The Methods and Materials of Demography,* Fourth Printing (rev.), (Washington: U.S. Government Printing Office, 1980), p. 771.

11. *Ibid.,* p. 805.

12. "Technical Notes: Brief Explanation of the CPI," *CPI Detailed Report* (January 1983): p. 179.

13. *Ibid.*

14. Ramon H. Meyers, "Government Statistics in China," *Reference Services Review* 10 (Fall 1982): p. 93.

15. John W. Ratcliffe, "International Statistics: Pitfalls and Problems," *Reference Services Review* 10 (Fall 1982): p. 94.

16. *Ibid.*

17. *Ibid.,* p. 95.

18. Joe Morehead, "The Uses and Misuses of Information Found in Government Publications," *Collection Development and Public Access of Government Documents: Proceedings of the First Annual Library Government Documents and Information Conference,* (Westport, CT: Meckler Publishing, 1982), pp. 70-71.

19. *Ibid.,* pp. 63-64.

20. Eugene P. Sheehy, *Guide to Reference Books,* 9th edition, (Chicago: American Library Association, 1976), p. 479.

21. U.S. Bureau of the Census, *Statistical Abstract of the United States,* (Washington: U.S. Bureau of the Census, 1878-). United Nations. Statistical Office, *Statistical Yearbook,* (New York: United Nations, 1949-).

22. *American Statistics Index,* (Washington: Congressional Information Service, 1973-). *Statistical Reference Index,* (Washington: Congressional Information Service, 1980-). *Index to International Statistics,* (Washington: Congressional Information Service, 1983-).

23. U.S. Office of the Federal Register, *U.S. Government* Manual, (Washington: U.S. Government Printing Office, 1934-). *Federal Regulatory Directory,* (Washington: Congressional Quarterly Inc., 1979-1980-).

24. Joe Morehead, *Introduction to United States Public Documents,* 3rd edition, (Littleton, CO: Libraries Unlimited, 1983), pp. 285-287.

# The NASA Industrial Applications Centers: Fee Based vs Free Information Services

Lynn Heer

In 1962 NASA initiated a technology transfer program to encourage the secondary utilization of the scientific and technical information that it had developed during the course of its aerospace research and development program. The space program itself was a combined government and private sector partnership, and that cooperative effort was continued in order to share this jointly-produced information.

Technology transfer agents known originally as regional dissemination centers were established to achieve this goal. The first was the Aerospace Research and Applications Center (ARAC) at Indiana University. The concept proved to be successful, and other centers were established around the country, usually associated with universities. Today there are nine comprised of two categories known as State Technology Applications Centers (STAC's) and Industrial Applications Centers (IAC's). The two STAC's (Florida and Kentucky) operate within one state; and the IAC's operate on a multi-state or regional basis. Table 1 lists their names, addresses and telephone numbers.

The primary purpose of the Centers is to promote the secondary use of NASA-developed technology and computer programs. Their broader mission now is also to provide access to the world's technical information resources. By performing these services they can help prevent the wasteful and costly duplication of research already performed and to build upon existing information.

NASA-generated technical information represents a major contri-

The author is at the State Technology Applications Center at the University of Florida, Gainesville, FL 32611.

## TABLE 1
### THE NASA APPLICATIONS CENTERS

NASA/Florida State Technology Applications Center (STAC)
University of Florida
307 Weil Hall
Gainesville, FL 32611
(904) 392-6626

NASA/University of Kentucky Technology Applications Program
(NASA/UK TAP)
University of Kentucky
109 Kinkead Hall
Lexington, KY 40506
(606) 258-4632

New England Research Applications Center (NERAC)
Mansfield Professional Park
Storrs, CT 06268
(203) 486-4533

NASA Industrial Applications Center
701 LIS Building
University of Pittsburgh
Pittsburgh, PA 15260
(412) 624-5211

North Carolina Science and Technology Research Center
(NC/STRC)
P.O. Box 12235
Research Triangle Park, NC 27709
(919) 549-0671

Aerospace Research Applications Center (ARAC)
1201 East 38th Street
Indianapolis, IN 46205
(317) 264-4644

Kerr Industrial Applications Center
Southeastern Oklahoma State University
Durant, OK 74701
(405) 924-6822

Technology Applications Center
University of New Mexico
2500 Central Avenue, S.E.
Albuquerque, NM 87131
(505) 277-3622

NASA Industrial Applications Center
University of Southern California
Denney Research Building
University Park
Los Angeles, CA 90007
(213) 743-6132
(formerly known as WESRAC)

bution to the world's scientific and engineering literature. A substantial amount of this may be useful to those outside of NASA. In fact, it has been estimated that as many as 200,000 end-users work might benefit from the sophisticated technology found in the NASA/RECON database.[1]

The Applications Centers are a vital part of the Technology Utilization Program whose purpose is to provide information and assistance with the development of secondary applications of NASA technology. They explore user's needs, and search for a technology which will match those needs. The Centers provide the data and expertise to re-design and re-engineer aerospace technology for the solution of problems encountered by private industry and other government agencies. These secondary applications are known as "spinoffs" and are described in annual NASA publications entitled *Spinoffs*. The latest, *Spinoff 1983*, also chronicles the silver anniversary of NASA and the U.S. space program.[2]

## RECON DATABASE

An essential part of the success of NASA's technology transfer program was the development of a comprehensive computerized database of the world's aerospace and related information. Its establishment was similar to the joint government-industry operation of the space program. There was no private sector information service that could provide the type of online computer-based bibliographic service. Available resources in both the private sectors were examined, and the decision was made to to contract the operational aspects of the program and to ask the American Institute of Aeronautics and Astronautics (AIAA) to share in the design and production of the database. It was named RECON (remote console), and the output from AIAA's journal literature indexing and abstracting and NASA's coverage of the report literature were merged into the database. NASA's Scientific and Technical Information Division provided overall direction and planning and the acquisition of reports from other Federal agencies, government contractors, foreign governments and intergovernmental organizations.[3]

RECON is now one of the oldest and most imitated of the online bibliographic databases, serving as the precursor and model for many of the online databases that reference librarians around the world use today. It includes books, journal articles, NASA contractor reports, reports of other Federal agencies, patents and patent applications, dissertations and theses, conference papers and translations. A searcher can access the system by subject from the controlled vocabulary using the *NASA Thesaurus*, author, contract number, report number and through free-text searching. For most citations there is an abstract from one of two semi-monthly NASA journals: STAR (Scientific and Technical Aerospace Reports) and

IAA (International Aerospace Abstracts). STAR covers world-wide report literature on space and aeronautics, and IAA covers scientific and trade journals, books and conference proceedings. Approximately 15% of NASA-generated information is printed and may be ordered either from GPO or NTIS. The remaining 85% is available on microfiche or hard-copy from microfiche from NTIS, NASA libraries and selected public and special libraries. A list of these libraries appears in STAR. There is also classified material in RECON that is not available to the public and cannot be displayed in the form of a citation on a RECON terminal except for facilities having the proper clearance. For further details about RECON's coverage and organization see item four in the references at the end of this article.

Access to the RECON database has historically been available through being a prime contractor with NASA or by submitting a request to a regional IAC or STAC. This has proven to be a very effective method for NASA to transmit information to private sector technologists.

## *OPERATION*

The NASA Applications Centers are a key part of NASA's Technology Transfer System (see Fig. 1) of personnel and facilities that extends from coast to coast and provides geographical coverage of the nation's primary industrial concentrations. The Centers are nonprofit service agencies which are jointly funded by NASA, user fees and the university (or state agency) which sponsors them. They are staffed by engineers, scientists and technical information retrieval specialists and provide a wide range of information services for business, industrial and governmental clients.

Online databases such as RECON are powerful tools for technology transfer and for information retrieval. They offer tremendous advantages in speed, flexibility and access to large quantities of data. One of the basic client services is retrospective searching of both governmental and commercial databases for relevant citations and statistical data. Government-produced databases such as NASA/RECON, DOE/RECON and Medline and commercial services such as Dialog, BRS, SDC Infoline, Questel and Mead Data are utilized. Some Centers also have access to European databases such as ESRIN (European Space Agency), Finsbury, ECHO and

FIGURE 1
NASA'S TECHNOLOGY TRANSFER SYSTEM

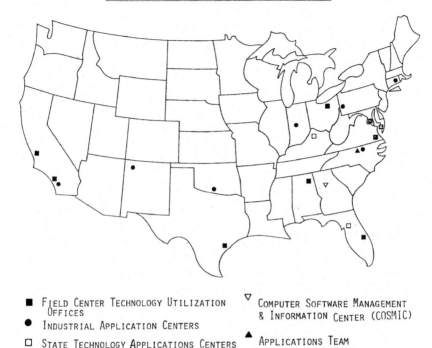

- ■ Field Center Technology Utilization Offices
- ● Industrial Application Centers
- □ State Technology Applications Centers
- ▽ Computer Software Management & Information Center (COSMIC)
- ▲ Applications Team

SAMSOM. Not all of the Centers offer the same databases so one should check with the nearest for further information about available resources.

In addition to retrospective searches most Centers offer some type of current awareness service (SDI) to keep key executives and/or engineers up-to-date in their areas of interest. Awareness can be maintained of the latest books, journal articles, patents and research trends.

Another service is providing demographic data based on census reports and tapes for the location of various types of business such as retail and service outlets. Detailed data from the census tapes on the characteristics of the population such as income levels, educational attainment and areas where people work and live can be used for more accurate planning, marketing and forecasting. Business can develop a demographic profile of their potential customers, analyze their market penetration, evaluate new sites and target their advertising.

Skilled assistance in selecting appropriate services and in interpreting the results of whatever service is provided is a valuable part of the services offered to clients. Assistance in applying the information located to the client's problem makes the Centers' approach more useful to the client. Work is performed for all sizes of organizations from one-person companies to Fortune 500 firms.

Document delivery is another important service; most Centers will obtain documents from sources all over the world. Copies of journal articles, conference proceedings, patents and technical reports are supplied from requests resulting from online searches and from other sources.

Fast turn-around time is an important consideration to many clients who are business people involved in tight schedules and require immediate response to their information requests. The Applications Centers appeal to such clients because they can provide the service required without delay. And many prefer to deal with a technically-oriented staff that can assist them in defining and focusing their questions to achieve the desired results.

And there is another important consideration—confidentiality. Many clients are concerned that competitors not know what research they are involved in. They can be sure that the Centers will keep their interests in strictest confidence. This is especially important during preliminary patent infringement search for a client who has not yet applied for a patent. The searcher is perhaps one of the first to whom the client has disclosed information about the idea or design that may be patentable.

Marketing of the services of the Applications Centers is accomplished through several methods such as speeches to business groups, associations, exhibit booths at national and regional professional and trade shows and conventions. Advertisements in newspapers and journals, brochures and newsletters are all used to increase awareness of the advantages of utilizing the services and expertise of the staff of the Centers. Articles in various professional and trade journals, airline flight magazines and newspapers have also contributed to the visibility and recognition of the NASA technology transfer activities. Demonstrations of online database searching have been performed at user facilities and group presentations have also been made to explain the uses and advantages of online databases in the retrieval of technical information. Some Centers have encouraged users to be present during searches in order that they may participate in the development of the search strategy, assist in reviewing initial output and agree to modifications until the final strategy is run and the output is generated (either online or offline).

The Centers also market NASA's computer software of more than 1300 high-tech programs from COSMIC (Computer Software Management and Information Center) located at the University of Georgia. Originally generated during the course of NASA projects this software is now available to business and industry. Time and money can be saved if the software meets the clients needs in such areas as CAD/CAM, robotics, structural analysis, image processing, data management and analysis and many other specific topics.

## *COMPETITION*

In the past few years there has been a steady growth of information brokers and libraries who offer information retrieval services in competition with the NASA Applications Centers. Libraries—public, academic and special—are also going into the online searching business on a fee-based basis. They are acquiring computer terminals or microcomputers and modems in order to offer information services through their reference departments or special service units. Academic libraries which have traditionally offered free reference services are beginning to charge outside users for any type of reference services requiring more than brief ready-reference assistance.[5] Examples also abound in the literature of charges for online reference services to both students and faculty. Fees for reference services even seem to be spreading to public libraries, especially for information services to business and for online bibliographic searching. Large public libraries such as the Cleveland Public Library are taking an aggressive and entrepreneurial approach to soliciting business from corporate executives and hiring staff to service the special needs of business.[6]

That there is a demand for this type of service has certainly been proven. Both libraries and information brokers can be successful in providing fee-based information services. For libraries, which have previously offered only free reference services there will need to be a change of service philosophy with the realization that free and fee-based services need not be antagonists in the provision of quality information to its patrons. Carolyn Weaver in a previous issue of this journal has provided an excellent analysis of this trend with suggestions on how this apparent conflict of roles may be resolved.[7]

For internal special libraries the proliferation of computerized database searching has some advantages, especially for larger firms with a frequent need for information searches. These have to be weighed against the disadvantages of the cost of supporting such a capability and the possible lack of interdisciplinary expertise and industrial experience available at the NASA Centers.

## SUMMARY

The NASA Applications Centers represent a valuable national information resource. Their activities and services are not as widely known as they should be. They assist decision makers in business, industry and public agencies in obtaining the information needed for them to make decisions. The Centers are available to serve anyone who has a need for information and is willing to pay a fee for that service. Although some Centers have staff who are subject specialists the Centers provide information on all topics. As non-profit service agencies they focus on the process of making secondary application of NASA technology and on the dissemination of technical information.

Secondary utilization of aerospace technology can be very difficult, however, because it depends on a transfer process which crosses established academic disciplines and organizational lines of authority and expertise. As an example, a joint NASA/military project on helicopter rotors produced a vibration dampening technology which is now used in building guitars.[8] One cannot predict whether and how spinoffs may occur. For more examples of other spinoffs the annual NASA publication *Spinoffs* is an excellent source as is item nine in the bibliography at the end of this article.

In the early days of the NASA Applications Centers program the primary service was retrospective searching of the NASA/RECON database. As online computerized databases have grown, other vendors have developed database systems, and information retrieval methods have become more sophisticated the Centers' services have expanded in order to provide a variety of services and retrieval of information about almost anything anyone has ever written about. Access is now available to hundreds of databases and numerous online systems. Today the Centers not only provide searches relating to scientific and engineering topics, but they also answer queries on marketing, advertising, personnel, management and human relations. Their non-profit service approach is designed to bring technology and users together. They make the results of modern technological research available to the "widest practicable and appropriate" audience as is required by The Space Act of 1958 which created NASA.

## REFERENCES

1. National Aeronautics and Space Administration. *NASA STI-RECON Bulletin & Tech Info News*. Washington, D.C. (August/September 1983) p.1.
2. National Aeronautics and Space Administration. *Spinoff 1983*. Washington, D.C. 1983.
3. Day, Melvin S. "Politics and Publishing in Washington: Are Our Needs Being Met in the 80's? A Panel Presentation." *Special Libraries* 75(1) (January 1984) p.12.
4. Jack, Robert F. "The NASA/Recon Search System: A File by File Description of a Major—But Little Known—Collection of Scientific Information." *Online* 6(6) (November 1982) pp. 40-54.
5. Beaubien, Anne K. "Michigan Information Transfer Source: Fee-Based Information Service." *Library Hi Tech* 1(2) (Fall 1983) p.69.
6. Nyren, Karl. "News in Review: 1983." *Library Journal* 109 (January 1984) p.40.
7. Weaver, Carolyn G. "Free Online Reference and Fee-Based Online Search Services: Allies, Not antagonists." *The Reference Librarian* Number 5/6 1983, pp.111-118.
8. Haggerty, James J. *Spinoff 1978*. National Aeronautics and Space Administration. Washington, D.C. 1978.
9. *Space Benefits: The Secondary Application of Aerospace Technology in Other Sectors of the Economy*. Prepared for the NASA Technology Utilization Office by the Denver Research Institute. Contract NASW-2067. NASA Document N77-23010.

## SUGGESTIONS FOR FURTHER READING

Hlava, Marjorie M.K. "The NASA Information System." Oxford and New York, Learned Information, 1978; 2nd International Online Information Meeting, London, December 5-7, 1978, pp.251-256.
Losee, M.W. "The NASA Information System: Citations in Seconds." *Law Library Journal* 64(2) May 1971, pp.198-202.
Counts, Richard W. "Information Services and Operations of the Aerospace Research Applications Center (ARAC)." In Caroll, Dewey E., Ed. *Proceedings of the 1967 Clinic on Library Applications of Data Processing*. 1967. University of Illinois, Graduate School of Library Science, Urbana. pp.41-54.
Jensen, Rebecca J., et al. "Costs and Benefits to Industry of Online Literature Searches." *Special Libraries* 71(7) (July 1980) pp.291-297.
Grogan, Nancy M. "UNM General Library/Technology Applications Center Literature Search Service: An Experimental Program," FY 1974. ERIC Document ED 101720.
"Better Information Management Policies Needed: A Study of Scientific and Technical Bib-

liographic Services." Washington, D.C. Comptroller General of the United States, 1979. 74p. ERIC Document ED 179191.

Katz, Bill and Ruth A. Fraley, Editors. Video to Online: Reference Services and the New Technology. *The Reference Librarian,* Numbers 5/6. 1983.

Lunden, E. "Library as a Business: Conference on Fee-Based Research in Academic Libraries Finds Cost Recovery Mandatory in Serving Off-Campus Users. *American Libraries* 13 (July 1982) pp. 471-472.

"Financing Online Services." *RQ* 21 (Spring 1982) pp. 223-226.